D0908362

The Crowd in History

GEORGE RUDÉ's numerous books include *Wilkes and Liberty, The Crowd in the French Revolution* and, with Eric Hobsbawm, *Captain Swing*. One of the most innovative social historians of the twentieth century, his work has been translated into German, Japanese, Spanish, Italian, Portuguese and Hungarian. He was born in 1910 in Oslo to a Norwegian father and Scottish mother and died in 1993.

The Crowd in History

A Study of Popular Disturbances in France and England, 1730–1848

George Rudé

Serif

London

This edition first published 1995 by
Serif
47 Strahan Road
London E3 5DA

First published by John Wiley and Sons, Inc., 1964
Revised edition published by Lawrence & Wishart in 1981

British Library Cataloguing-in-Publication Data.
A catalogue record for this book
is available from the British Library.

Library of Congress Cataloging-in-Publication Data.
A catalog record for this book is available
from the Library of Congress.

ISBN 1 897959 21 4

Printed and bound in Great Britain by
Biddles of Guildford

CONTENTS

List of Illustrations

List of Maps

To Joan and Gwen

PREFACE TO THE 1981 EDITION

Much that is germane to my subject has been written since this book first appeared nearly seventeen years ago. But as most of the problems that I discussed in my Introduction of 1964 remain, I have not thought it necessary to to submit the work to a thorough revision. However, some change to the original text is called for, and I have thought it essential to revise such passages as are patently wrong or misleading, to bring the Bibliography up to date, and to add this Preface in order to take note of the considerable developments that have taken place, not only in the study of crowds but in labour and peasant history as well.

While these developments have been more marked in social history than in social or political science, it would be churlish not to acknowledge the importance of new interdisciplinary ventures like the *Journal of Peasant Studies* and *Social History* in Britain or the succession of research pieces published by Charles Tilly and his associates in the United States, culminating in such major studies as *The Rebellious Century 1830–1930* (1975). However, the strong impression remains that American sociology, for all its activity in the field of ethnic and conflict studies, persists in pursuing behavioral patterns while largely neglecting what Asa Briggs (after David Reisman) has called "the faces in the crowd".

Among historians, at least, there has been, during the past twenty years no dearth of attempts to unravel the past by viewing it "from below". In the United Kingdom in particular, we have seen the birth of a "new" labour history, initiated by E. P. Thompson's *The Making of the English Working Class* (1963), followed a year later by E. J. Hobsbawm's *Labouring Men*. What was novel about these new labour historians was that instead of placing their emphasis on institutions and "movements", as the earlier historians had done, they placed theirs squarely on the lives and activities of working men and women themselves.

If this has been the major contribution made by Englishmen to the study of history "from below", in France and America the focus has been more often placed on the popular classes in revolutions. French scholars, having previously devoted their main attention to the revolution of 1789, have more recently switched to the study of the common people in the revolutions of the nineteenth century, in that of 1848 in particular. Here the great innovator has

1

been Maurice Agulhon, whose *La République au village* (1970) has traced the development of a revolutionary ideology, suited to the times, among the peasants and rural artisans of the South, notably of the Var. The Americans, for their part, have thrown a new light on their own revolution and on some of the French revolutions as well. In the first place on the revolution of 1830 and its aftermath in which they have established something like a closed reserve. The trend was inaugurated, fifteen years ago, by David Pinkney's article "The Crowd in the French Revolution of 1830" (*American Historical Review*, 1965), followed by Pinkney's *The French Revolution of 1830* and the work of younger scholars, such as John Merriman's collections of articles on France in 1830 (1975) and of others on "Class Consciousness and Class Experience"(1979), and Robert Bezucha's *The Lyons Uprising of 1834* (1974). In addition, American scholars have turned to the popular element in their own revolution and to "crowd" studies of the pre-Revolution and post-Revolution years. The most successful of the results have been those achieved by a group of young historians variously influenced by Bernard Baylin and Alfred Young (though from differing perspectives) in the United States, and the English socialist historians of the 1950s and 1960s: among them mention may be made of Jesse Lemisch, Garry Nash, Dirk Hoerder, Eric Foner, Pauline Mayer and Lionel Richards.*

Equally important perhaps in shaping the "new ways" in history have been the tumultuous events of the past fifteen years. On the one hand, there has been the traumatic experience of the generation of students growing up in the 1960s under the shadow of the Vietnam War and the threat of a nuclear conflict. On the other, there has been the succession of revolutions and near-revolutions in South-East Asia, Latin America, Spain, Portugal and Iran. So far, the creative work in the historical and social sciences that these experiences have engendered has been only the tip of an iceberg; but it is hoped that the new and expanded Bibliography pays adequate attention to such of it as is relevant to the subject of this book.

---

* Three of these—Nash, Hoerder and Foner—have pieces in Alfred Young's volume *The American Revolution*. Explorations in the History of American Radicalism (1976).

INTRODUCTION

The Subject and Its Problems

Perhaps no historical phenomenon has been so thoroughly neglected by historians as the crowd. Few would deny that the crowd has, in a rich variety of guises, played a significant part in history. Yet it has, over many years, been considered a subject fit to be studied by the psychologist or the sociologist rather than by the historian. This book is a historian's attempt to do something to redress the balance.

Of course, I have no intention of attempting to deal with the crowd as a whole, and I shall begin by explaining my subject and defining its limits. In the first place, I am assuming the crowd to be what sociologists term a "face-to-face" or "direct contact" group[1] and not any type of collective phenomenon, such as a nation, a clan, caste, political party, village community, social class, the general "public," or any other "collectivity too large to aggregate." This would seem evident enough, had not some writers in the field (and there are eminent names among them) chosen to extend the crowd's boundaries to encompass far wider horizons. Gustave Le Bon, for example, the founding father of modern crowd psychology, being preoccupied with mental states rather than physical phenomena, includes in his crowd not only castes, clans, and classes but electoral "crowds," criminal juries, and parliamentary assemblies.[2] And Dr. Canetti, an occasional intruder in the field, discusses "the crowd in history" (such is the subheading to one of his chapters) in terms of the various national symbols that he considers most appropriate to Englishmen, Frenchmen, Dutchmen, Germans, Jews, and Italians.[3]

This, however, can only be a first step in the process of delimitation. Any sort of crowd may, exceptionally, be termed suitable material for history; yet the "historical" crowd is more likely to be found among some of the sociologists' neat categories than among others. I say "more likely" quite deliberately, as we shall see that one type of crowd is liable, by the intrusion of the unexpected or of forces outside itself, to be converted into another. Nevertheless, in general, we may exclude from our present considerations crowds that are casually drawn together, like sight-seers; crowds assembled on purely ceremonial occasions or crowds taking part in religious or academic processions; or "audience" crowds (as they have been termed) who gather in theaters or lecture halls, at baseball matches or bullfights, or who used to witness hangings at Tyburn Fair or in the Place de Grève in Paris. Equally, we should generally exclude those more active, or "expressive" crowds that come together for Mardi Gras, participate in dancing orgies or student "rags," or attend revivalist meetings to hear Billy Graham or Father Divine, as they listened two hundred years ago to George Whitefield and the Wesleys. Certain "escape" or "panic" crowds (again to use the sociologist's jargon) are more likely to fall within our province: such manifestations have sometimes accompanied food riots and runs on banks, and these may be the very stuff of social history. Other outbursts of mass hysteria—from the convulsions around St. Médard's tomb in eighteenth-century Paris or the self-immolating orgies of Russia's Old Believers to the more recent frenzies stirred by Orson Welles' "Martian" broadcast—are fascinating material for the student of crowd psychology, but they may be of only casual interest to the historian. In fact, our main attention will be given to political demonstrations and to what sociologists have termed the "aggressive mob" or the "hostile outburst"[4]—to such activities as strikes, riots, rebellions, insurrections, and revolutions.

Even now, without further limitation, the subject would be far too vast to cover in a single volume. It is not the "crowd in history" in general that I propose to deal with, but the crowd within a limited period and within a limited area. For this purpose, I have chosen the period of the 1730's to 1840's in French and English history: apart from their importance as having seen the great political revolution in France and the industrial revolution in England, they were years of transition leading to the new "industrial" society.

Some may object to so arbitrary a division of what I am calling the "pre-industrial" and the "industrial" ages. Admittedly, my starting point is a somewhat arbitrary one, and the 1730's are chosen as much for convenience as to mark any sudden change in the pattern of social and political development. There is, however, a stronger case, in considering these two countries, for drawing a line somewhere around the 1840's. By then the effects of both the political and industrial revolutions were (earlier in the city and later in the village) transforming old institutions, uprooting the old society, changing old habits and modes of thinking, and imposing new techniques. To name only a few innovations, factory towns, railways, stable trade unions, a labor movement, socialist ideas, and the new Poor Law and police force in England were evidence that a new age was not only in the making but in being.

Such breaks with the past could not fail to leave their mark on the form and content of the crowd's activities; and we may as sharply (or as broadly) distinguish the typical popular disturbance of the new industrial society from that of the "pre-industrial" age as we may distinguish the latter from that of earlier times. In industrial society, the disturbances most prone to be historically significant take the shape of strikes and other labor disputes, or of public mass meetings and demonstrations conducted by political organizations; their objects tend (though by no means always) to be well defined, forward looking, and rational enough, even if only acceptable, in the first instance, to one side in the dispute; and participants tend, except in distinct peasant communities, to be wage earners or industrial workers. Similarly, the "pre-industrial" age has its own type of disturbance whose objects, behavior, forms of actions, and participants are, more or less, peculiar to the times. In our transitional period the typical form of social protest is the food riot, not the strike of the future or the millenarial movement or the peasant *jacquerie* of the past. Those engaging in popular disturbances are sometimes peasants (as in the past), but more often a mixed population of what in England were termed "lower orders" and in France *menu peuple* (or, for a short period in the 1790's, sans-culottes); they appear frequently in itinerant bands, "captained" or "generaled" by men whose personality, style of dress or speech, and momentary assumption of authority mark them out as leaders; they are fired as much by memories of customary rights or a nostalgia for past utopias as by present grievances or hopes of material improvement; and they dispense a rough-and-ready kind of "natural justice" by breaking windows, wrecking machinery, storming markets, burning their enemies of the moment in effigy, firing hayricks, and "pulling down" their houses, farms, fences, mills, or pubs, but rarely by taking lives. The riot, then, is the characteristic and ever-recurring form of popular protest which, on occasion, turns into rebellion or revolution.

It would be ridiculous, of course, to press this general distinction too far. Strikes were frequent enough in the eighteenth and early nineteenth centuries in France and England, particularly after the 1770's; and, on occasion, they assumed forms almost identical with those of more recent times. Londoners demonstrated and signed petitions in St. George's or Copenhagen Fields, and Parisians in the Champ de Mars or Place de Grève, as they might today in Trafalgar Square or Downing Street, around the "Bastille Column" or in the Place de la Concorde. Race riots today are not unlike religious riots of an earlier period. Outbursts of mass hysteria provoked by rumors of Flying Saucers or Martian invaders, recall similar manifestations in the past. Revivalist orgies and the antics of "Holy Rollers" (though little known in present-day Western Europe) are by no means strangers to modern industrial society. Again, in 1914, German bakers' shops in the East End of London were pillaged and wrecked as they might have been in Paris in the Revolution; and mythical Russians with "snow on their boots" were then as much a figment of popular imagination as the dreaded "brigands" of the Great Fear of 1789. And, if we need any further reminder that past or "archaic" forms may spill over into the present, we have but to turn to Dr. Hobsbawm's studies on millenarial, "populist-legitimist," and "Robin-Hood" types of movement in southern Europe today.[5] The overlap between periods is, then, considerable and extends into fields that are as much the concern of the historian as of the sociologist; yet, in my view, they are not sufficient to invalidate the general distinction that I am seeking to establish.

The "crowd" of the "industrial" age has the advantage of having been relatively well served by historians (and, more recently, by sociologists): labor history and popular movements of this period have attracted a fair crop of reputable historians from the Webbs and Cole in England to Duveau, Sée, and Dolléans in France. The "pre-industrial" crowd has, in this respect, been less fortunate. There are honorable exceptions: the Hammonds in England and Jaurès and Lefebvre in France come to mind. But, generally, the treatment of such movements has been bedeviled by one or other of two stereotyped approaches. The one—the more liberal, humane, and "democratic"—has taken one of two forms. The first is to read history backwards and ascribe such activities, without further investigation, to the "working class": J. M. Thompson in England, Tarlé in the Soviet Union and Levasseur in France have all, in one form or another, done this. More frequently, the writer shows his sympathy for the objects of a movement by labeling its participants "the people." In France, the great protagonist of this school of writing was Michelet, whose generous impulses led him, quite simply and in defiance of all sociological niceties, to see *le peuple* as the sole agent of revolutionary action. Who captured the Bastille? he asks: not Marat's *pauvres ouvriers* or Dickens' *Saint-Antoine;* but, even less specifically, *"le peuple, le peuple tout entier."* [6] The tradition has survived. Similar approbatory labels are appended by liberal historians to Greek, Italian, and Spanish nationalist rebels of the nineteenth century and, if their cause is considered just (but then alone), to the "patriots" and "freedom fighters" of today.

The other stereotype—more fashionable among conservative writers—is to pin the label "mob" or "rabble" without discrimination on all participants in popular disturbance. The usage goes back to the seventeenth century at least, but we shall not attempt to trace its origins. It was certainly already fashionable in this "pre-industrial" age in France and England, when rioters and other disturbers of the peace were generally dismissed by contemporaries as "banditti," "desperadoes," "mob," "convicts," or "canaille";* and even a revolutionary democrat like Robespierre, though passionately devoted to "the people," was inclined to

* For an interesting exception, see Lord Granville's speech in the House of Lords on February 10, 1737, when commenting on the popular disturbances of 1736: "The People seldom or never assemble in any riotous or tumultuous manner, unless they are oppressed, or at least imagine they are oppressed" (*Gentleman's Magazine,* 1737, p. 374). But Granville, like Michelet in 1847, was in opposition to the government.

see food rioters (as on a famous occasion in February 1793) as agents of the English or the aristocracy. Burke, to whom the "lower orders" were a "swinish multitude," could not fail to look on the revolutionary crowds of 1789 as being composed of the most undesirable social elements: thus the Parisians invading the royal château at Versailles in the October "days" become "a band of cruel ruffians and assassins, reeking with . . . blood"; and the King and Queen, on their return journey to the capital, are escorted by "all the unutterable abominations of the furies of hell, in the abased shape of the vilest of women." [7] Yet Burke's invective, colorful as it is, is far surpassed by the French historian Taine, who, though a liberal in 1848, had, before he wrote his account of the Revolution, been soured by his experience of the Paris Commune. To him the revolutionaries of 1789 and the captors of the Bastille were the lowest social scum: "dregs of society," "bandits," "savages," and "raggamuffins"; the insurgents of October were "street-prowlers," "thieves," "beggars," and "prostitutes"; and those of August 1792, who drove Louis XVI from the Tuileries palace, were bloodthirsty adventurers, "foreigners," "bullies," and "agents of debauchery." [8] So rich a flood of expletives has never, it is true, been matched by later historians; but the tradition launched by Burke and Taine has found its more recent echoes in such generalized labels attached to "No Popery" rioters, English Jacobins, political demonstrators, rural incendiaries, machine wreckers, and strikers as "criminal elements," "the slum population," or, more usually, just "the mob." [9] And the "mob" in question, having no ideas or honorable impulses of its own, is liable to be presented as the "passive" instrument of outside agents—"demagogues" or "foreigners"—and as being prompted by motives of loot, lucre, free drinks, bloodlust, or merely the need to satisfy some lurking criminal instinct.

Of course, there is all the difference in the world between these two approaches—that of Michelet, which sees the crowd as "the people," and that of Burke and Taine, which presents the crowd as "rabble"—and I do not hide my own preference for the

---

[9] Even serious students of popular movements are not immune from this: see, for example, J. P. de Castro, *The Gordon Riots* (London, 1926); and M. Beloff, *Public Order and Popular Disturbances 1660-1714* (London, 1938).

first rather than the second; yet, in relation to my present argument, they have an important element in common. It is that they both are stereotypes and both present the crowd as a disembodied abstraction and not as an aggregate of men and women of flesh and blood. In short, they both reduce the participants in crowds and popular movements to what Carlyle called a "dead logic-formula" and thus, for the purpose of our present study, beg all the relevant questions.

Sociologists, having learned from Marx and Weber, have, on the whole, a better record. This is hardly surprising; the crowd has often been their particular field of study and, in recent years, American sociology in particular has done invaluable work on mixed communities, racial minorities, and racial riots. To them the crowd has not been, as it so often has to the historian, a merely generalized abstraction: they have rather tended to break it down and classify it according to its goals, behavior, or underlying beliefs.[9] Again, their concern for the collective attitudes of crowds is a salutary reminder to those liberal historians to whom the crowd has appeared as merely an aggregate of individuals that the whole is often not simply the sum total of its parts. Yet the crowd psychologists among them have often been guilty of creating their own stereotypes. Le Bon allowed that crowds differed according to "race" (most often, he appears to mean nationality) and that a crowd could be heroic as well as cowardly and might even possess virtues denied to many of the individuals who composed it. But he was inclined to treat the crowd in *a priori* terms: as irrational, fickle, and destructive; as intellectually inferior to its components; as primitive or tending to revert to an animal condition.[10] His prejudices led him to equate the "mob" with the lower classes in society; and, though critical of Taine in some respects, he took from him his fanciful picture of the French revolutionary crowd, which (as Le Bon claimed) tended to be formed of criminal elements, degenerates, and persons with destructive instincts, who blindly responded to the siren voices of "leaders" or "demagogues."[11] So, in spite of the author's profession to distinguish between one type and another, he arrives at a generalized conception of the crowd that, disregarding all social and historical development, would be equally appropriate to all times and to all places.

It would, of course, be absurd to suggest that the study of crowd behavior has stood still since Le Bon wrote over sixty years ago; and, though he is still revered for his pioneering efforts, many of his aristocratic prejudices and racial notions have been discarded by his successors. Even his insistence on the crowd's "irrational" behavior (though it has been further developed by Freud and Pareto), has been questioned: Dan Katz has been inclined to identify crowds according to class and has urged that account be taken of such stubborn historical realities as hardship and persecution in determining the collective actions of feudal serfs and working men; and Alexander Mintz has gone so far as to find reason in the actions of "panic" crowds.[12] More recently, Professor Smelser has turned his back even more firmly on the old shibboleths and urged that the defining characteristics of collective behavior should be seen as social rather than psychological, and he has stressed the importance in such matters of what he terms "generalized beliefs."[13] These are welcome signs and are, at least, the beginning of wisdom; for to be content to classify the crowd—and certainly the *historical* crowd—by mere patterns of behavior is rather like classifying political leaders according to their tricks of oratory, their sartorial habits, or their amatory exploits. And yet one of the old stereotypes still remains: the social psychologist, like the historian, continues to show reluctance to abandon the old concept of the crowd as "mob," * with all its disparaging connotations. He has a better excuse than the historian, as much of his "live" material, concerned with lynchings, crazes, and panics, may condition him to see humanity in its collective manifestations as fickle, irrational, and destructive. For his knowledge of the past he has to rely on the historian; and if the latter sees fit to relay the hoary old preconceptions of those nurtured in the tradition of a Burke or a Taine, he can only expect to have them served back to him in double measure.

How, then, do we escape from these stereotypes; and how, in particular, do we propose to study the crowd in the "pre-industrial" age? In the first place, by asking a number of questions, beginning with: what actually happened, both as to the event

---

* See L. L. Bernard's definition of "mob" as "a highly excited form of crowd" in the *Encyclopaedia of Social Sciences*, X, 552.

itself, and as to its origins and its aftermath? That is, we should attempt from the start to place the event in which the crowd participates in its proper historical context; for, without this, how can we hope to get beyond the stereotypes and probe into the crowd's outlook, objects, and behavior? Next: how large was the crowd concerned, how did it act, who (if any) were its promoters, who composed it, and who led it? Such questions are important, as they will help us to determine not only the general nature of the crowd and its behavior but also its components—by picking out what Asa Briggs has called "the faces in the crowd" in terms of the individuals and groups that compose it, their social origins, ages (sometimes), and occupations. Next: who were the target or the victims of the crowd's activities? This is also important, as it may help to throw further light on the event itself and tell us something of the social and political aims of those that took part in it.* But, more specifically, we need also to enquire: what were the aims, motives, and ideas underlying these activities? This is where Professor Smelser's "generalized beliefs" come in: without such enquiry we shall have to fall back on the purely "psychological" and "behaviorist" explanations of the crowd. A further relevant question is: how effective were the forces of repression, or of law and order? It is evident that in strikes, riots, or revolutionary situations the success or failure of the crowd's activities may largely depend on the resolution or reluctance of magistrates or on the degree of loyalty or disaffection of constables, police, or military. Finally: what were the consequences of the event, and what has been its historical significance? And so, having dissected the crowd and its components, its leaders and its victims, we return to the question from which we started—the nature and importance of an event in history.

It is, of course, one thing to ask such questions and quite another to find reasonably adequate answers to them. The degree to which our curiosity may be satisfied will depend both on the event itself and on the availability of suitable records. Obviously, we cannot afford to neglect the traditional sources, the historian's stock in trade: memoirs, correspondence, pamphlets, provincial

* For its relevance to the study of the London Gordon Riots of 1780 and the English agrarian disturbances of 1830, see Chapters 3 and 10.

and national newspapers, parliamentary reports and proceedings, the minutes and reports of local government and political organizations, and the previous findings of other historians, chroniclers, and antiquarians. Yet, even if we have the patience to consult them all, they may not take us very far; for they will often tend to present the question exclusively from the point of view of the government, the official political opposition, the aristocracy, or the more prosperous middle class—in short, from the angle of more elevated groups and classes than those to which the participants will generally belong. They will, in fact, rarely tell us much about the identity of either the rioters or their victims and remarkably little (as a rule) about the more detailed pattern of events, or about the motives or behavior of those most actively involved. These participants, unfortunately, rarely leave records of their own in the form of memoirs, pamphlets, or letters; and to identify them—and their victims—and probe into their motives and behavior, we shall have to rely on other materials. They may include police, prison, hospital, and judicial records; Home Office papers and Entry Books and the Treasury Solicitor's reports; tax rolls; poll books and petitions; notarial records; inventories; parish registers of births, deaths, and marriages; public assistance records; tables of prices and wages; censuses; local directories and club membership lists; and lists of freeholders, jurymen, churchwardens, and justices of the peace. The record is by no means exhaustive: in fact, in considering this kind of history it would be foolish to attempt one. It is intended rather to give an idea of the sort of document where answers may be sought.

Yet, in their use, we must be prepared for disappointments. For one thing, such records are often housed in local depots, where they have not been classified or preserved with the same diligent care as those in central archives. Many have, in the course of time, tended to disappear or to fall victim to fire or flood, civil disturbance, enemy action, local ignorance, the misplaced zeal of collectors, or even (in the case of some judicial and transportation records) to the desire of some to cover up the seamy past. In England, few parliamentary petitions have been preserved; some were destroyed in the House of Commons fire of 1834. Similarly, in Paris, taxation and municipal records up to 1870 were largely destroyed by fire during the street-fighting at the time of the

Commune;* others, in French provincial collections, have been obliterated in the course of two World Wars. Australian transportation records (invaluable for the study of English and Irish social movements of the early nineteenth century) have not escaped the attentions of collectors or other interested parties. English judicial records are piecemeal and incomplete for quite another reason; respectable enough in itself but with frustrating consequences for the researcher. Whereas the French police system of the eighteenth century was already highly developed, the English system was not; and whereas the French have accumulated substantial records of the cross examination of prisoners before trial, the English system, being concerned to protect the defendant from self-incrimination, did not allow him to be cross examined even in open court. As a result, English records of Assizes, quarter sessions, and consistory courts are not comparable in value for the researcher in this field with those that may be found in French national and departmental archives.

Even where such records are reasonably complete, however, they cannot possibly help us to identify all "the faces in the crowd." This can only be done on those rare occasions when the names and descriptions of all the persons concerned appear on some contemporary list or register. We know, for example, from lists in the French National Archives, the names, addresses, and occupations of all the 800-odd citizens who were able to establish their claim to have been actively engaged in the final assault on the Bastille. Again, if we are willing to follow Le Bon in stretching the meaning of "crowd" beyond our earlier limitation, we can tell from the poll books of 1768 and 1769 the names and parishes of every one of those who voted for the radical John Wilkes in the Middlesex elections of those years, and from the Land Tax or Poor Rate books we may tell what properties they owned or rented. But these are quite exceptional cases. To identify the crowd, we usually have to supplement what we can learn from the one-sided accounts of eyewitnesses with such samples of those killed, wounded, or arrested in disturbances as we may find in police,

---

* An interesting survivor is the rolls of the Poor Tax (*taxe des pauvres*) of 1743, discussed by F. Furet in "Structures sociales parisiennes au XVIII⁰ siècle", *Annales (Economies-Sociétés-Civilisations)*, 1961, pp. 939-58.

judicial, and hospital records. Such samples have to be treated with caution as they are often too small to permit us to draw general conclusions; and there is often little to tell us whether those shot down or arrested were curious bystanders or active participants. Moreover, even if the sample is adequate, we may be left in doubt, as in studying English sessions papers, whether the term "laborer" denotes a journeyman, a domestic servant, or a small tradesman, or the term "yeoman" a small farmer, a shepherd, or an agricultural laborer.[14] To say the least, the task of identifying "faces" is beset with obstacles and problems.

Even greater problems may face us when trying to establish the causes, motives, and mental and social attitudes underlying the crowd's activities. But these will no doubt become evident from what appears in later chapters, and I shall not elaborate them here. Enough has perhaps already been said to convince the reader that, in such a field of enquiry, the historian needs to tread warily, to look out for constant pitfalls, to avoid snap judgments, and to be more tentative in his conclusions than the historian of later labor movements and, even more, the modern field worker whose materials are not elusive parchment but living human beings. Yet the historian must use what evidence he can lay his hands on; and documents such as these, with all their imperfections, enable him, at least, to fill in a part of his picture and to answer some, if not all, of the questions with which he started.

In this book, it is with the help of similar materials, drawn from my own researches and from those of others,* that I have attempted to portray the "pre-industrial" crowd in action and to analyze its components and characteristics. To do this, I have, in the first place, divided its activities into a dozen selected categories and then in turn treat French and English rural and provincial riots of the eighteenth century, French and English city riots, industrial disturbances, the crowd in the French revolution of 1789, "Church and King" riots, English rural movements of the early nineteenth century, the crowd in the French Revolution of 1848, and Chartism in England. No particular virtue is claimed for these precise divisions, which are bound to be some-

---

* My considerable debt to other writers in this field will be evident from the references and bibliography.

what arbitrary and to reflect "values" and conceptions that may be acceptable to some and not to others. Besides, they are evidently those of a historian rather than of a sociologist. Where some might prefer to classify crowds solely according to their modes of behavior or motives and beliefs, I have chosen to take account not only of these factors but of others, such as the country and period in which disturbances took place and the composition of their participants: for example, were they peasants or city dwellers? This will at least help to place the crowd in its geographical and historical as well as in its purely behaviorist or sociological setting; besides, it is not a rigid classification, and the reader will easily see for himself where there is an overlap between one selected category and another. This will appear more clearly in Part 2, where I have attempted a critical analysis of the crowd in its various manifestations, discussed the part played by the forces of law and order and the crowd's allies in other social classes, and drawn some general conclusions from the whole field of my enquiry. Such conclusions certainly do not claim to have any universal validity: at most, they are relevant to the crowd at a single stage of its history. Yet I hope that they may also encourage others to study the crowd in other periods and in other places.[15] So, by such combined efforts, the crowd may eventually appear not as an abstract formula but as a living and many-sided historical phenomenon.

REFERENCES

1. See articles by L. L. Bernard on "Crowd" and "Mob" in *Encyclopaedia of Social Sciences* (15 vols. New York, 1931-5), IV, 612-13; X, 552-4.
2. Gustave Le Bon, *The Crowd: A Study of the Popular Mind* (English translation, 6th impression, London, 1909), pp. 181 ff.
3. Elias Canetti, *Crowds and Power* (London, 1962), pp. 169-200. Neither of these two authors can claim much following today.
4. See R. W. Brown, "Mass Phenomena," in *Handbook of Social Psychology* (2 vols. Cambridge, Mass., 1954), II, 847-58; and N. J. Smelser, *Theory of Collective Behavior* (London, 1962), pp. 222-69.
5. E. J. Hobsbawm, *Primitive Rebels: Studies in Archaic Forms of Social Movement in the 19th and 20th Centuries* (Manchester, 1959).
6. J. Michelet, *La Révolution française* (9 vols. Paris, 1868-1900), I, 248.
7. E. Burke, *Reflections on the Revolution in France* (London, 1951), pp. 66-9.

8. H. Taine, *Les origines de la France contemporaine. La Révolution* (3 vols. Paris, 1878), I, 18, 53-4, 130, 272.

9. See R. W. Brown, *op. cit.*, pp. 840-67 (especially the table of "varieties of crowds" on p. 841); and N. J. Smelser, *op. cit.*, pp. 4-22. Dr. Canetti (perhaps hardly a sociologist) has his own peculiar method of classification (*op. cit.*, pp. 48-63.)

10. Le Bon, *op. cit.*, pp. 25-88.

11. Le Bon, *La Révolution française et la psychologie des révolutions* (Paris, 1912), pp. 55-61, 89-93.

12. See Brown, *op. cit.*, pp. 842-5.

13. Smelser, *op. cit.*, p. 16.

14. For the foregoing, see my article, "The Study of Popular Disturbances in the 'Pre-Industrial' Age," *Historical Studies* (Melbourne), May 1963, pp. 457-69.

15. For the changes that have taken place in this respect, particularly among historians, see the Preface.

PART ONE

The Crowd in Action

ONE

The French Rural Riot
of the Eighteenth Century

The seventeenth century in France had been rent by popular disturbance, above all by the periodic rebellions of disaffected peasants. In Richelieu's time, there had been the desperate uprisings of the *croquants*—or "poor countrymen"—of the 1620's, '30's and early '40's, involving whole provinces in bloody clashes with tax collectors and recruiting sergeants; and the peasants' war in Normandy, known as that of "Jean Va-Nu-Pieds," which aimed to abolish all new taxes levied in the past thirty years. After the dissident princes and *parlements* had had their turn in the civil wars of the Fronde (1648-52), peasant disturbances broke out again in the early years of Louis XIV, culminating in the great insurrection of the 1670's, which, starting over the salt tax (the hated *gabelle*) in the region of Bordeaux, carried the torch of rebellion through ten provinces in the south and west of France. A final wave attended the last twenty-five years of the "Great Monarch'"s reign, with its wars, famines, and religious persecution. This was the age of the great peasant insurrection in Calvinist Languedoc, known as the war of the *Camisards*, the last of the French religious wars. But it was more than that, because it was also fought over the peasant's manorial obligations to his lord; and, soon after, in Catholic Quercy and Périgord, peasants were challenging the whole existing order by refusing to pay taxes to the King, tithe to the Church, or to perform servile manual labor (*corvée*) for the upkeep of the roads. Louis' long reign ended in a final outburst of peasant riots over the disastrous harvest and famine of 1709 and the further exactions of tax collectors for the War of the Spanish Succession.[1]

Surprising as it may seem, the eighteenth century, which ended in the great social and political upheaval of the Revolution, was rarely marked by disturbances of such violence, scope, or magnitude. In the seventy-odd years separating Louis' death from the pre-revolutionary crisis of 1788, such fundamental questions as those raised by the peasants of Normandy, Languedoc, and Périgord in Richelieu's and Louis' time far more rarely appeared as issues in popular disturbances.[2] Basically, peasant claims remained unsatisfied: the most onerous of the royal taxes—the *gabelle* and *taille* (land tax)—continued to be levied on unwilling peasants; and the holders of seigneurial fiefs continued to exact feudal obligations (though rarely servile labor other than the *corvée*) from their tenants; and in fact, aided by their lawyers, they were able to revive old claims, or to invent new ones, as the century progressed. So fundamental rural discontents continued to simmer beneath the surface; yet more peasants acquired land as freeholders or tenants, rural incomes rose, and Louis XV's reign, in particular, saw a degree of general agrarian prosperity unknown in earlier times.

In one sense, the great turning point was 1709, the year of the last great famine of the Old Régime: after this, nationwide starvation disappeared as a recurring phenomenon from the French countryside. Admittedly, rural distress continued, and agricultural prices, which had begun to fall about 1660, continued to fall till 1730; and there was a final backlash of widespread peasant disturbance, reminiscent of earlier years, that convulsed large parts of the country in hunger riots during the Regency in the 1720's. Soon after, however, the rural producer began to find a continuously expanding market for his grain and wine; and Professor Labrousse has convincingly shown us that the forty-five years between 1733 and 1778 were years of steadily advancing prices and prosperity for rural proprietors and tenant farmers, or anyone else in the countryside whose holding was large enough to enable him to sell in the market.[3] For ten years after 1778, partly because of France's entry into the War of American Independence, prices tended to fall again, with results that were often disastrous to wine-growers; but only in 1787 was France afflicted by a series of bad harvests and other attendant calamities that stirred the whole countryside into a renewed outbreak of rebellion, which played a vital part in the revolutionary crisis of 1789.

In 1789, then, it was once more economic distress that forced the old traditional and basic grievances of the whole rural population to the surface; and, as Alexis de Tocqueville has insisted, the explosion may have been all the more violent because of the comparative prosperity and freedom enjoyed by many peasants in the preceding sixty or seventy years.[4] Even in the prosperous years, however, when age-old discontents due to tithe, tax, and seigneurial exaction were dormant rather than active, a large part of the peasantry, even if cushioned against actual starvation, could still only scrape a meager existence from the cultivation of the soil. These included not only the hosts of landless laborers, cottagers, and *métayers* (sharecroppers)—accounting between them for over half the rural population—but many thousands of small proprietors who, even though they owned their land outright, did not possess the thirty acres or more that alone would yield a surplus for sale on the market. Such persons, therefore, like the bulk of the wine-growers and the people of the cities, depended for their survival on the purchase of bread or grain. Many cottagers and stripholders might be vitally concerned at the tendency of the larger proprietors and farmers to enclose the commons and encroach on their traditional rights of gleaning and pasture; but all, being buyers rather than sellers of food, would be concerned with the need for cheap and plentiful bread—indeed, this was their overriding preoccupation. As bread was the staple diet and accounted, even at its normal price of 2 sous a pound, for something like 50 percent of the poor man's budget,[5] he was naturally alarmed, and might even suffer serious hardship, when it rose appreciably higher. In fact, whenever harvests were bad, or when the needs of war or a breakdown in communications led to shortage, hoarding, or panic buying, a large part of the rural population, like their fellows in the cities, were threatened with hunger; and on such occasions many would demonstrate in markets or at bakers' shops, or resort to more violent action by stopping food convoys on roads and rivers, pillaging supplies, or compelling shopkeepers, millers, farmers, and merchants to sell their wares at lower prices, or the authorities to intervene on behalf of the small consumers. As long as the peasant proprietor was relatively satisfied, there could be no question of a general rural conflagration, and the old issues underlying peasant rebellion lay muted; but the food riot remained as the typical and constant expression of popular discontent; and this was true of the village as it was of the city and market town.

France being a largely agrarian community, outbreaks of rioting (outside Paris, at least) corresponded fairly closely to the years of bad harvest and shortage. The lean years, between 1709 and the pre-revolutionary crisis of 1788, were 1725, 1740, 1749, 1768, 1775, and 1785. With the exception of 1749, these were also the major years, though by no means the only years, of popular disturbance. There were food riots at Caen in Normandy and throughout the Paris region in 1725. In 1739-40, the Marquis d'Argenson, one-time Foreign Minister, reported in his journal the desperate condition of the western provinces and successive outbreaks at Bordeaux, Caen, Bayeux, Angoulême, and Lille: at the latter, the Intendant was threatened with assassination. In 1747, he recorded disturbances at Toulouse and in Guyenne and, in 1752, at Arles, Rennes, Bordeaux, Metz, Le Mans, Caen, Rouen, Fontainebleau, and in Auvergne and Dauphiné: at Rouen, the cotton workers held the city for three days, raided granaries and warehouses and suffered the loss of ten lives by bullets and five more by execution before being silenced by three regiments of dragoons. In 1768, when the price of bread rose higher in some provinces than at any time since 1725, there were riots at Le Havre and, at Mantes, crowds sacked a warehouse and sold its contents at half the market price. In 1770, spinners and weavers performed a similar operation at Rheims. In 1774, the Parisian bookseller-diarist, Sébastien Hardy, recorded food riots at Tours and Bordeaux; they were followed early the next year by further outbreaks at Dijon, Metz, Rheims, Bordeaux, and Montauban which led, in turn, into the more extensive and protracted movement known to historians as *la guerre des farines* (the "flour war") of April–May 1775.[6]

This was by no means the last of such disturbances before the Revolution: there were bread riots at Grenoble and Toulouse in June 1778, others in Normandy in 1784 and 1785, and many more in the critical year of 1788. Yet the riots of 1775, which, for two weeks and more, gripped Paris and its neighboring provinces and caused considerable alarm at Court, have a special claim on our attention. They were the last of the great popular movements before the Revolution; they occurred before such movements had

begun to be impregnated with the new ideas of the Enlightenment; and, in some respects, they look forward to similar types of
outbreak during the revolutionary years. Above all, they afford a
classic (and richly documented) example of a particular type of
food riot that had begun to emerge over the past century: the imposition of an unofficial price control by collective action, or what
the French call *taxation populaire*.[*] It is proposed, therefore, to
devote the remaining pages of this chapter to a description and
discussion of this movement.

Turgot had been made Comptroller General of Finance by
Louis XVI shortly after his accession to the throne, in August 1774.
His record was a good one and, except by a small but influential
group of aristocratic diehards, the appointment was well received.
The new minister was a "Physiocrat" and a firm believer in free
trade; and, in September, he took steps to restore the freedom of
trade in grain and flour in the home market. This was not in itself
an unpopular move: his predecessor, the Abbé Terray, who had
regulated the trade by means of a monopoly of bulk purchase
and stocking of markets, had won notoriety and odium by en-
trusting his operations to a couple of shady and unscrupulous
dealers. The climate was, therefore, favorable for a change; and
had the harvest been good (after a succession of failures), it
might well have succeeded. But, unfortunately for Turgot, the
harvest of 1774 turned out to be even worse than those immediately before it; and, with the depletion of stocks in the spring of
1775, the free entry of merchants and speculators into the markets,
and the panic buying of the wealthier consumers, the price of
grain, flour, and bread began to rise at an alarming pace. At
Rozoy-en-Brie, one of largest markets in the Paris region (it was
one of some sixty from which the capital drew its supplies of
grain), the price of wheat rose, on April 1, from 25 to 30½ francs
a *setier* (approximately 12 bushels), while in the Paris bread
markets the price of the 4-pound loaf, normally 8–9 sous but recently 11, rose to 11½ sous in March, to 13½ sous at the end of
April and to 14 sous in early May. In parts of Normandy and
Picardy, prices rose even higher; so much so that some local officials begged the minister to intervene. But Turgot was obsti-

[*] For earlier examples, see Rose, *op. cit.*, pp. 433–34.

nately committed to his Physiocratic ideas and refused to compromise. So the poor, faced with a mounting threat to their means of livelihood, resorted to their traditional mode of protest; but, this time, it was to be more persistently sustained and to be on a larger scale than any similar commotion in the last fifty years.

It began on April 27 at Beaumont-sur-Oise, a market town twenty miles north of Paris. According to the senior magistrate, who was later charged with complicity in the affair, the riots arose from the bakers' refusal to bake more bread and the high prices demanded by the grain merchants. He himself was asked to intervene; but, although entitled as a last resort to adjust the price of bread, having no authority to reduce the market price of wheat, he refused. So the local people, with the porters of Beaumont at their head, and peasants from neighboring villages took the law into their own hands, invaded the market, and compelled the dealers to sell their wheat at a "just" or reasonable price—in this instance, at 12 francs a *setier*.

The initiative taken by the Beaumont porters proved to be the "spark" that set the whole movement alight. It also set the pattern for the disturbances that followed in the Ile de France around Paris and four of its bordering provinces.* The area covered was essentially enclosed by the rivers encircling the capital: the Oise and the Somme to the north, the Eure to the west, the Seine to the northwest and southeast, and the Marne to the east. Generally, the riots followed the course of these rivers or crossed them at strategic points, spreading from one market town to the next, and fanning out on either side of the rivers into the farms and villages of the surrounding countryside. In each market and village touched by the disturbances the news had got around— and it needed no specially hired agents or messengers to spread it—that, in other places, something was being done, either by the authorities or, failing them, by the people themselves, to impose a "just" ceiling on the exorbitant prices being charged by merchants, farmers, millers, and bakers; and it was urged that they, too, should follow this example. Usually, the "just" price in question followed the pattern set at Beaumont, and the men and women

---

* The affected provinces were the Ile de France, Normandy, Picardy, Champagne and (marginally) the Orléanais.

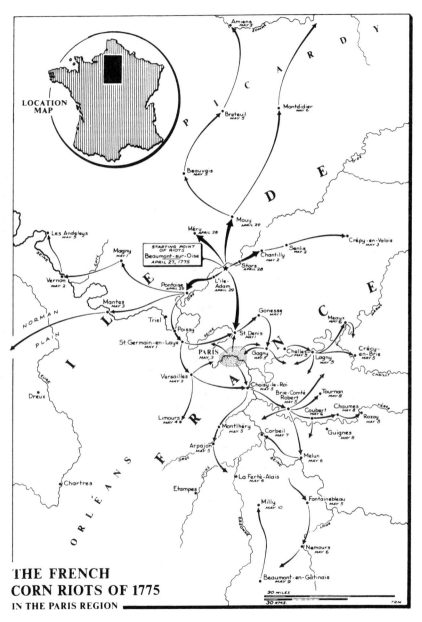

LOCATION
MAP

STARTING POINT
OF RIOTS
Beaumont-sur-Oise
APRIL 27, 1775

THE FRENCH
CORN RIOTS OF 1775
IN THE PARIS REGION

who flooded into the markets, bakers' shops, or farms of the
laboureurs, refused to pay more than 12 francs for a *setier* of
wheat, 20 sous for a bushel of flour, and 2 sous for a pound of
bread.° Admittedly, these proceedings afforded the opportunity
for many to engage in indiscriminate pillage, or to undercut the
"popular" price; but this was not a typical feature, and it is remarkable how many who had underpaid in the heat of the moment made up the difference later.

It was perhaps natural that contemporaries, especially Turgot's
supporters (Voltaire among them), should have seen these disturbances as the outcome of a plot designed to starve the capital
of its food supplies and overthrow the government by force.
Miromesnil, the Keeper of the Seals, for example, told the Paris
parlement, with all the authority of his high office, that "a plan
had been devised to strip bare the countryside . . . to starve the
cities, Paris in particular." Turgot, indeed, had enemies at Court,
among them the powerful Prince de Conti, whose ancestral seat
of L'Ile-Adam lay suspiciously near the place where the trouble
had started. There were also the Jesuits and the Church party, for
whom Turgot's free-thinking principles and known association
with *philosophes* and Encyclopaedists were matters of public
scandal and reproach; and was it not significant that a number of
parish priests had been arrested, and several more suspected, as
alleged instigators of these riots? Was it not also strange that the
Abbé Terray's former trusted agents, Doumerc and Sorin de
Bonne, should as soon as the disturbances were over, have been
confined, with several others, in the Bastille?

Such suspicions were widely held and have been inherited, in
one form or another, by Turgot's biographers and other historians.
Yet they have little basis in fact. The Prince de Conti himself
proved to be a minor victim of the very riots that he was supposed
to have incited, and his estates were to be the scene of further
peasant disorders both before and during the Revolution of 1789.
Sorin and Doumerc, it later appeared, were being charged solely
with squandering public funds during the Abbé's administration;

° In practice, there were considerable variations in the prices offered for
wheat and flour; and the variations were greatest and the prices offered
highest (and this was no doubt significant) in areas furthest removed from
Paris or the scene of the original outbreak.

and the most that could be found against the parish priests, who were soon released from custody, was that they had been too ready to believe the current rumors that wheat was being sold at a reduced price in nearby markets. Even so, if the riots had been a more or less simultaneous explosion, or if any of the emissaries said to have been moving around with specimens of mouldy bread or bags of *louis d'or* had been arrested and questioned by the police, there might seem to have been some substance in the charge that the "flour war" was fostered by a conspiracy rather than by the fear of hunger.

But there were no such arrests, and the pattern and the time table of the riots suggest that the charge was false. Starting at Beaumont on April 27, they spread in four directions: southwestwards down the Oise to Pontoise and St. Germain; eastwards to St. Denis and Gonesse north of Paris; northwards up the Oise to the villages of the Beauvaisis; and eastwards to the market towns of Senlis and Crépy-en-Valois. The first of these currents reached Pontoise on the twenty-ninth and St. Germain on May 1; the second reached St. Denis and Gonesse on May 1; the third reached Stors, a riverside port, and Méru, a small market town, on April 28, and the villages of Mouy and Mours on the twenty-ninth; while the fourth reached Senlis and Crépy on their respective market days, on May 2 and 3. This was only a start. These early currents divided in turn, the northerly stream reaching up through the valley of the Oise to Breteuil and Montdidier in Picardy (May 5 and 6) and the easterly stream turning southwards into the plain of Champagne and the Brie; while the southwesterly stream split into two at Pontoise, one branch continuing south to St. Germain and the other turning westwards into the Norman plain at Magny (May 1), Vernon, Mantes, and Les Andelys (May 2, 3, and 5).

Yet these were comparatively minor affairs, and, occurring at a safe distance from the capital, they excited little comment. From Pontoise and St. Germain, however, the main southwesterly stream flowed on to Versailles, which it reached on May 2. Here villagers from miles around joined with the townspeople in besieging bakers' shops, looting the flour market, and compelling dealers to sell their flour at 20 sous a bushel. According to one account, the King appeared on the balcony of the palace and addressed 8,000 demonstrators; Hardy noted in his journal that the

Queen shed tears and Louis had to forego a day's hunting. Of greater moment, however, was the decision taken by the city's governor, the young Prince de Poix, to order bakers "in the name of the King" to sell their bread at 2 sous a pound. Although countermanded the same evening by Turgot, the measure was to have important consequences: by associating the King's name with one of the rioters' main demands, it appeared to many to set the stamp of royal approval on their activities. The fact soon became evident as the movement spread eastwards to Choisy in the Seine valley and northeast to Paris; in more than one village on the approaches to the capital, men and women demanding bread at 2 sous a pound invoked the price fixed by royal command at Versailles.

The next day—Wednesday, May 3—was market day in Paris. That same morning (such was the folly of authority), the price of the 4-pound loaf was raised from 13½ to 14 sous in the bread markets. Almost simultaneously, bands of men and women from the outer suburbs and nearby villages swept through the customs posts into the central grain and flour markets and pillaged or bought wheat, rye, and flour at reduced prices. Meanwhile, the city's wage earners and poor had joined in the fray: having cleared the bakers' stalls in the bread markets, they stormed or laid siege to every baker's shop in the city center and the inner faubourgs. The general demand was for bread at 2 sous a pound, often accompanied by the claim that it was "by order of the King"; but often, in the scurry that ensued, bread was simply pilfered from shelves and ovens and hurled unceremoniously through the windows to waiting hands outside. In one Paris district alone, that of St. Benoit on the Left Bank of the Seine, twenty-eight bakers reported a combined loss of 20,000 pounds of bread, or an average of 700 pounds each. The military had been slow to muster but, by evening, Turgot had managed to order troops to the markets and bakers' shops; and the movement in the capital subsided. But it spread south and east of the city; and it was in the Brie—in the markets, farms, and villages enclosed by the Seine and the Marne—that it attained its greatest force and momentum. In fact, only a week later did Turgot succeed in bringing the disturbances to an end—by a massive concentration of troops and militia, many hundreds of arrests, two public executions in the capital, and synchronized appeals from the village pulpits.

The progression and chronology of these riots, tedious as they may appear to the reader, help us to fathom their nature. They show us that far from being a simultaneous eruption touched off at some central point of control, they were a series of minor explosions, breaking out not only in response to local initiative but to the force of example. Quite apart from the chronological sequence, this is amply attested by the police records relating to the affair. At Magny, for example, it was reported that the people had been "excited by the revolt at Pontoise" (17 miles away); at Villemomble, south of Gonesse, it was argued in support of the lower prices offered by buyers "that the price of bread had been fixed at 2 sous in Paris and wheat at 12 francs at Gonesse"; and other such cases could be cited. Perhaps more important was the fact that local magistrates had, in a number of market towns, felt compelled to meet at least a part of the rioters' demands by reducing the price of bread or of wheat. At Beaumont, as we have seen, the official in charge was not empowered to interfere with the market price of wheat, but he later agreed to sanction the sale of bread at 2½ or 2 sous a pound. At other strategic points along the course of the riots, magistrates, either from fear of disaster or from a genuine sympathy for the plight of the poor, made similar concessions to popular demands. At Pontoise the municipal officers, finding themselves without troops to restore order, tried to appease the angry peasants invading the market by ordering wheat to be sold at 12½ francs a *setier*. At Montdidier in Picardy, where the prices offered by the rioters were higher than in the Ile de France and the Brie, the mayor and *procureur* agreed to reduce the price of wheat to 18 francs. At Brie-Comte-Robert, to the east of the capital, the magistrate in charge of the market not only fixed the price of wheat at 12 francs, as demanded by the rioters, but opened up to them the reserves in the local granaries. And we have noted the measures taken in the King's name by the Prince de Poix at Versailles.

It would be unreasonable to charge these magistrates with complicity in the riots (though Nicolas Bailly, *procureur* of Beaumont, was so charged at the time), yet their acts undoubtedly served to spread the disturbances by giving them an appearance of official sanction; and even where magistrates refused to follow the example set at Pontoise or Versailles, the voice of rumour often insisted that they had done so. This, of course, helps to explain why such "respectable" persons as curés, schoolmasters, farmers, and petty local officials frequently failed to restrain the laborers or others in their charge, and even sent them out to buy cheap grain for their own accounts or led foraging parties against local farmers and granaries. One such person was Thomas Blaison, *procureur fiscal* of Villemomble in the Ile de France, who at first expressed surprise that the price of wheat should have fallen so suddenly from 33 to 12 francs, but was comforted by the reflection that the King, in his wisdom, had probably decided "to compensate the farmers by a reduction of the *taille*" !

There is other evidence besides to suggest that these disturbances were a genuine, and largely spontaneous, expression of popular alarm at the rising price of food. There were many hundreds of persons arrested: 145 in Paris, 260 in the Brie and Ile de France, and 183 at Beaumont, Pontoise, and in the Beauvaisis; a further 170 or more suspects were described in detail by local farmers and shopkeepers. Apart from a handful of farmers, gamekeepers, petty officials, and curés, these were almost without exception (and here the documents are remarkably precise) typical wine-growers, market gardeners, farm laborers, porters (as at Beaumont and Paris) and village craftsmen of the Paris region and market towns and villages of Champagne, Picardy, and Upper Normandy. They were nearly all local people, well known to farmers and tradesmen; few were vagrants, and only a handful had previous criminal records. In fact, they hardly deserve the title of "brigands" so liberally applied to them in official correspondence.[7]

The grain riots of 1775 have other noteworthy features. For one thing, they form an interesting link between the popular disturbances of the past and those of the French Revolution.[8] In the Revolution, too, after the initial revival of the peasant war of former times, we shall find similar outbreaks of *taxation populaire* in the great food riots of 1789, 1792-3, and 1795. This is not surprising, as the Revolution did nothing to destroy—in fact, it further promoted—the hostility of the small people of town and countryside to the newfangled doctrine that the price of the necessities of life should be regulated by supply and demand rather than by a traditional concern for "justice." Yet there are important differences. Similar movements in the Revolution achieved a considerable measure of success, whereas that of 1775 (like those of

1725 and 1752) ended in almost total failure. This was due to the isolation of these earlier rioters, who found themselves confronted, once its forces had been marshaled, by the combined opposition of army, Church, government, urban bourgeoisie, and peasant proprietors: their few supporters or sympathizers among parish priests, farmers, and local officials were quite insufficient to redress the balance. Again—and this of the greatest importance—the new ideas of "liberty," popular sovereignty, and the Rights of Man, which were later to align the lower and middle classes against a common enemy, had not yet begun to circulate among the urban and rural poor. There is, in fact, not the slightest indication in these riots that such ideas were already abroad. Even the peasants' traditional hostility to manorial dues, tithes, game laws, and feudal obligations are not expressed in any way whatsoever in the course of these disturbances: although a number of seigneurs and priests were among their victims, this was simply because, like other rural proprietors and substantial tenants, they had grain to spare in their barns. The sole target was the farmer or prosperous peasant, the grain merchant, miller, or baker; and the appeal made, where the King himself did not appear to intervene to protect his people, was to precedent and ancient custom. There was no question of overthrowing the government or established order, of putting forward new solutions, or even of seeking redress of grievances by political action. This is the eighteenth-century food riot in its undiluted form. Similar movements will appear under the Revolution, but they will never have quite the same degree of spontaneity and political innocence.

REFERENCES

1. For a convenient summary, see B. F. Porchnev, "Jean Meslier at les sources populaires de ses idées," in *Rapports de la délégation soviétique au Xe Congrès international des sciences historiques, 1955* (Moscow, 1955), pp. 42-6.
2. For some of the rare exceptions see J. Nicolas' study of the neighbouring territory of Savoy (to become French in 1792) in the century before the Revolution: in *Annales historiques de la Revolution française*, no. 214, 1973, pp. 593-607; no. 215, 1974, pp. 111-53.
3. C. E. Labrousse, *Esquisse du mouvement des prix et des revenus en France au XVIIIe siècle* (2 vols. Paris, 1933); *La crise de l'économie française à*

la fin de l'Ancien Régime et au début de la Révolution (Paris, 1944), pp. ix-xli.

4. A. de Tocqueville, *The Old Régime and the French Revolution* (New York, 1955), pp. 176-7.

5. Labrousse. *Esquisse,* II, 597-608.

6. See *Journal et Mémoires du Marquis d'Argenson* (9 vols. Paris, 1859), I, 54; II, 149-59, 184, 213; III, 61-2, 131-73; V, 124; VII, 81-7, 206-29, 333. E. J. F. Barbier, *Journal historique et anecdotique du règne de Louis XV* (4 vols. Paris, 1847), III, 376-7. S. Hardy, "Mes loisirs, ou Journal d'événements tels qu'ils parviennent à ma connaissance," (8 vols. in MS., Bibliothèque Nationale, fonds français, 6680-87), II, 303; IV, 9. See also R. B. Rose, "18th-Century Price Riots, the French Revolution and the Jacobin Maximum," *International Review of Social History,* III (1959), 432-45.

7. For the foregoing and for sources, see my articles, "La taxation populaire de mai 1775 à Paris et dans la région parisienne," *Annales historiques de la Révolution française,* no. 143 (April-June 1956), 139-79; and "La taxation populaire de mai 1775 en Picardie, en Normandie et dans le Beauvaisis," *ibid.,* no. 165 (July-Sept. 1961), 305-26.

8. The late Vladimir Lublinski, in a recently published work, has argued that the "link" was even closer that I have suggested here. (See his "La guerre des farines", *Documents et mémoires,* Univ. of Grenoble, 1980.)

TWO

The English Country Riot
of the Eighteenth Century

Unlike France, England had long since shed her feudal survivals. The old medieval village had gradually been transformed by the impact of trade, civil war, sales of land, enclosure, and the invasion of domestic crafts. There were no longer lords and peasants; and peasant rebellion, which in France though dormant would explode again in 1789, had not, in England, been heard of since the days of Elizabeth. In place of the old feudal lord of the manor, the squire ruled in the village, sat on the county bench, appointed the Church of England parson, leased land to the tenant farmer, and, like him, employed the wage labor of rural workers. These landless laborers formed a far higher proportion of the country population than in France, and even more than in France were engaged in the spinning and weaving of cottage industry. Here the master was the merchant manufacturer, who hired out looms and brought the finished cloth to market; the newer type of industrial employer would only come into his own with the factory system and the Industrial Revolution. The merchant also owned land in the village and sat beside the squire in Parliament; and here squire and merchant gave proof of their basically common interests by jointly voting Enclosure Acts, subsidies, and Corn Laws; promoting tolls and turnpikes, Militia Acts, and measures against smuggling; and upholding the Poor Law and Acts of Settlement for the better policing and regulation of the poor.

Such issues rarely divided the upper classes or the political parties, but they were of considerable concern to the "lower orders" or "laboring poor"—the cottagers, small freeholders, weavers,

33

colliers, tinners, craftsmen, and village poor—who, having no political rights, had no other means of redress of grievance than resort to the traditional riot. On such occasions, market towns, miners' villages, and country lanes echoed to the sound of marching feet, crashing timber, or broken glass, as working men and women settled accounts with corn factors, religious dissenters, mill owners, farmers, or enclosing landlords. Such riots were frequent in the eighteenth century, yet they rarely assumed a political form. Popular rebellion had lost its sharp edge since Monmouth's defeat at Sedgemoor and, since the demise of Lord Shaftesbury's *Green Ribbon Club,* London's popular radicalism had lain quiescent and would remain so for many a year. Yet there were exceptions: the Sacheverell riots in London (1710) and the "High Church" attacks on dissenters' chapels and government offices in 1715 and 1716 remind us that, in cities at least, popular protest might still on occasion be harnessed to a political cause. But these outbreaks took place in periods of general political excitement: we shall find similar popular-political manifestations (both of a radical and of an antiradical kind) in the "Wilkes and Liberty" riots in London and, in Birmingham, in the Priestley riots of 1791.° Such movements were confined to large cities, and even when the long-slumbering battle of parties was stirred to new life at Westminster (as between 1709 and 1716 and after the 1760's), they were by no means typical of eighteenth-century popular disturbance.

The absence of politics from popular riots has led historians to treat them as a matter of small importance: G. M. Trevelyan even concluded that there lay behind them "little or no social discontent." [1] This is a remarkable judgment in view of the frequency of riots which, though rarely political, were essentially a form of social protest. This was more obviously so when they arose, as they most often did, over such bread-and-butter issues as prices and wages; but it was equally true of the other forms and disguises that they occasionally assumed. There were, for example, "religious" riots as when Roman Catholic chapels were "pulled down" in Sunderland and Liverpool in 1746, and in London and Bath in 1780,† and the numerous occasions when Methodist preachers

---

° See Chapters 3 and 9, respectively.
† See Chapter 3.

were shouted down and their congregations dispersed. There were the attacks on the Irish—often a disguised form of industrial dispute—in Spitalfields in 1736, in Covent Garden in 1763, and, as part of a far broader conflagration, in 1780. The Militia Acts stirred massive protests: in 1757 they provoked riots in East Anglia, Lincoln, Northampton, and the Yorkshire East Riding; and in March 1761, 5,000 Northumberland miners, marching to Hexham to stop the ballot for recruits, were fired on by the Yorkshire militia, who killed 42 of them and wounded 48. Turnpikes and toll gates aroused intense popular opposition. There were riots against turnpikes around Hereford and Worcester in 1735-6; in 1727, and again in 1753, there was a mass destruction of turnpikes and toll gates on all roads leading into Bristol; and in June 1753, every turnpike was pulled down near Leeds, Wakefield, and Beeston in the West Riding of Yorkshire: on this last occasion, there were 10 arrests and 10 rioters were killed and 24 wounded. Hostility to enclosure was even more sustained, and disturbance on this account (though mainly after 1760) was scattered throughout the century: we may instance the riots in Northamptonshire in 1710, in Wiltshire and Norwich in 1758, Northampton and Oxfordshire in 1765, Boston (Lincs) in 1771, Worcester in 1772, Sheffield in 1791, and the Nottingham district in 1798. There were attacks on workhouses in several Suffolk villages in 1765. Attempts to impose excise and to stop smuggling met with staunch resistance, as on the grim occasion in 1736 when Captain Porteous, who had fired on a crowd attending a smuggler's execution and been reprieved after sentence of death, was hanged by the people in the Grass Market at Edinburgh. But such physical violence is quite exceptional. More typical of popular proceedings is the incident related by the *Annual Register* in 1766:

> The colliers from the Cleehill, near Ludlow, assembled in a body and pulled down the still-house in that town. They entered the town in a very orderly manner, proceeded to the house, pulled it down, and then returned without offering any other violence to any person whatever.[2]

But by far the most numerous of the riots of the eighteenth century, the most persistent, widespread, and stubbornly promoted, were those occasioned by a shortage or a sudden rise in the price of food. Of some 275 disturbances that I have noted between 1735 and 1800,[3] two in every three are of this kind; and it is unlikely that the proportions are any different for the remaining years of the century. Nor is the reason hard to find. In England, even more than in France, the bulk of the population were small consumers dependent on the cheap and plentiful supply of bread, and also of meat, butter, and cheese. When harvests were bad, when wartime needs imposed a heavy strain on stocks, or when wheat was exported abroad in times of growing shortage,° prices rose in villages and market towns and, as in France, the fear of famine provoked disturbance. On the whole, harvests were good and prices were low during the first part of the century: between 1713 and 1764, the average price of wheat was 34s. 11d. per quarter (¼ hdwt.) and bread sold at 5 or 6d. the quartern (or 4-pound) loaf. But there were bad periods in 1709, 1727-8, 1740, and 1756-7. In 1709, a cold winter was followed by a rainy summer, and the quarter of wheat rose from 27s. 3d. to 81s. 9d. in eighteen months. In 1727-8, a rainy summer caused wheat to rise from 32s. 11d. to 49s. 2d. In 1740, a bad harvest followed a severe winter, and the price of wheat at Oxford rose, over two years, from 20s. 2d. to 59s. In 1756, the outbreak of the Seven Years' War was succeeded by a deficient harvest; and by the middle of 1757, wheat, which a few months earlier had sold at Mark Lane for 22 to 26s, was selling for 67 to 72s.[4] On each of these occasions considerable disturbances took place: among Essex housewives, Kingswood colliers, and Tyneside keelmen in 1709-10; and among Cornish tin miners and Gloucestershire colliers in 1727. In 1740 and 1756-7, food riots spread over large parts of the country. Dr. Wearmouth records eighteen incidents between April 1740 and January 1741 and thirty-five between August 1756 and November 1757.[5] Respectable opinion was becoming alarmed; and after this last bout of outbreaks a Carmarthenshire correspondent was moved to send the following to the *Gentleman's Magazine:*

If the Legislature don't speedily use some method effectually to suppress the present spirit of rioting, which is become general among the

---

° By the Corn Law of 1689, wheat might be exported and a bounty of 5s. a quarter be paid to the exporter if its price at the port of exit did not exceed 48s. By the law of 1733, the figure was reduced to 44s.; but in 1791, owing to the high prices prevailing, it was raised to 54s. (D. G. Barnes, *A History of the English Corn Laws from 1660 to 1846* (New York, 1961), pp.11, 43, 59.)

lower sort of people . . . , there will be no protection from the plundering mob . . . The Mob must be conquered!! [*]

The "mob," however, not only remained unconquered, but resumed its riotous activities with even greater zeal in the second half of the century; for harvests, far from getting better, tended to become considerably worse, and fifty years of relatively cheap food were followed by a half-century of high and generally rising prices. Thus, between 1765 and 1800, there were harvest failures in 1766-7, 1770-74, 1782, 1789, 1794, and 1799-1800; and the effects of those after 1793 were made the more disastrous by England's entry into the European war. The average price of the quarter of wheat over these 36 years was no less than 55s. (compare the 34s. 11d. of the period 1713-64)—the peak years being 1767, 1774, 1783, 1789, 1795, and 1800, when the price of wheat reached respective upper limits of 60, 64, 64, 62, 92, and 128 shillings.[7] Not surprisingly, such peaks were attended by renewed outbursts of food rioting. Probably the most widely spread were those of 1766, when something like sixty incidents were reported in the press in a dozen weeks.[*] Though prices rose far higher in the next thirty years, riots never reached the same degree of intensity: Dr. Wearmouth instances nine food riots in 1772-3, seven in 1783, eight in 1792-3, fifteen in 1795, and a dozen or more in 1800.

Two general points apply to all the food riots of the century and are perhaps worthy of mention here. One is the large numbers of industrial workers that took part in these disturbances. We constantly read, in this connection, of the activities of Kingswood colliers, Cornish tinners, Staffordshire potters, Tyneside keelmen, and Wiltshire and Somerset weavers. It is another reminder that in England as in France the typical form of social protest at this time, even among wage earners, was the food riot rather than the strike.[†] Another point to note is that food riots tended to break out more frequently in the north and west than in the south and east. This is not really surprising, as the main wheat-growing areas lay in the south and east while their produce, when the export of grain was permitted, was more often shipped from northern and western ports.[8]

[*] See pp. 38-43.
[†] See also Chapter 4.

Food riots were by no means all of one kind. They might take the forms of simple looting of warehouses, attacking the homes of merchants, or stopping grain vessels bound for foreign parts. Or again they might, as in France, take the more sophisticated form of imposing a ceiling on prices, or *taxation populaire*. In fact, this appears to have been a more frequent phenomenon in England than in France—and not only in the eighteenth century: Mr. R. B. Rose, who has written a paper on the subject, gives examples ranging over a period of 150 years, from 1693 to 1847.[9] In the eighteenth century, such price-fixing riots tended to occur in the peak periods of general food rioting and appeared in 1709, 1740, 1756-7, 1766-7, 1772, 1782-3, 1795 and 1800. On such occasions the commodities generally singled out by the rioters were wheat, flour, and bread; and numerous instances are recorded of farmers and grain merchants being made to sell the wheat at the "normal" or "fair" price of 5s. or 5s. 6d. a bushel, of millers being made to sell flour at ls. 6d. a peck or l-3d. a pound, or bakers their bread at 6d. for the quartern loaf. But, more frequently than in France, butter might be seized and sold for 4½, 5, 6, or 7d. a pound, cheese for 5 or 6d., or meat for 2½, 3, or 4d.; and Mr. Rose adds further examples of forced sales at reduced prices of potatoes, bacon, malt, candles, and soap.[10]

It is now time to look more closely at one particular set of riots. I have chosen those of 1766, as they are among the most extensive in England and afford interesting parallels with the French *guerre des farines* of 1775. Unfortunately, in this case the sources consulted do not permit an exact time table of their origins and progress. A close study of the county and Assizes records would, no doubt, yield richer information; but here I have followed their course and pattern mainly in the monthly bulletins of the *Annual Register* and *Gentleman's Magazine*.[11]

Of one thing we may be reasonably certain: these disturbances, whatever their exact point of origin, were strictly related to the shortage and rising cost of grain. No one, even among those most ill-disposed to the rioters, suggested, as in France in 1775, that they had been stirred up by interested political factions.[12] There had been a poor harvest in 1765, and others followed in 1766 and 1767. The poor crop of 1766 was ascribed by the *Gentleman's Magazine* to "much of it being smutty, much blighted, and very much choked with weeds"; and, a week later, a correspondent wrote from East Anglia (normally one of the richest grain-producing regions of the Kingdom) that "the crops of wheat were very bad in Norfolk and Suffolk; bad to a degree not known to us, nor perhaps to our forefathers."[13] The price of wheat at Cambridge rose from 45s. a quarter at Michaelmas (September 29) 1765 to 50s. in 1766 and 60s. in 1767, and remained high until the summer of 1768.[14] In other markets it followed a similar course.

But such figures based on annual returns, although pointing to the general causes of distress, do little to explain the suddenness with which so many small consumers panicked and poured into the markets to seek redress by common action. To explain this, we must look at the monthly returns form certain markets, which show a sudden rise from an almost normal level in the late summer of 1766. At Gloucester, for example, one of the largest of the west-country markets, the bushel of wheat rose from 5s.9d.-6s.1d. in June and July to 7s.-8s.1d. in August and September; at Tewkesbury it rose from 5s.-5s.3d. to 6s.6d.-7s. (and later to 6s.-7s.8d.) and, at Hereford, from 5s.6d.-6s. to 6s.9d.-7s. (and later to 7s.6d.-8s.). Meanwhile, the prices of butter, meat, and cheese also spiraled upwards: at Stourbridge fair, for example, we learn that on September 18 "cheese sold dearer than has been known."[15] And so it seems likely that this sudden increase in the summer and autumn months, rather than the severity of the peak itself, touched off the riots that, in the course of twelve weeks, spread over large parts of the west country (Gloucestershire, Wiltshire, Somerset, Devon, Cornwall, Hampshire, Dorset, Hereford, Worcestershire); the Home Counties of Berkshire, Buckingham, and Oxford; the Midland counties of Leicester, Nottingham, Derby, Warwick, and Stafford; and the East Anglian counties of Norfolk and Suffolk. Like the south and southeast, the north, for once, was largely left untouched. There was one "outrageous" incident at Berwick-on-Tweed, on the Scottish border, in late September; but this appears to have been a defensive measure "on account of the vast quantities of corn that had been bought up for exportation." A report in a London newspaper of riots at Carlisle was flatly refuted by a Yorkshire correspondent. The fact is easily explained. While in late October the price of wheat at Cambridge ranged from 48 to 50s. a quarter, at Carlisle it varied between 29 and

THE ENGLISH FOOD RIOTS OF 1766

36s.,[16] and generally prices were lower in the north than in the Midlands, east, and west.

Riots appear to have begun in Devonshire in the last week in July. On the thirty-first, it was reported that the poor had risen near Honiton, seized the farmers' wheat and sold it in the market at 5s. 6d. a bushel (the current price being around 7s.), "paying the money and returning the bags to the owners." Disturbances followed at Crediton, Ottery, Tipton, and Sidbury, where mills were destroyed and damage done to the value of £1,000. Flour mills were burnt down at Exeter and Stoke. To check the riots, it was reported, local gentry were buying large quantities of flour and selling it to the poor at 3½d. a pound. A week later, farmers at Barnstaple, in North Devon, were compelled to sell their wheat at 5s. a bushel.

On August 7, riots broke out in Berkshire. At Newbury, the market was invaded by "a great number of poor people," who "ripped open the sacks and scattered all the corn about, took butter, meat, cheese and bacon out of the shops and threw it into the streets; and so intimidated bakers that they immediately fell their bread 2d. in the peck-loaf and promised next week to lower it to 8d. per gallon." At neighboring flour mills damage was done to the value of £1,000.

A six-week lull followed, possibly because of the remedial action taken by certain farmers and gentry and the slowness of some markets to reflect the growing shortage of grain. The next report is from September 23; and then no less than eighteen separate outbreaks are grouped together. Somerset, Gloucester, Wiltshire, and Worcester now come into the picture. At Bath, "a great deal of mischief" was done in the market before the crowds dispersed; and at Beckington nearby, a miller who had shot down two rioters had his mill burned down. Gloucestershire was more widely affected. At Malmesbury, the people seized the farmers' wheat, sold it at 5s. a bushel, "and returned the farmers the money." At Tetbury, a crowd carried off cheese and bacon from the warehouses and sold the cheese for 3d. and the bacon for 4d. a pound. At Stroud, a huckster's shop was leveled to the ground; and at Gloucester, the principal farmers, to forestall trouble, supplied the market with wheat at 5s. a bushel. At Hampton, houses were "pulled down," and at Lechlade 6 tons of cheese were unloaded from wagons bound for London. From Wiltshire it was reported that "the whole country are flocking to join the rioters." Near Trowbridge, the county capital, a riotous crowd destroyed a mill and divided the grain among them. At Salisbury, after a preliminary bout of "very serious" disorders, the magistrates agreed to lower the price of wheat and thus averted further trouble. In all, fifty-one Wiltshire rioters were arrested and charged with stealing bacon, cheese, flour, wheat, wine, geese, shoes, and clothes, destroying flour mills and setting fire to ricks.[17]

Further north, in Worcestershire, prices were also reduced by riot. At Kidderminster, farmers were made to sell their wheat at 5s. a bushel; and at Bewdley and Stourbridge (across the Staffordshire border), "they lowered the price of butter, meat and wheat." In Cornwall, the tinners of Redruth and St. Austell joined the movement and "compelled the farmers and butchers to lower their prices." At Oxford, crowds raided flour mills and sold the flour cheap in the market. There were cheese riots at Leicester, Newbury, Exeter, and Lyme in Dorset. Further disturbances broke out in Berkshire; and an informant reported that, on September 26,

> Thomas James with a great Number of other disorderly persons were at John Lyford, the younger, at Drayton and then declared they were Regulators and would lower the Prices of Corn and swore they would be dam'd if they wou'd not take away his wheat and threaten'd to break open his Cottage if he wou'd not open the Doors, and accordingly they went to Lyford's dwelling house and demanded and got the keys of the Cottage and took the wheat away. . . .[18]

The next report comes a fortnight later. On October 11, we read, the inhabitants of Alton in Hampshire were so alarmed by a threatening letter that, "in great consternation," they consented to lower the prices of provisions to the poor. On October 30, a single report in the *Gentleman's Magazine* lists no less than thirty-three separate outbreaks ranging from Devon to Wolverhampton in the west, to Norwich in the east, and passing north as far as Derby, Nottingham, and Leicester in the center. It would be tedious to relate each incident, as the pattern was much the same as before: the same raids on flour mills in country districts; the same invasion of markets and forced sales of wheat and flour at 5s. a bushel, of bread at 2d. (or even 1d.), butter at 6 or 7d., meat at 2½d., and cheese at 2½ or 3d. a pound. There are occasional variations from the common pattern, as at Nottingham, where the rioters only seized cheese from the factors, "leaving the farmers' cheese unmolested"; at Dunnington, where, offered cheese at 2d. a pound, they preferred to have it "for nought"; or at Marlow, where riotous bargemen extorted money from local farmers and gentry and "got themselves intoxicated with liquor" before being clapped into Reading jail. The largest demonstrations appear to have taken place at Nottingham, Derby, Norwich, Birmingham, and other Warwickshire market towns. We may cite the example of Norwich, where:

> a general insurrection began, when the proclamation was read in the market place, where provisions of all sorts were scattered about by the rioters in heaps; the new mill, a spacious building, which supplies the city with water, was attacked and pulled down; the flour, to the num-

ber of 150 sacks, thrown, sack after sack, into the river; and the proprietor's books of account, furniture, plate, and money, carried off or destroyed; the bakers' shops plundered and shattered; a large malt-house set fire to, and burnt; houses and warehouses pulled down; and the whole city thrown into the greatest confusion. During this scene of confusion, the magistrates issued out summonses to the housekeepers in their respective districts, to assemble with staves to oppose the rioters. The conflict was long and bloody, but, in the end, the rioters were overpowered. . . .[19]

On November 15, we read, the Ludlow colliers marched into town to "pull down" a local still-house (Parliament had already forbidden distilling from wheat). But this was an isolated incident and, to all intents and purposes, the riots were over by the end of October. Prices, though generally high until the summer of 1768, had by now taken a temporary downward turn. In part, no doubt, this decrease was due to the measures taken belatedly by the government to assure more plentiful supplies. On September 26, it was ordered by the King in Council that no further wheat should be exported, and soon after licenses were issued for the importation of wheat from overseas. Private initiative also played a part; we have seen how certain magistrates and farmers responded to the riots by reducing the prices of grain and flour. Again, we read of a certain William Hanbury of Kelmarsh in Northamptonshire who, hearing of the riots while on a trip abroad, purchased 100,000 quarters of wheat in Flanders for sale in English markets at 5s. a bushel.[20] But this was only one side of the medal: repression was also used to curb the riots. County militia and military were mobilized, and in some towns and villages farmers took up firearms and householders were issued staves to bring the rioters to heel. One rioter was shot dead at Stroud, two each at Frome and Beckington, and eight on the road to Kidderminster. There were several arrests at Aylesbury, thirty at Norwich, and thirty-four at Derby, and ninety-six were brought to trial at Gloucester. Apart from those tried and sentenced at quarter sessions, larger numbers were tried by the special commissions set up, at an estimated cost of £100,000, in Berkshire, Norfolk, Wiltshire, and Gloucestershire. Three were sentenced to death at Reading, eight at Norwich, and four at Salisbury. At Gloucester, nine were sentenced to be hanged and seven to transportation.[21]

Repression seems, therefore, to have been more severe in England than it was in France in 1775. Other instructive parallels may be drawn between these movements. In both, there was the same quick response to the rising price of bread and wheat. In both, the main center of activity was the market; and it is possible that in England, as in France, the market place was the main center for the purveying of news and rumor to and from other districts. In both, the target of the crowd's hostility was the grain factor or the farmer, though in England, at least, the former was strikingly more so than the latter. In both, a central feature was the forcible reduction of the price of food by riot, in France, exclusively of wheat, flour, and bread; in England, frequently of cheese, butter, meat, and bacon besides. Of the sixty incidents reported in 1766, at least half (though possibly more) were of this kind. In France, this *taxation populaire* almost always took the form of compelling farmers, bakers, and merchants to reduce their prices; in England, as often as not the crowd itself conducted the sale. In either case, the normally determined price of 5s. for a bushel of wheat corresponded remarkably closely to the French "just" price of 30 francs a *setier* (or 2½ francs a bushel). Nor was this a mere coincidence. In both countries, the price was that prevailing in years of good harvests and of normal plenty; and, in both, the old practice of official intervention to protect the poor against famine prices had been abandoned sufficiently recently to live on in popular memory—sufficiently recently, too, for many local magistrates to hanker after the old methods. This was strikingly evident in France in 1775, and in England too the spirit of the old protective Tudor statutes was by no means dead.*

The differences between the two movements, although not so remarkable, are also worthy of note. The French grain riots of 1775 were a single "snowball" movement, spreading in a series of consecutive eruptions from one market to another. The English riots lacked this unity; though having a common origin and purpose and linked in time, they appear rather as a series of separate eruptions. At most (and this is not certain), they may be reduced

* A late eighteenth-century example was the "Speenhamland System" of 1795 (not fully abandoned until 1834), whereby magistrates guaranteed the poor a living wage by subsidizing wages from the poor rate in cases where farmers failed to pay the recommended rates.

to three distinctive "pockets" of disturbance—the west-country outbreaks with a center somewhere about Wiltshire and reaching northwards into Worcester, southwards into Devon and Cornwall, westwards into Hereford, and eastwards into Oxford and Buckingham; an East Anglian "pocket" based on Norwich; and a Midlands "pocket" reaching into the north-central market towns of Leicester, Nottingham, Birmingham, Derby, and Wolverhampton. Yet this is somewhat hypothetical, and the riots may correspond more closely to the separate outbursts in Dijon, Metz, Bordeaux, and other French cities that heralded the *guerre des farines* of May 1775 in the Paris region and adjoining provinces. But there is a more important difference. The composition of the rioters of 1775 and 1766 were not the same. In France, apart from Paris, they were mainly peasants: wine-growers, farm laborers, and village craftsmen. In England, those most frequently mentioned in reports, as in most English eighteenth-century disturbances, were weavers, tinners, colliers, bargemen, or merely "the poor." Nor in England was the same touching faith revealed in the protective role of the monarch: such faith, of course, could hardly be placed in a constitutional King enthroned by consent of Parliament. All of which suggests that the English movement, though traditional, was of a more sophisticated type than the French; but above all, it reflects the different stage of social development that had been reached by the English countryside.

For all this, both movements belong to a similar popular tradition; and both, in their varying ways, are typical of a form of social protest which, in England, survived (as we have seen) until 1847 and in France made its final bow during the revolution of 1848.

REFERENCES

1. G. M. Trevelyan, *England in the Age of Johnson* (London, 1920), p. 7.
2. *Annual Register*, IX, (1766), 149. For my other examples, see *Gentleman's Magazine*, 1731-1800; R. W. Wearmouth, *Methodism and the Common People of England in the Eighteenth Century* (London, 1945), pp. 19-91; M. Beloff, *Public Order and Popular Disturbances 1660-1714* (London, 1938), pp. 77, 139; and T. S. Ashton, *An Economic History of England: The Eighteenth Century* (London, 1955), p. 227.
3. Mainly from *Gentleman's Magazine*, 1731-1800; and Wearmouth, *loc. cit.*

4. T. S. Ashton and J. Sykes, *The Coal Industry in the Eighteenth Century* (Manchester, 1929), pp. 116-22.

5. Wearmouth, *loc. cit.*

6. *Gentleman's Magazine*, XXVIII, 591 (Dec. 22, 1757).

7. T. S. Ashton, *An Economic History of England*, p. 239.

8. D. G. Barnes, *A History of the English Corn Laws from 1660 to 1846* (New York, 1961), p. 13.

9. R. B. Rose, "Eighteenth-Century Price Riots and Public Policy in England," *International Review of Social History*, VI (1961), Pt. 2, 277-92. And, above all, see E. P. Thompson's "The Moral Economy of the English crowd in the Eighteenth Century", *Past and Present*, no. 50, Feb. 1971, pp. 76-136.

10. Wearmouth, *loc. cit.*; Rose, *op. cit.*, pp. 284-5.

11. Public Record Office, T. S. 11/1116/5728, T. S. 11/995/3707; *Gentleman's Magazine*, XXXVI, 385-8, 436, 438, 492-4, 549, 598 (Aug.-Dec. 1766); *Annual Register*, IX (1766), 119, 124-5, 134, 137-40, 150-51.

12. In a recent study, however, Dr. Walter Shelton has argued that the riots, while not being initially incited by the magistrates, were prolonged by the hostility of many to the "forestalling" practices of the grain merchants ("The Role of the Local Authorities in the Hunger Riots of 1766", *Albion*, V, i, Spring 1973, 50-56).

13. *Gentleman's Magazine*, XXXVI, 389 (Aug. 27, 1766), 415 (Sept. 2, 1766).

14. T. S. Ashton, *An Economic History of England*, p. 239; *Economic Fluctuations in England 1700-1800* (Oxford, 1959), p. 181.

15. *Gentleman's Magazine*, XXXVI, 296, 344, 392, 436, 440, 496, 552.

16. *Ibid.*, XXXVI, 436, 438, 504.

17. P.R.O., T.S. 11/1116/5728.

18. P.R.O., T.S. 11/995/3707.

19. *Annual Register*, IX, 139.

20. *Gentleman's Magazine*, XXXVI, 599 (Dec. 30, 1766).

21. *Ibid.*, XXXVI, 598-9 (Nov. 15; Dec. 5, 6, 18, 1766); *Annual Register*, IX, 151; *Gloucester Journal*, Dec. 8, 16, 22, 1766; P.R.O., T.S. 11/995/3707, T.S. 11/1116/5728. According to the *Annual Register*, most of those capitally convicted were reprieved.

THREE

The City Riot
of the Eighteenth Century

If the rural riot was marked by its sensitivity to the rising price of food, the city riot was distinguished by its greater variety. Clearly urban dwellers, among whom wage earners formed so large a part, were as concerned as their fellows in the village or market town with the supply of cheap and plentiful bread. Potentially, therefore, food rioting was as constant a threat to public order in large cities as it was in the countryside; and, in many of Europe's capitals, the "lower orders" or *menu peuple* were as liable to riot in protest against famine prices at times of shortage as for any other cause.[1] But authority, which might be sanguine about periodic outbursts of popular anger in country districts, was less inclined to be so in capital cities and, in consequence, tended to limit such outbreaks by devising special measures to keep the larder stocked. In London, civic authorities and magistrates ensured that markets were well supplied, kept a close watch on the prices of wheat and bread, and reduced their fluctuations in all but the leanest years. In Paris, elaborate steps were taken to supply wheat to suburban millers and flour to the city's bakers: in fact, the preferential treatment given to Parisians was a constant source of irritation to their neighbors and provoked frequent riots among angry villagers along the capital's supply routes.[2] In addition, the policing of large cities, though grossly inadequate by nineteenth-century standards, was taken far more seriously than that of country towns. This was particularly true of Paris; so much so that a chronicler of the early 1780's wrote that, while London might be wracked by serious civil commotion, in Paris this was almost impossible to contemplate.[3]

One way or another, such measures appear to have kept food rioting in abeyance. In London, at any rate, they were remarkably successful. London was certainly not without its riots, and in them, as we shall see, concern for the price of food often played its part even when other issues were more obviously involved. But the undiluted food riot as we have seen it in Chapters 1 and 2 plays virtually no part whatsoever in the record of the city's popular outbreaks. There were, no doubt, minor exceptions: for example, during the Wilkite riots in 1768, a crowd besieging the House of Lords included some who cried "that bread and beer were too dear and that it was as well to be hanged as starved." [4] Yet this was in a year of strikes and general disturbance in which political factors played as large a part as concern for the price of bread.

England was, in fact, in this respect as in so many others, in a quite peculiar position. She had virtually ceased to be a peasant country, and London was, at its most vulnerable point, cut off from the countryside by the protective shield of the near-urban county of Middlesex. Paris, on the other hand, was ringed round by and exposed to the frequent invasion of peasant communities that came to sell or to buy their stocks of vegetables, fruit, grain, flour, and bread in the city's markets. So, in Paris, despite the special measures taken to supply and to police the capital, the food riot might be imported from the neighboring countryside: we have noted the case of May 1775. This, of course, could only happen in years of bad harvest, drought, hail, or frost, or when "monopolists" cornered, or were believed to have cornered, the market. But on such occasions the whole elaborate system would temporarily break down, and panic buying in the market would lead to steep rises in the price of wheat and bread and to outbursts of anger and violence by the Parisian *menu peuple*. This happened in August 1725, when the price of bread rose even higher than in the famine year 1709 and riots became so menacing that the minister responsible was compelled to resign his post. In September 1740, the price of the 4-pound loaf rose to 20 sous (equal to the daily wage of an unskilled laborer); Louis XV was assailed with cries of "Bread! Bread!"; Cardinal Fleury, his Chief Minister, was mobbed by crowds of women; and fifty prisoners at Bicêtre were shot dead after protesting against a cut in their bread ration.

In December 1752, bread riots were coupled with protests against the Archbishop of Paris; and in 1775, as we have seen, Paris had its last taste of a major popular disturbance due to a shortage of food before the outbreak of the Revolution.[5]

Impressive as these demonstrations were, however, even in Paris the food riot was not the predominant type of popular disturbance. There were other forms of protest in which the poorer classes, though by no means challenging the existing order, laid claim to better living standards or to a fuller measure of social justice. In July 1720, the crisis provoked by the Scotsman John Law's financial operations touched off massive riots in the business quarter: 15,000 people gathered in the Rue Vivienne, sixteen were trampled to death, Law's coachman was lynched, and the Palais Royal, home of the Regent, was threatened with destruction. In 1721, a succession of disturbances was caused by the severity of the punishments inflicted on domestic servants: on one occasion, a crowd of 5,000 formed to protest at the whipping, branding, and exhibition in the stocks of a coachman; five were killed and several were wounded. In 1743 in Paris and nine years later at Vincennes, riots broke out in protest at the manner of balloting for the militia. In 1750, a panic followed the arrest of a large number of children, rounded up by the *archers* (armed police) on charges of vagrancy. It was widely believed (and with some justification, as this had in fact happened thirty years before) that the children of the poor were being shipped to the colonies. In the course of a week's rioting four to eight *archers* were killed; and, after sentence by the *parlement* of Paris, three men were executed in the Place de Grève amid scenes of violent disorder. There was even talk—such were the feelings aroused—of marching to Versailles to burn down the royal château.[6]

On this last occasion, the Marquis d' Argenson, who had witnessed the disturbances, deplored the fact that the *parlement*, which had ordered the executions, must now have lost all credit with the common people.[7] His fears proved to have little substance. It was, in fact, the *parlement* which, more than any other body, first drew the Parisian *menu peuple* into political agitation and taught them political lessons that they later, in 1789, turned against their teachers. Quite apart from its judicial functions, the Paris *parlement* claimed, by ancient usage, to be the guardian of the nation's "liberties" and under weak or indolent monarchs re-fused to register royal edicts until its "remonstrances" were satis-fied. It became the firm champion of the Gallican Church against the Jesuits and Ultramontanes; it resolutely opposed the opera-tion of the Bull *Unigenitus* against Jansenist heresy within the Church; and, in the name of "liberty" (a term often synonymous with "privilege"), it resisted the government's attempts to reform the finances by encroaching on the fiscal immunities of aristocracy and clergy. But the magistrates, though largely concerned to safe-guard their own particular interests, were past masters at playing on popular passions in their war on Ultramontane claims or minis-terial "despotism." Already in 1727, the *parlement* headed a com-mon front, composed of the parish clergy, the Parisian *bourgeoisie*, the lawyers, and the common people of the streets, against the Jesuits. The next popular explosion of this kind came in 1752, when the Archbishop of Paris was condemned by the *parlement* and mobbed in the streets of the city for ordering the refusal of the sacrament to dying nuns and clergy who were not prepared to make formal renunciation of their Jansenist beliefs. Soon after, the political battle of the *parlement* against the royal government, largely dormant since the 1720's, began again in earnest. Having studied the "philosophers" (first Montesquieu and later Rousseau), the magistrates translated their political speculations, hitherto re-served for the more fashionable society of the *salons*, into a lan-guage intelligible to the streets and markets, and, in the course of a protracted pamphlet war, indoctrinated Parisians in the use of such catchwords as "citizens," "nation," "social contract," and the "general will." The *parlement's* remonstrances of 1753, 1763, 1771, and 1776 evoked a considerable response among the people. These years were studded with minor disturbances in support of the *parlement's* claims; they reached a climax on the very eve of the Revolution when, in 1787 and 1788, great demonstrations of city craftsmen and journeymen from the faubourgs rioted in sympathy with the exiled *parlement* and acclaimed its return to the capital.[6, 8]

In London, too, the typical eighteenth-century riot was either a form of social protest or a political demonstration; but more often its was compounded of the two. Apart from industrial disputes,[*]

---

[*] Discussed in Chapter 4.

the undiluted social protest without political undertones was comparatively rare: probably rarer than in Paris, at least before the 1750's. There were, however, such occasions: in July 1736, the dismissal of English workmen and the employment of cheaper Irish labor touched off violent rioting against the Irish in Shoreditch, Spitalfields, and Whitechapel; and in August 1794, "a mixed multitude of men, women, boys and children" (to quote one of the Lord Mayor's dispatches) defied the militia and Guards for three days and attacked and destroyed "crimping houses," or houses used for recruiting to the army, in Holborn, the City, Clerkenwell, and Shoreditch. On both occasions, there were sinister rumors of enemy agents at work—in the first case Jacobites, in the second Jacobins—but in neither case do the motives for rioting appear to have been any other than those that were proclaimed.

More often, however, London riots were attached to a political cause. Even if there was no such thing as a "Tory mob" (a term used by some historians), it seems evident that Tory influences were at work behind the riots of 1715 and 1716, when London crowds paraded the streets of the city, Holborn, and Whitechapel to shouts of "High Church and Ormonde," smashed the windows of government supporters, and attacked a Presbyterian Meeting House in Highgate. Yet it was not the dwindling band of Tory politicians, but the Common Council of the City of London, that most often gave the lead. The city, which prided itself on its political independence, opposed the policies of Westminster and St. James's almost continuously throughout the century, and more particularly between 1730 and 1780; and, like the *parlement* in Paris, it became the real political educator of London's "lower orders." It was the city that, in 1733, led the campaign against Sir Robert Walpole's Excise Bill and forced him to withdraw it, after London crowds had besieged Parliament and mobbed the minister to cries of "No slavery—no excise—no wooden shoes!" Three years later, a similar fate befell Walpole's Gin Act, which, though passed by Parliament, became impossible to operate. This time, riots were only threatened—in the form of mock funerals to celebrate "Madam Geneva's lying-in-state"—and actually came to nothing. The same thing happened in 1753, when a combination of City interests, country Tories, and opposition Whigs compelled the

Pelham Ministry, by means of a nationwide agitation and the threat of London riots, to defeat its own Bill for the easier natural-ization of alien Jews.[9]

Up to now, the City Corporation had been allied, in order to wage its political battles, with a group of opposition Tory lead-ers: to that extent, at least, each one of these movements, if not wholly Tory, may be said to have had Tory undertones. This was no longer the case after 1756 when, in clamouring for war with France (and later Spain), the Common Council adopted William Pitt as its champion, helped him into office, and after his dismissal in 1761 conferred on him the City's Freedom, while London's "lower orders" hailed Pitt and booed and pelted the King's favor-ite, the Earl of Bute. The same year, Pitt's principal lieutenant in the City, William Beckford, in standing for election to Parliament, denounced "rotten boroughs" and thereby fired the opening shot in the City's campaign for electoral reform. Thus City radicalism, which challenged the principles of both parliamentary parties, came to birth.[10] From the City's radicalism there stemmed, in turn, the wider movement that rallied to the cause of John Wilkes; and "Wilkes and Liberty" became for a dozen years the political slogan uniting the diverse activities of City merchants, Middlesex free-holders, and the small shopkeepers, craftsmen, and workmen in the London streets and boroughs. After the Wilkite riots came the last and the most violent of London's great upheavals, the Gordon Riots of 1780, when "No Popery" crowds held the streets of the metropolis for a week and caused widespread destruction to both private and public property. This last outbreak was not strictly speaking "political"; but in this case too the rioters drew their initial inspiration, though not their mode of behavior, from a solid body or respectable City opinion.[11] [12]

Let us now follow the same procedure as before and look more closely at a number of these London episodes—the anti-Irish out-break of 1736, the Wilkite riots of 1768, and the Gordon Riots of 1780. At first sight, they may appear to have little in common. The disturbance of 1736 began as a dispute over the employment of Irish labor in the parishes of Shoreditch and Spitalfields, spread-ing later into Whitechapel.[13] In Shoreditch, a certain William Goswell, who was in charge of the rebuilding of St. Leonard's Church, had dismissed a number of his English workmen, who

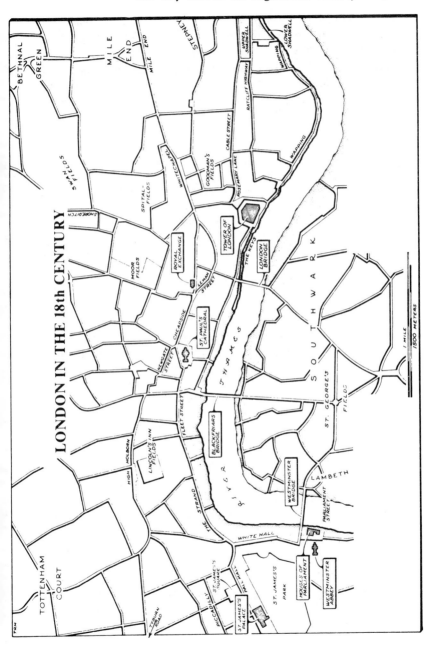

were asking for higher pay, and employed in their place Irish labor at one-half or two-thirds of their wages. A further grievance was that master weavers in both Shoreditch and the adjoining parish of Spitalfields were also employing large numbers of Irish. From this double irritation sprang a two-day riot in the two parishes. It was graphically described by Sir Robert Walpole in a letter to his brother Horace:

> On Monday night last (26 July), there was an appearance of numbers being assembled in a very disorderly manner at Shoreditch, near Spitalfields. Their cry and complaint was of being underworked, and starved by the Irish: *Down with the Irish, etc.* But that night the numbers were not very great, and they dispersed themselves without doing any mischief. . . . On Tuesday evening they assembled again in bodies, and were about 7 o'clock thought to be 2,000 in number. They now grew more riotous; they attacked a public house kept by an Irishman, where the Irish resorted and victualled, broke down all the doors and windows and quite gutted the house. Another house of the same sort underwent the same fate. By this time (those places being within the jurisdiction of the City), the Mayor and Deputy Lieutenant of the Tower Hamlets were assembled in order to disperse them. The proclamation was read; but the mob, wholly regardless of the proclamation, increased every minute, and were thought to be about 4,000 strong. . . . Upon the appearance of the Guards the mob retired, shifted from one street and alley to another, and gave no resistance, and by break of day were all dispersed. All Wednesday things seemed very quiet till evening, when the mob rose again to as great a number; but the Militia of the Tower Hamlets being then raised, marched against them; but the mob in the same manner retired before them wherever they came, and gave not the least resistance . . . and so dispersed themselves before the morning.[14]

Walpole believed that this was "the end to this bustle," but he was over-sanguine. These earlier rioters now joined with others who, on the evening of July 30, attacked Irish dwellings and alehouses in Goodman's Fields and Rosemary Lane in Whitechapel. By later standards, the damage done was comparatively slight: half-a-dozen victims, including Austin Allen of the *Gentleman and Porter* in Leman Street, had their houses "broke"; John Walden, publican of the *Bull and Butcher* in Cable Street, had his shutters and windows smashed; while Ann Pool was robbed of a leg of lamb and two knuckles of legs of mutton. The riots had repercussions in other districts, as we learn from a note in the *Gentleman's Magazine* of August 1 that

> Mobs arose in Southwark, Lambeth and Tyburn-road, and took upon 'em to interrogate people whether they were for the English or Irish? but committed no Violence; several Parties of Horse Grenadiers dispers'd the Mobs which were gathering in Ratcliff-highway, to demolish the Houses of the Irish.[15]

But this was virtually the end of the affair. By August 20, nine prisoners had been secured, of whom five were later brought to trial at the Old Bailey; and Sir Robert Walpole wrote to Horace that "the tumults and disorders here are quite at an end—the industry of the Jacobites was not able to improve this truly Irish incident into a more general confusion."[16]

The Wilkite riots of the 1760's and '70's, of which those of 1768 were the most substantial, were of a very different kind. They were not only political, as those of 1736 were not, but spread over a number of years and inspired by a single unifying slogan. This they owed in part to the extraordinary career and personality of John Wilkes himself, and in part to the political passions aroused in the early years of George III. It all started when Wilkes, having been committed to the Tower of London for libeling the King, was released by order of Chief Justice Pratt at Westminster Hall in May 1763; his discharge was greeted with a shout of "Wilkes and Liberty!", which for a dozen years became the rallying call of his supporters. The same year, when Parliament commanded that Wilkes's offending journal, *The North Briton,* be solemnly burned at the Royal Exchange, the "lower orders" of London's citizens pelted the sheriffs with dirt and refused to allow the public hangman to do his duty. Wilkes, however, was compelled to seek refuge in Paris, was expelled from Parliament, and was declared an outlaw. On his return in 1768, he was elected as their Member by the freeholders of Middlesex; his victory was greeted by tumultuous riots in the Cities of London and Westminster which, for two days on end, the forces of law and order were quite inadequate and unable to contain. The Austrian Ambassador was dragged from his coach; and every lamp and window of the Mansion

Wilkes' supporters in the City of London prevent the burning of No. 45 of his journal, *The North Briton*, at the Royal Exchange (December 3, 1763).

House was smashed, as were the windows of those who, when called to do so, refused to "put out lights for Mr. Wilkes." Having surrendered to his outlawry, Wilkes was confined in the King's Bench prison; its approaches became, for two weeks on end, the scene of further riots, culminating on May 10, 1768, in the "massacre" of St. George's Fields, when the Guards shot into a vast crowd surrounding the prison, killing eleven and wounding a dozen others.

In March 1769, when Wilkes was still in prison, his supporters broke up a cavalcade of City merchants, who were trying to present a "loyal" address to George III; only a bedraggled handful were able to get through to St. James's Palace. Further noisy celebrations attended Wilkes's birthday, his defeat of Luttrell in Middlesex (after a second expulsion from Parliament), and his release from prison in April 1770. Unable to take his seat in the Commons, he now flung himself into City politics; and, as a City Alderman, he played an important part in the great battle that broke out in 1771 between City and Commons over the reporting of parliamentary debates in the public press.[17] In the course of the dispute the Lord Mayor, Brass Crosby, was committed to the Tower, and huge crowds demonstrated at the approaches to Parliament, assaulted government supporters, and hailed George III himself with shouts of "No Lord Mayor, no King!" Three years later, Wilkes's election as Lord Mayor was greeted by a final salvo of broken windows in the City of London. It was the last of the Wilkite riots. The same year, he was able to take his seat in Parliament, and he gradually lost his connections with London's "inferior set of people."[18]

Four years after the last of the Wilkite disturbances, Parliament passed the Catholic Relief Act, which repealed a number of the restrictions imposed on Roman Catholics. It was not a radical measure, and it passed through both Houses without a division. But the attempt to apply the Act to Scotland met with stern resistance; and after violent rioting in Edinburgh and Glasgow it had to be abandoned. Resistance now spread south of the Border. In London a Protestant Association was set up to conduct a campaign for the repeal of the Act. Lord George Gordon, the Association's president, launched a petition that collected 60,000 signatures; and on June 2, 1780, he addressed a vast assembly in St. George's Fields

Rioters set fire to Newgate Prison on the night of June 6, 1780: a dramatic episode in the Gordon Riots.

before proceeding by coach to Westminster, followed by his supporters, who marched in orderly contingents and were said to be
composed of "the better sort of tradesmen." When Parliament,
alarmed by the throng of demonstrators besieging its approaches,
refused to consider the petition, uproar broke loose; and a part of
the crowd moved off to the nearby private chapels attached to the
Sardinian and Bavarian embassies, ransacked them, and burned
their contents in the streets. There followed a week of rioting in
the Cities of Westminster and London, and in Spitalfields, Wapping, Bermondsey, and Southwark, in the course of which Catholic
chapels, schools, dwellings, and pubs, and the houses of both government and opposition supporters, were damaged or destroyed,
half-a-dozen prisons were set ablaze and their inmates released,
and assaults were made on Blackfriars Bridge and the Bank of
England. At the height of the disorders, on the night of June 7,
London appeared to onlookers to be a sea of flames. "I remember,"
wrote Horace Walpole on the eighth, "the Excise and the Gin Act
and the rebels at Derby and Wilkes' interlude and the French at
Plymouth, or I should have a very bad memory; but I never till
last night saw London and Southwark in flames!"[19] It was only on
the seventh day, after 100 houses had been damaged or "pulled
down" to a value of over £100,000, that the military took full
control. Retribution was heavy; 285 rioters had been killed and
another 173 wounded. Lord George Gordon was clapped in the
Tower before being tried and acquitted on a charge of High
Treason. Some of his followers were less fortunate. Of 450 prisoners taken, 160 were brought to trial; and of these twenty-five were
hanged and another twelve were imprisoned. Such were the
Gordon Riots, perhaps the most violent and the most savagely repressed of all the riots in London's history.[20]

I have said that these movements may appear to have little in
common; yet in some respects they all conform to the common
pattern of the eighteenth-century city riot. First, as to the methods of the rioters. In all three episodes (if we limit our picture of
the Wilkite riots to those of 1768), they operated in itinerant
bands, marching (or running) through Shoreditch, the City of
London, Westminster, or Southwark, gathering fresh forces on
the way, but generally they were local men who were perfectly
recognizable to publicans and other local witnesses. These bands

were frequently "captained" by men enjoying temporary authority —men like Tom the Barber, who led a contingent in Goodman's Fields in July 1736; or Thomas Taplin, a coach master, who directed the collection of money "for the poor Mob" in Great Russell Street during the Gordon Riots; and similar leaders were described to the police in the Wilkite riot of March 1768. These men may also have passed on to their followers the slogans of the day: "Down with the Irish!" in 1736, "Wilkes and Liberty!" in 1768, and "No Popery!" in 1780. They may, too, have been bearers of "lists" of houses that were to be "pulled down" or whose windows were to be smashed. Whether such "lists" existed in fact (I have found none among judicial records) or were merely figments of the imagination of informants, it is certain enough that the houses of selected victims were picked out for special treatment. By such direct-action methods considerable damage was done, as we have noted; but it is also important to note that it was strictly discriminating and was directed against carefully selected targets. In the Gordon Riots, considerable care was taken to avoid damage to neighboring property,* and where the wrong targets suffered it was due to the wind rather than to the rioters' intentions. Violence was discriminating in another sense as well. It was limited to property and, of all the lives lost in 1780, it is remarkable that all were from the side of the rioters and not one from among their victims.

Nor were the rioters, on any of these occasions, the "criminal elements," social riff-raff, or "slum population" imagined by those historians who have taken their cue from the prejudiced accounts of contemporary observers. An anonymous informer of 1780 gave the following description of the Gordon rioters:

200 house brakers with tools;
550 pickpockets;
6,000 of alsorts;
50 men that . . . gives them orders what to be done; they only come att night.

---

* While buildings marked for destruction were "pulled down," their movable contents were burned in the street.

But, for all its apparent authenticity, this turns out to be a largely fanciful picture. From the records of those brought up for trial at the Old Bailey, in Southwark, and at the Surrey Assizes we may be reasonably confident that the rioters were a fair cross section of London's working population: two in every three of those tried were wage earners—journeymen, apprentices, waiters, domestic servants, and laborers; a smaller number were petty employers, craftsmen, or tradesmen. In the anti-Irish riots of 1736, as we might expect from their nature and origins, wage earners formed an even larger proportion; whereas in 1768 the Wilkite rioters appear again to have been a similar mixture of wage earners, small employers, and independent craftsmen. Such elements, too, although rarely appearing on the lists of householders assessed for the parish poor rate, were rarely vagrants, rarely had criminal records of any kind, generally had settled abodes, and tended to be "respectable" working men rather than slum dwellers or the poorest of the poor. It is also perhaps a surprising fact that the most riotous parts of London, not only on these occasions but on others, were not the crowded quarters of St. Giles-in-the-Fields or the shadier alleys of Holborn but the more solid and respectable popular districts of the City, the Strand, Southwark, Shoreditch, and Spitalfields.

Other bonds in common between these groups of rioters may be found in the motives that impelled them. Clearly, the ostensible objects of these riots were very different in one case from another: in 1736, to prevent the employment of cheaper Irish labor; in 1768, to celebrate Wilkes's return to Parliament; in 1780, to compel Parliament to repeal the Catholic Relief Act; and these objects were not only overtly proclaimed but genuine enough. But motives in such affairs (and we discuss this point far more fully in Chapter 14) are generally mixed and far from simple: in this sense, the underlying motive may be even more worthy of attention than that more obviously apparent. For the moment, we may discount the often-repeated charge of a "hidden hand"— whether of Jacobites, High Church, or of French or American agents—lying behind such riots: this, too, we shall have occasion to discuss more fully later. Here we are concerned with the genuine interests of the crowd itself. Evidently, crowds so composed would feel the pinch of hunger in times of shortage and, in moments of social tension, might wish to settle accounts with those more prosperous and better favored than themselves. In fact, the short-term economic motive appears to have played a certain part in some of these disturbances, though not in all. In July 1736, the price of the quarter of wheat in London rose sharply to 26-36s. from 20-25s. in June; in March-May 1768, the prices of wheat and bread were high, and had been so for many months; on the other hand, in June 1780, prices were low, as they had been for some time past.* So, in the first two cases, the fear of hunger may have been an inducement to rioting, while it seems unlikely in the third.

A more constant element, perhaps, than hunger is that of a class hostility of the poor against the rich. There is no obvious evidence for this in the riots of 1736, though it may be implicit in the observation made, a month after the anti-Irish riots, by one of Walpole's agents: "It is evident that there are great discontents and murmurings through all this Mobbish part of the Town." But it appears more explicitly in our other two examples. In March 1768, Wilkes's supporters celebrated his election to Parliament by smashing the windows of lords and ladies of opulence and fashion with gay abandon; and they made little distinction in picking out their victims between government and opposition members. This concern to settle accounts with the rich is even more strikingly displayed in the Gordon Riots. Overtly, the rioters proclaimed their hostility to Roman Catholics without distinction; but, as it turned out, the Catholics whose houses were attacked were not those living in the most densely populated Catholic districts (whether in St. Giles-in-the-Fields, Saffron Hill, or the dockside parishes of East London), but in the more fashionable residential areas of the West; and it was not the Catholic craftsmen or wage earners—men similar to themselves—that engaged the rioters' attention, but gentleman, manufacturers, merchants, and publicans. Such evidence of social discrimination might, no doubt, be found, if it were looked for, in other city riots of the time.

---

* Prices of wheat and bread are from the *Gentleman's Magazine*. In London, wheat prices were high and appreciably above average (though fluctuating less violently than in certain country markets) in 1736, 1740, 1756-7, 1766-8, 1772-3, 1775, 1777, and 1793-5.

Another common element among London's "mobbish" population, also noted by Dr. Hobsbawm in the case of other European cities,[21] was hostility to foreigners, or a militant type of chauvinism. "Foreigners" in this sense would include Scots and Irish as well as Frenchmen, Spaniards, Jews, and Roman Catholics. Such feelings are evident in the frequent proclamation of the free-born Englishman's "liberties" and hostility to "slavery" and "Popery and wooden shoes." Irishmen and Catholics were, of course, readily associated with each other, as they were on more than one occasion in the Gordon Riots. Frenchmen and Spaniards were, in addition to being Catholics, the traditional national enemy and therefore obvious targets of popular dislike; and in June 1780, we read of a Portuguese householder (possibly taken for a Spaniard) being assailed as an "outlandish bouger."

The case of the Scots was somewhat different, and here hostility, though intense for a time, was shorter lived. It was largely due, no doubt, to the long association of Scotland with an alien Jacobite cause: in fact, the last of the severed Scottish Jacobite heads of the "forty-five" was still grinning down from its perch on Temple Bar as late as 1772. This antipathy was particularly strong in the early 1760's, when the unpopular Bute became the favorite of George III, and was cleverly exploited by Wilkes and the City radicals. Yet it appears to have died by 1780, for Lord George Gordon, the new popular hero of the hour, was a Scot and it was the Scots that set the English the example of "pulling down" Catholic schools and chapels. At this time, however, England was at war with France and Spain, and London's chauvinism could vent its spleen—and it was by no means confined to the riotous "lower orders"—on Catholics, whether Irish, French, or English. Although some of these antagonisms tended to diminish, others survived to serve as fuel for future riots. Francophobia was one survival: it reappears in the English "Church and King" disturbances of the 1790's* and receives a fresh lease of life in the French Revolutionary and Napoleonic Wars.[22]

In brief, the eighteenth-century city riot arose over issues far more varied than those of the countryside. Yet, beneath the sur-

* See Chapter 9.

face, there were common elements—no less in the methods than in the motives and "generalized beliefs" of its participants. These, even more than the issues themselves, give it its peculiar and distinct identity.

REFERENCES

1. See E. J. Hobsbawm, *Primitive Rebels* (Manchester, 1959), "The City Mob," pp. 10-16.
2. See L. Cahen, "La question du pain à Paris à la fin du XVIIIᵉ siècle," *Cahiers de la Révolution française*, no. 1 (1934), 51-76; and R. C. Cobb, *Les armées révolutionnaires* (2 vols. Paris and The Hague, 1961-3), II, 370-81.
3. L. S. Mercier, *Tableau de Paris* (12 vols. Amsterdam, 1783), VI, 22-5.
4. See my *Wilkes and Liberty: A Social Study of 1763 to 1774* (Oxford, 1962), p. 53.
5. See my *The Crowd in the French Revolution* (Oxford, 1959), pp. 22-4.
6. For Parisian disturbances of the eighteenth century, see *Journal et mémoires du Marquis d'Argenson*, vols. I-IX; E. J. F. Barbier, *Journal historique et anecdotique du règne de Louis XV*, vols. I-IV; D. Mornet, *Les origines intellectuelles de la Révolution française* (Paris, 1933), pp. 439, 444-8, 498-9; M. Rouff, "Les mouvements populaires," in *La vie parisienne au XVIIIᵉ siècle* (Paris, 1914), pp. 263-92.
7. D'Argenson, *op. cit.*, VI, 241.
8. For the Parisian riots of 1787 and 1788, see my *The Crowd in the French Revolution*, pp. 29-33.
9. For the first of these two episodes, see my article " 'Mother Gin' and the London Riots of 1736," *The Guildhall Miscellany*, no. 10 (September 1959); and, for the second, see Thomas W. Perry, *Public Opinion, Propaganda and Politics in Eighteenth-Century England: A Study of the Jew Bill of 1753* (Cambridge, Mass., 1962).
10. Lucy S. Sutherland, *The City of London and the Opposition to Government, 1768-1774* (London, 1959).
11. For a summary of these riots and further sources, see my *Wilkes and Liberty*, pp. 13-14. For the riots of 1736, 1763-74, and 1780, see references 9, 17, 19.
12. For the view that London plebeians had a greater degree of independence, even early in the century, than I have allowed for, see Nicholas Rogers, "Popular Protest in Early Hanoverian London", *Past and Present*, no. 79, May 1978, pp. 70-100.
13. See my article, " 'Mother Gin'."
14. Archdeacon William Coxe, *Memoirs of the Life and Administration of Sir Robert Walpole* (3 vols. London, 1798), III, 348-9.
15. *Gentleman's Magazine*, VI (1736), 484.

16. Coxe, *op. cit.*, III, 357.
17. See Peter D. G. Thomas, "John Wilkes and the Freedom of the Press (1771)," *Bulletin of the Institute of Historical Research*, May 1960, pp. 86-98.
18. See my *Wilkes and Liberty*, pp. 26-7, 33-4, 41-56, 62-6, 155-65, 168-71, 191-2.
19. *The Letters of Horace Walpole, Earl of Orford*, ed. P. Cummingham (9 vols. London, 1891), VII, 388.
20. See my article "The Gordon Riots: A study of the Rioters and Their Victims," *Transactions of the Royal Historical Society*, 5th series, VI (1956), 93-114.
21. Hobsbawm, *op. cit.*, pp. 112-13.
22. For a fuller discussion of these and similar factors, see my article "The London 'Mob' of the Eighteenth Century," *The Historical Journal*, II, i (1959), 1-18.

FOUR

Labor Disputes
in Eighteenth-Century England

We have seen in earlier chapters that in the eighteenth century the typical and ever recurring form of social protest was the riot, and that in English riots it was wage earners rather than others who were the most actively engaged. We have noted, in particular, how frequently industrial workers—Kingswood colliers, Tyneside keelmen, Cornish tinners, silk weavers of Spitalfields, and woolen weavers of Norwich, Yorkshire, and the western counties—took part in such events. But these workers, although more prone in times of hardship to seek redress from grain factors and millers than from their own employers, were also on occasion involved in purely industrial disputes. In modern times such disputes most commonly take the form of a simple withdrawal of labor, and although "blacklegs" may be severely handled, little is done to intimidate employers or to molest their property or persons. Even in the eighteenth century, such peaceable proceedings, though relatively infrequent, were not entirely absent. In 1750 the keelmen of Newcastle, and in 1751 the London tailors, struck work for higher pay; and though both disputes lasted several weeks, in neither case do we read of the strike being attended by violence or disturbance. In Manchester, in 1753 and 1758, there were two remarkably "modern" wages movements: in the first, carpenters and joiners, followed by the bricklayers and their laborers, stopped work for higher pay; and in the second, 10,000 workmen downed tools, forced their more reluctant comrades to join them, and raised funds to conduct the defence of their imprisoned leaders.

In 1765, the opening stages of the great miners' strike in the north-eastern coalfield, which paralyzed the export trade in coal and threw 100,000 colliers and seamen out of work, was of a similar peaceful nature.

Such movements, like all industrial disputes, tended to become more frequent with the industrial revolution in the century's closing years. In 1792, we read, there were similar strikes of Staffordshire potters, Nottingham cordwainers, shoemakers in London and Nottingham, and sailors at Shields and Ipswich; while the first great strike of factory hands, organized on almost modern lines, was that of the Manchester cotton spinners of 1810, in which several thousand men took part and strike pay was distributed, amounting to £1,500 a week.[1]

Another form of peaceful industrial agitation was the petition, addressed to Parliament, to the magistrates, or to the King himself. This remained a fairly common practice as long as the memory, if not the practice, of the old Elizabethan Statute of Artificers, whereby wages were determined by the justices in the counties, still survived. In 1721, it was in response to such representations that Parliament authorized the magistrates to regulate hours and wages in the tailoring trade. In 1764, the London journeymen tailors petitioned the Middlesex justices for an increase in wages and won a small concession. In 1768, a year of high food prices and great industrial disputes in London, not only tailors but glass grinders, coopers, and sailors assembled to present their various petitions to Parliament. Some sailors marched to St. James's Palace "with colours flying, drums beating and fifes playing" and petitioned George III; others, 5 to 15,000 in number, marched to the House of Commons in Palace Yard, left their petition, "gave three cheers," and then dispersed. Two thousand tailors followed suit and petitioned Parliament for a further rise in pay: having received a few encouraging words, "they went away very quickly and peaceably." Five years later, we find a similar combined movement of the trades in London: in that year, silk weavers, coal heavers, watermen, carmen, and porters drew up petitions to the King. This time the magistrates, fearing disorder, forbade the march; but the weavers, at least, received some benefits: their wages were raised and, as we shall see, a system of arbitration for the future was devised.[2]

But such methods were, by their very nature, more appropriate to the capital than to the provinces; or they might, like the peaceful type of strike, be more readily undertaken by trades more skilled or highly organized than others, or at least by those more able to find support in Parliament. Trade unions, or "combinations," were, however, expressly forbidden by Act of Parliament—among tailors in 1721 and 1767; in the woolen trades in 1726; in 1749, in the silk, linen, cotton, fustian, iron, and leather trades and others; and, universally, by the notorious Combination Act of 1799. Under such conditions, to combine in unions was a precarious venture. Unions were generally secret or disguised, sporadic, and short lived; more stable and permanent forms of organization could only be attempted (as indeed they were) by highly skilled and relatively highly paid workers like tailors, curriers, hatters, woolcombers, brushmakers, basketmakers and calico printers.[3] Besides, under the old domestic system and small-workshop method of production prevalent before the industrial revolution, workers generally worked in small groups and found it difficult to concert their efforts except in moments of acute distress caused by rising prices or a sharp decline in trade.

To all such workers, neither the peaceful strike nor the leisurely petition to Parliament appeared as the most appropriate weapon for winning their demands. Acts of violence tended, therefore, to be the rule rather than the exception, and trade disputes tended to develop into riots. To coerce his employer, the worker would on such occasions join with his fellows in "pulling down" his house or in injuring his business by wrecking his workshop, mine, or mill. Thus in December 1738, the Wiltshire weavers and shearmen, in the course of one of the most violent and protracted of all their numerous disputes, succeeded in forcing their terms on the clothiers after engaging in widespread riots and attacking their victims' houses and destroying their property. Similarly, in London in 1739 the journeymen weavers gathered in large numbers before a master weaver's house in Spital Square and attempted to destroy it before the Riot Act was read and they were dispersed by the Guards. In February 1744, we read in the *Gentleman's Magazine*, "a mob of Nailers, consisting of several Thousands, having got together in Staffordshire, in order to raise their Wages, . . . plundered Houses." In July 1763, the journeymen coopers of Liverpool resorted to a more novel form of intimidation: incensed by the conduct of a master cooper, they carried him round the streets on a pole. In the same city, twelve years later, the sailors, when on strike for a 40-shilling monthly wage, paraded through the streets armed "with cannons, guns, muskets, musquetoons, blunderbusses, pistols, swords, cutlasses, knives, clubs, sticks, stones, bricks, and other offensive weapons." [4]

Such violent proceedings might lead to attacks on persons as well as on property. A case in point is that of the East London coal heavers' dispute of 1768.[5] The coal heavers of Shadwell and Wapping were mainly Roman Catholics and, no doubt for that reason as well as for others, were viewed with the utmost suspicion by the authorities. "A few . . . are quiet laborious men," wrote the Treasury Solicitor in preparing a brief against a number of them, "the rest are of a riotous disposition and ready to join in any kind of disorders." The disturbances of 1768 had a dual origin. On the one hand, the men were demanding an increase of 4d. (later 8d.) on every score of sacks unloaded; and when the employers refused to comply, a total stoppage followed in the port of London. The other aspect of the dispute was a protracted "war" between two groups of agents operating rival schemes for registering coal heavers, the one administered by Pitt's City friend, William Beckford, the other by a Middlesex justice, Ralph Hodgson of Shadwell. Besides competing for members, the two agencies took opposing sides in the coal heavers' dispute. Beckford's agents, who were anxious to break the strike, advertised in the press in early April, inviting men willing to work to report to their office. In consequence John Green, one of Beckford's principal lieutenants, was besieged in his public house in Gravel Lane by angry coal heavers armed with cutlasses and bludgeons, who demolished his windows but were repulsed by musket fire. The next day, Hodgson's men resorted to more violent measures: they made an armed assault on Green's house, taunted him with shouts of "Green, you bouger, why don't you fire?," and swore that "they would have his heart and liver, and cut him to pieces and hang him on his sign." Green defended himself stoutly and before escaping to safety over the roofstops shot two of his assailants dead. As a result of this affray, seven coal heavers were sentenced to death at the Old Bailey and hanged in Stepney before a crowd of 50,000, attended by three hundred soldiers and "a prodigious number of peace officers."

The focus now shifted to the other aspect of the dispute. A settlement appeared to be in sight in early May; but the masters refused to consent to a rise in wages and engaged sailors to load and unload their colliers on the Thames. Further violence followed. On May 23, coal heavers boarded the *Thames and Mary,* lying in Shadwell Dock, and threatened to murder any sailor who continued to load. They were as good as their word; and the next day, when sailors came ashore from another collier, the *Free Love,* they were attacked with bludgeons and cutlasses. Two were wounded and a young sailor, John Beatty, was stabbed to death. At Wapping, a week later, two collier captains who had come ashore to buy provisions were beaten up by fifty coal heavers. Soon after, however, the military were called in to help the magistrates, several of the rioters were captured and brought to trial, Beatty's murderer was hanged at Tyburn, and the movement appears to have collapsed.

Far more frequent in the course of such disputes than assaults on persons and private dwellings were attacks on industrial property, workshops, and machinery. This form of "collective bargaining by riot," as it has been called,[6] is to the eighteenth-century industrial dispute what popular price fixing, or *taxation populaire,* is to the contemporary food riot. Both forms of direct action, the one by small producers, the other by small consumers, appear over a similar span of years: attacks on machinery are recorded at least as early as 1663 and as late as 1831.[7] Such attacks, in turn, were of two kinds and had two different (though related) purposes in view: the one to protect the worker's livelihood against wage cuts or rising prices; the other to protect his livelihood against the threat, or the believed threat, of new machinery. They have often been confused and placed under the common label of "Luddism," a term which applies more particularly to the English machine-wrecking riots of 1811-17; though even these, as we shall see, were by no means confined to protests against technical innovation.[*] Such protests played their part, however, as they did

[*] See Chapter 5.

also in these earlier disputes. Particularly was this the case in the opening stages of the industrial revolution: we may instance the destruction by irate spinners of Richard Arkwright's new "water frames" in his Chorley works in 1779 and similar attacks on cotton mills in Blackburn and Bolton and, the following year, at Leeds. An earlier example comes from London where, in 1768, Charles Dingley's new mechanical sawmill in Limehouse was attacked and partially destroyed by a "mob" of five hundred sawyers. Their motives appear clearly from the evidence later given at the Old Bailey by Dingley's principal clerk, who reported that, when he asked the rioters what they wanted,

> They told me the saw-mill was at work when thousands of them were starving for want of bread. I then represented to them that the mill had done no kind of work that had injured them, or prevented them receiving any benefit. I desired to know which was their principal man to whom I might speak. I had some conversation with him and represented to him that it had not injured the sawyers. He said it partly might be so, but it would hereafter if it had not; and they came with a resolution to pull it down, and it should come down.[8]

These, then, are early examples of machine wrecking in its convential "Luddite" sense. But they are by no means typical of the eighteenth-century machine-breaking riot, which, far more frequently, was merely a method of bringing pressure on employers by damaging, or threatening to damage, their economic interests and which displayed no marked hostility to machinery as such. This was a frequent proceeding among the most turbulent of all London's groups of workers, the Spitalfields silk weavers, who from 1663 onwards (and no doubt before) conducted their disputes by cutting the silk in the frame or destroying the looms in their masters' workshops.[*] The West of England clothiers had frequent cause for complaint on the score of similar activities by the domestic cotton workers: in 1718 and 1724 they protested to Parliament that weavers "threatened to pull down their houses and burn their work unless they would consent to their terms." There were such outbreaks in Somerset, Wiltshire, Gloucester, and Devon in 1726-7; in Wiltshire again in 1738, when the weavers

[*] See pp. 72-7.

and shearmen "cut all the chains in the looms belonging to Mr. Coulthurst . . . on account of the lowering of the Prices"; and at Bocking (Essex) in 1740, when spinners threatened to destroy a mill and kill a master webster who had reduced their piecework rates.[9]

Miners' disputes also tended to take this form. In the riots of the 1740's, the colliers of Northumberland burned machinery at the pit head; and the strikes of 1765, having begun as a perfectly peaceable withdrawal of labor, developed into an orgy of destruction, in the course of which the miners cut the ropes of the gins, smashed machinery, flung it down the shaft, and set fire to the coal above and below ground. It was to protect the owners against similar depredations by their colliers that Parliament passed a long series of measures, from the middle years of George II to the later years of George III, imposing heavy penalties for incendiarism in mines.[10]

Of all the groups of workers who used such devices to coerce their employers, none had so long a history of struggle, none were so remarkably persistent, and, maybe, none so violent as the silk weavers of Spitalfields, Moorfields, Stepney, and Bethnal Green in London.[11] On some occasions, when trade as a whole was threatened, masters and journeymen combined in common protest, as when, in May 1765, 8,000 weavers marched to Parliament with black flags and besieged Bedford House because the Duke had defeated a Bill designed to protect the London silk weavers' livelihood by excluding French silks from the English market. Again, in January 1768, masters and journeymen joined in a great march to St. James's Palace to thank the King for reducing the period of Court mournings. Another joint approach to Parliament occurred in 1773. But such demonstrations of solidarity, though in their own way characteristic of eighteenth-century industrial relations, were more often overshadowed by bitter disputes over wages or over the conflicting methods used by rival groups of tradesmen. So it was in the last violent phase of the weavers' stormy history—that of the 1760's and early 1770's. In October 1763, during a wages dispute, 2,000 journeymen weavers disguised themselves as sailors and armed with cutlasses broke into the houses of journeymen who had refused to join them, smashed their looms, wounded several, and burned a master weaver in effigy. Such "cutting" and destruction of looms had by now become a common form of reprisal, and Parliament in 1765, in addition to excluding French silks (as requested by the weavers), tried to end the abuse by making "cutting" a capital offence; but we read in an official report that the journeymen,

knowing their fate, if apprehended, . . . disguised themselves and performed all their exploits in the dead of night, procured arms and offensive weapons of all kinds, beat and abused persons of all ranks and denominations, whom they thought fit to visit for the purpose of cutting their looms and work.[12]

And this was a constant feature of the weavers' outbreak of 1767-9, which will be related in the following pages. It started with a dispute between two groups of journeymen: the single-hand (or "narrow") weavers and those operating the engine loom, which had been introduced from Holland. From a report in the *Gentleman's Magazine* of November 30, 1767 we learn that

A body of weavers, armed with rusty swords, pistols, and other offensive weapons, assembled at a house of *Saffron-hill,* with an intent to destroy the work in the looms of an eminent weaver near that place, but were happily dispersed without much mischief. Some of them were apprehended, and being examined before the justices at *Hick's-hall,* it appeared that two classes of weavers were mutually combined to distress each other, namely the *engine* and *narrow* weavers. The engine-weavers were supposed to be ruinous to the narrow weavers, because, by means of their engines, one of them could do as much in one day as six of the other, and the same kind of work equally good; for which reason the narrow weavers were determined to destroy them.[13]

In the following January there were three cases of assault by single-hand weavers on their opponents' looms in Stepney; one of the assailants was later hanged for the offence. Meanwhile, to add fuel to the flames, the masters had reduced the price of work by 4d. a yard; so a three-cornered fight ensued, in which it is often difficult to distinguish one aspect from the other. After a few months' lull, we read that, on July 26, 1768,

a great number of evil-disposed persons, armed with pistols, cutlasses and other offensive weapons, and in disguise, assembled together about

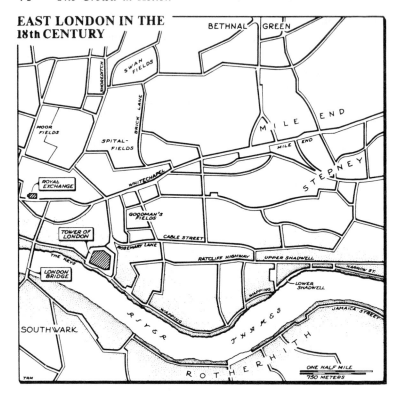

EAST LONDON IN THE 18th CENTURY

the hour of twelve in the night . . . and entered the houses and shops of several journeymen weavers in and near Spitalfields . . . and cut to pieces and destroyed the silk works then manufacturing in nine different looms there.[14]

And, on August 20, the Spitalfields weavers "rose in a body," broke into the house of Nathaniel Farr in Pratt's Alley, cut to pieces the silk in two looms and shot dead Edward Fitch, a lad of seventeen. Rewards were offered, but no prosecution followed.

Shortly after, a partial agreement was reached between masters and journeymen, and some firms drew up new price lists allowing for earnings of 12 to 14s. weekly and more. But as the Middlesex justices refused to endorse the agreement, it was soon broken by a number of the masters and reprisals began again. To promote their cause the journeymen weavers had formed committees for the different branches of the trade, called themselves the Bold Defiance, and levied a monthly contribution of 2 to 5s. a loom to build up a strike fund and meet all expenses. These contributions were collected in conspiratorial fashion at a number of public houses in the weaving districts, to which committee members came in disguise and armed with pistols, swords, and cutlasses. Summonses were sent out to masters and journeymen couched in such terms as:

> Mr. Hill, you are desired to send the full donation of all your looms to the Dolphin in Cock Lane. This from the Conquering and Bold Defiance, to be levied at 4s. per Loom;

and contributors were handed receipts made out as follows:

> Independent and Bold Defiance
> Received . . . shillings . . . Looms.
> Success to Trade.

The "cutters" reopened their campaign in the spring of 1769—both, it would seem, to bring wage-cutting employers to heel and to intimidate those defaulting on their subscriptions. On March 10, we read that Spitalfields throwsters had "extorted money from the masters and committed many outrages." On April 10, William Tilley of St. Leonard, Shoreditch, cut and destroyed a loom and "a warp of thread therein of the value of ten shillings," the property of Lydia Fowler. Further attacks followed in the summer and autumn. During the night of August 7, Thomas Poor, self-employed journeyman weaver of Stocking-Frame Alley, Shoreditch, was visited by a number of "cutters," headed by two of their leaders and committeemen, John Doyle and John Valline. Though Poor protested that he had paid his weekly contribution of 3s. 6d. for the seven looms that he worked with his journeymen for the master weavers, the intruders "cut a large quantity of bombazine silk in the loom," his looms were "cut" again on two subsequent occasions, and, for fear of more drastic reprisals, he was eventually compelled to leave his house and seek nightly refuge "under hedges in the fields." Another target of the "cutters'" animosity was Peter Auber, weaver of Spital Square, who refused to pay the weekly levy demanded. He had his windows broken and was left a number of threatening letters, one of which had an almost lyrical quality:

> Mr. Obey, we give you now an Egg Shell of Honey, but if you refuse to comply with the demands of yesterday, we'll give you a Gallon of Thorns to your final Life's End.

A more substantial victim was Lewis Chauvet of L. Chauvet & Co., silk handkerchief weavers, of 39, Crispin Street, Spitalfields Market. Chauvet's house was besieged by John Valline at the head of a crowd of 1,500 weavers, who "cut" seventy-six of his looms for his failure to contribute to the committee's funds. He only escaped further damage by paying out £2-2s. in beer money and consenting to pay his subscription.

Meanwhile, the authorities had decided to take more vigorous action. At the end of September, the magistrates, supported by the military, made an armed raid on the Dolphin Ale-House in New Cook Lane, in the course of which a soldier was shot dead by the weavers, two "cutters" were killed in the taproom and one of their leaders, Daniel Murphy, found in the landlord's bed, was arrested and later sentenced to death. Publicans who put their houses at the disposal of the "cutters'" committees were threatened with the loss of their licences. Troops were quartered in Spitalfields, and Lewis Chauvet and 150 other master weavers undertook to lodge the officers at their own expense and to feed their men at the Three Tuns Tavern at a cost of 9d. a head per day. The City radicals were incensed and the sheriffs, James Townsend and John Sawbridge—at this time both firm Wilkites—protested energetically and held a meeting with Sir John Fielding, the Bow Street police magistrate. Radical opinion was further outraged by the decision to terrorize the weavers by hanging two of their leaders, Doyle and Valline, in the neighborhood of their crimes. The sheriffs at first refused to execute the warrant; but they were overruled and on December 6, 1769, Doyle and Valline were hanged before a great crowd of weavers near the Salmon and Ball, Bethnal Green.

This was the end of the silk weavers' affair of the 1760's; but their distress continued, and none of their problems had been settled. In 1773, when there were 12,000 unemployed journeymen weavers in Spitalfields, Bethnal Green, and Shoreditch, there was a revival of riots and of joint approaches to Parliament. Under this combined pressure, Parliament passed the Spitalfields Act, which virtually gave a fresh lease of life to the old Tudor protective legislation by empowering magistrates to fix the rates of wages and to enforce their observation. But it also led to a remarkable innovation. To keep the magistrates fully apprised of the state of trade, the weavers formed a permanent organization, known as the "Union"; and it was through this body that both masters and men presented their case before the justices; and it was as a result of these representations that piecework rates were periodically determined.[15]

And so the London weavers' riots, which are as typical as any of the eighteenth-century industrial dispute, ended in the creation of a novel form of negotiating machinery that anticipates the arbitration procedures of more recent times.

REFERENCES

1. T. S. Ashton and J. Sykes, *The Coal Industry in the Eighteenth Century* (Manchester, 1929), pp. 89-91; T. S. Ashton, *Economic Fluctuations in England 1700-1800* (Oxford, 1959), p. 167. P. Mantoux, *The Industrial Revolution of the Eighteenth Century* (London, 1948), pp. 461-2; R. W. Wearmouth, *Methodism and the Common People of England of the Eighteenth Century* (London, 1945), pp. 19-50.
2. See my *Wilkes and Liberty: A Social Study of 1763 to 1774* (Oxford, 1962), pp. 91-5; Wearmouth, *loc. cit.*
3. T. S. Ashton, *An Economic History of England: The Eighteenth Century* (London, 1955), pp. 23-31; S. and B. Webb, *The History of Trade Unionism* (London and New York, 1896), Chapters 1 and 2.
4. R. B. Rose, "A Liverpool Sailors' Strike of the Eighteenth Century," *Transactions of the Lancashire and Cheshire Antiquarian Society*, LXVIII (1958), 85-92.
5. See my *Wilkes and Liberty*, pp. 95-8.
6. By E. J. Hobsbawm in "The Machine Breakers," *Past and Present* (Feb. 1952), pp. 57-70.
7. M. Beloff, *Public Order and Popular Disturbances 1660-1714.* (London, 1938), p. 87; John Prest, *The Industrial Revolution in Coventry* (London, 1960), pp. 30, 48.

8. Old Bailey *Proceedings,* 1768, p. 256; quoted in *Wilkes and Liberty,* pp. 93-4.

9. Contemporary accounts cited by Hobsbawm, *op. cit., p.* 59; Wearmouth, *loc. cit.*

10. Hobsbawm, *loc. cit.;* Ashton and Sykes, *op. cit.,* pp. 89-91.

11. For most of what follows and for sources consulted, see my *Wilkes and Liberty,* pp. 98-103. (My thanks are due to the Clarendon Press for allowing me to reproduce pp. 100–102 almost *in extenso.*)

12. Public Record Office, Treasury Solicitor's Papers, 11/818/2696: "The Case against Daniel Murphy for the wilful murder of Adam McCoy."

13. *Gentleman's Magazine,* XXXVII (1767), 606.

14. *Annual Register,* XI (1768), 139.

15. S. and B. Webb, *op cit.,* pp. 48-9; Ashton, *Economic Fluctuations,* pp. 75, 158; P. Mantoux, *op. cit.,* p. 83.

FIVE

Luddism

The years of the Regency were among the most disturbed and
riotous in England's recent history. Radical agitation revived; and
the City of London, quiescent since the early 1780's, resumed its
duel with the Ministers of the Crown. In May 1812, the Prime
Minister himself, Spencer Perceval, was assassinated in the lobby
of the House of Commons. The same year there were food riots
and a recrudecence of *taxation populaire* in places as widely dispersed as Falmouth, Bristol, Sheffield, Nottingham, Bolton, and
Carlisle; and Londoners rioted against the Corn Law of 1815.
There were the Spa Fields riots in London and agricultural disturbances of the following year. It was a period of minor rebellions
and risings of the poor: such as the march of the so-called "Blan-
keteers" from Manchester, the Pentridge "revolution," and the
Huddersfield "rising" of 1817; and, two years later, the yeomanry
cut down a great reform meeting in the massacre of "Peterloo" at
Manchester. As sensational as any of these episodes, while they
lasted, were the Luddite riots in the midlands and northern counties. They proved remarkably destructive and tied up a considerably larger military force than Wellington took with him on his
first expedition to Portugal in 1808. At the height of the disturbances in the summer of 1812, there were more than 12,000 troops
stationed in the Luddite districts between Leicester and York;
and the machinery and property destroyed may, when all was
over and done with, have amounted to a value of over £100,000.[1]

Broadly speaking, there were several types of Luddite* activity.

---

* The name "Luddite" is said to derive from a certain Ned Ludlam, a
Leicester stockinger's apprentice, who, being reprimanded, lost his temper
and smashed his master's frames with a hammer. F. O. Darvall, *Popular Disturbances and Public Order in Regency England* (London, 1934), pp. 1-2.

79

There were, in the first place, the two types of machine breaking that have already been discussed in the previous chapter: the type directed against employers to force them to make concessions, and that directed against the use of machinery as such. In addition, there were food riots, which on occasions but by no means always overlapped with the Luddites' machine-wrecking activities; there were conspiracies involving "twisting-in" or the administration of illegal oaths; and there were so-called "Luddites" —self-styled or so named by the authorities—who took advantage of the general commotion to extort money, rob farmhouses, or search for arms. All these riotous activities tended to attract a common label; but it is only with the first two kinds of Luddism that we are here primarily concerned.

There were one major and three minor waves of Luddism. The major wave was that of 1811-12, which started in the lace and hosiery trades of the midlands counties of Nottingham, Leicester, and Derby and spread among the croppers and cotton weavers of Yorkshire, Cheshire, and Lancashire. The minor waves were those of the winter of 1812-13, the summer and early autumn of 1814, and the summer and autumn of 1816. The first wave of riots owed its origins to the calamitous state of trade and deplorable harvests of 1809-12; and all these disturbances whether of framework knitters or shearers, whether of machine wreckers or food rioters, had a common origin in the widespread distress of England's manufacturing districts during the closing stages and aftermath of the Napoleonic Wars. The industrial depression of 1811 was due not so much to the operation of Napoleon's Continental System— though this cut off trade with Europe—as to the sudden closure of the American market in response to Britain's retaliatory Orders in Council. Banks failed and the export trade collapsed. On top of this came a succession of bad harvests from 1809 to 1812. The price of wheat, which averaged 107s. 3½d. per quarter for the period 1800-1813, rose, in August 1812, to the unprecedented peak of 156s. in London and to 180s. in Yorkshire. Thus a stockinger, who even when fully employed might earn as little as 7s. to 14s.6d. a week, or a handloom weaver, whose weekly wage in 1812 was 9 to 12s., now paid as much as 1s.5d. or 1s. 8d. for his daily quartern loaf.[2]

While distress was general, it was markedly more severe in the areas producing for the export market than in others. A case in point was the home of the lace and hosiery trades in the midlands counties, centered around Nottingham and branching out into Derbyshire and Leicestershire. Here the merchant hosier rented his frames to the master stockinger, who in turn employed framework knitters to carry out his work. It was an industry with a long and stormy history: machine breaking was a recognized form of industrial action, and cases are recorded as early as 1710. Disputes arose over wages, frame rents, the number of apprentices employed, and the promotion of cheap and shoddy work. Such matters became the more urgent in times of trade decline; and, on such occasions, if negotiations with the hosier or petitions to Parliament failed to give early satisfaction, tempers became frayed and rioting might follow. So it was in 1811, when negotiations had long been going on over wages, frame rents, and "cut-up" stockings made on wider frames: the latter was a particular bone of contention as it led to shoddy work and called for unskilled labor at lower wages. And, when negotiations broke down, this was the issue that provoked disturbance and launched the mythical *Ned Ludd* on his stormy career.

The first outbreak occurred in February 1811 at Arnold, a small town near Nottingham, where "cut-ups" were being manufactured on the wider frames. Framework knitters broke into the workshop of the hosiers concerned and disabled their frames by removing the jack-wires. It served as a signal to the neighboring districts; and meetings began to take place, among them a rally of stockingers in the market place of Nottingham. A further riot followed at Arnold; and by early April, when the arrival of the military put a temporary stop to the disturbances, over 200 of the offending frames had been destroyed.

A lull followed, but in November a new outbreak occurred, as unexpected as the first. It took place in the village of Bulwell; and it was in Bulwell Forest, where framework knitters assembled and took their orders, that the name of their commander, Ned Ludd, first was heard. This time, although still largely confined to the area around Nottingham, the attacks were made over a wider field; and on the same night frames were broken in villages and

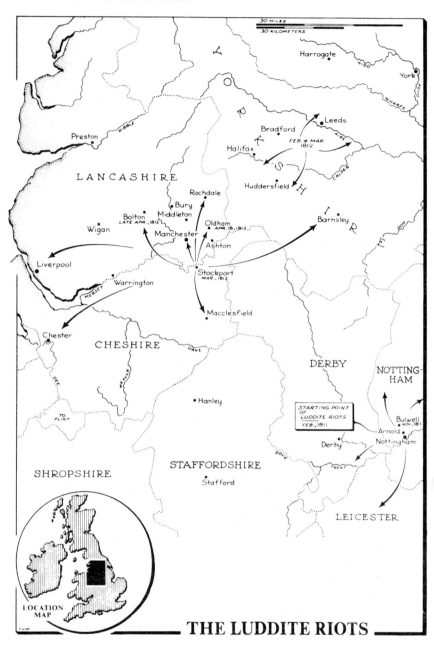

THE LUDDITE RIOTS

towns lying twelve or fifteen miles apart. The Luddites were well organized; they appeared in closely knit bands and evidently enjoyed the support of the local population; and certainly the master stockingers, whose frames they shattered, were more sympathetic to their claims than to those of the hosiers from whom they rented them. Besides, the Luddites acted with discrimination and chose selected targets: there was, as in other similar movements, talk of "lists" of persons whose frames should be destroyed. They also collected money to promote their cause; and to one stockinger whom they visited the following letter was read:

> Gentlemen all. Ned Ludd's Compliments and hopes you will give a trifle towards supporting his Army as he well understands the Art of breaking obnoxious Frames. If you comply with this it will be well, if not I shall call upon you myself. Edward Ludd.[3]

Meanwhile, further troops were summoned; and in December, General Dyott was ordered to Nottingham with a force of 2,000 men, "a larger force [it was announced in the Commons] than had ever been found necessary in any period of our history to be employed in the quelling of a local disturbance."[4] New constables and "specials" were sworn in, proclamations were read, and responsible citizens were alerted to help to round up malefactors. Such measures helped, after the first weeks of rioting, to check the movement in Leicestershire and Derbyshire; yet up to February 1812 cases of frame breaking in northwest Nottinghamshire and at Nottingham itself continued at the rate of 200 frames a month. In these districts the outbreaks ended as much as the result of conciliation as of repression. By early December, the town and country magistrates began to offer mediation. Meetings were held between representatives of the hosiers and framework knitters; and several hosiers offered to pay higher rates of wages, and even to give up making cut-up stockings. After several false starts and a temporary revival of disorders, the stockingers won a short-lived victory: there was no formal agreement, but hosiers found it expedient to abandon "cut-ups" and to pay higher wages. Besides, both sides had begun to seek redress through petitions to Parliament. The most striking outcome of this was the Frame-Breaking Bill, which Parliament adopted on February 14, 1812 and which made frame breaking a capital offence. But by this time the riots in the lace and hosiery districts had virtually ended. There was a short revival in the winter of 1812-13, yet this was on an altogether lesser scale; and, to all intents and purposes, by the spring of 1812, Luddism was already dead in the counties of its birth.

Meanwhile, however, the focus of disturbance had shifted to the northwestern counties of Lancashire and Cheshire. This was the home of the newly mechanized cotton industry, the center more than any other of England's industrial revolution, whose great commercial and manufacturing cities, Liverpool and Manchester, were second only to London in population. Yet the factory system was still in its infancy, having only been firmly established in cotton spinning; and the typical Lancashire worker was still as likely as not a handloom weaver, who worked at home in what was once a village and had hardly yet become a town. The steam loom, which would shortly transform and uproot this labor, had only made its first appearance: in 1806, four factories were so equipped, and by 1813, there were still barely more than a dozen. The new machinery was viewed with suspicion by the weavers; but, as long as trade was relatively good and food was in fair supply, their opposition had been half-hearted. Wages had, it is true, been steadily declining over a number of years, but there was no sudden cataclysmic crisis until the closure of the American market, the general trade depression, and succession of bad harvests threw men out of work and sent the prices of food rocketing in the manufacturing districts. At this point, it seemed as reasonable to blame the steam loom as the miller or provision merchant for the state of affairs; and it is hardly surprising that the disturbances that followed, whether in the form of food rioting or machine breaking, should have been mainly centered around Stockport, Bolton, Middleton, and Manchester, all towns in which the new mechanical devices had been introduced.[5]

Besides, there was the contagious example of the Nottinghamshire Luddites and already, by the end of 1811, there were reports in the cotton towns of secret meetings between the framework knitters' delegates and those of the Manchester and Stockport weavers. Manufacturers employing steam looms began to receive threatening letters, and late in February 1812 a Stockport magistrate wrote that the weavers "certainly do meditate the destruction of the Looms worked by Steam and employed in factories." In March, a first attack was made at Stockport on a warehouse belonging to a Mr. Radcliffe, described as "the original projector of the obnoxious looms": a few windows were broken, but an attempt to set fire to the building failed. At Bolton, meetings were held on the moors outside the town, and there was talk of men with blackened faces wandering around and administering illegal oaths by night. At Manchester, rioting assumed political overtones: a meeting of merchants convened at the Exchange Dining Room to vote a loyal address to the Prince Regent was broken up by invading crowds, while (adds a newspaper report) "the mob in the Square *were reading and passing the resolutions of the livery of London!*"[6] Food riots followed at Rochdale, Oldham, Barnsley, Bolton, and Macclesfield: at Macclesfield, rioters ransacked provision shops and stormed the jail to release a prisoner.

Properly speaking, however, these were not "Luddite" outbreaks: no specific attempt was made to damage machinery. The next outbreak of this kind came once more at Stockport, where, on Sunday, April 14, crowds milled about the town, broke windows, and threatened vengeance on the owners of steam looms. Led by two men disguised as women, who were hailed by their followers as "General Ludd's wives," they stoned the house of Joseph Goodair, an owner of steam looms, at Edgeley and later returned with reinforcements to fire his house and cut up the work in his looms before destroying the looms themselves. When, four days later, rioting was stopped by the military at Stockport, it broke out at Oldham. It began as a food riot, in which shopkeepers were called upon to sell their wares more cheaply, and developed into an attack on Daniel Burton's steam-loom factory at Middleton. The attack was repulsed, and five of the assailants were killed and eighteen wounded; but next day, headed by the colliers of nearby Holmwood, the crowds returned and completed their work. The riots spread to the neighborhood of Bolton. A few days later the *Annual Register* reported:

On Friday afternoon, about four o'clock, a large body of rioters suddenly attacked the weaving factory, belonging to Messrs. Wroe and Duncroft, at West Houghton, about thirteen miles from this town; of which, being unprotected, they soon got possession. They instantly set it on fire, and the whole of the building with its valuable machinery, cambrics, &c. were entirely destroyed. The damage sustained is immense, the factory alone having cost 6,000 l. The reason assigned for this horrid act is, as at Middleton, "weaving by steam." By this dreadful event, two worthy families have sustained a heavy and irreparable injury, and a very considerable number of poor are thrown out of employment. The rioters appear to level their vengeance against all species of improvement in machinery. Mistaken men!—what would this country have been without such improvements? No one of the incendiaries are taken, nor was there any soldier in that part of the country.[7]

Disturbances continued at Liverpool, Manchester, and in the Stockport district; but gradually magistrates who had been reluctant at first to summon the militia began to enroll special constables, to operate the old Watch and Ward, to organize substantial citizens in voluntary associations, and to cooperate with the regular forces arriving from other parts. General Maitland was placed in supreme command of a mixed force that included eight regiments of infantry and three of Horse Guards and Dragoons. Bodies of troops, operating in small units in association with constables and spies, moved rapidly around the disaffected area, broke up the Luddite bands, and made arrests. Over a hundred prisoners were brought to trial before Commissions of Assize at Lancaster and Chester at the end of May. At Lancaster, 8 were sentenced to death and 13 to varying periods of transportation. At Chester, of 15 sentenced to death, 4 were hanged; and a total of 17 were eventually shipped to New South Wales.[8] In June the Orders in Council were repealed, which brought some relief to the export trade. By July, Luddism in the cotton districts of the north was virtually at an end.

The third focal point of Luddism lay in the Yorkshire moors, in the Spen Valley between Huddersfield and Leeds. This was the center of the cropping or shearing branch of the woolen industry, in which the master cropper (like the master stockinger in Nottinghamshire) employed small groups of journeymen and apprentices to carry out the work farmed out to him by the wealthy clothier. No clear class division separated masters and journeymen, who shared a tradition of sturdy independence and were generally on cordial terms. Like the framework knitters of the midlands and the weavers of the northwestern counties, the Yorkshire shearmen were suffering from the effects of poor harvests and trade depression; and like them they resorted to machine breaking to protect their livelihood. In their case the machine was a comparatively simple device, a double pair of shears working on a frame, far simpler to handle than the traditional hand shears, and not repugnant to the craftsman like the hosier's "cut-up" frame; but, as a means of saving labor, it endangered his employment when trade was bad and work was scarce.[9] The new machine had been resisted by the croppers since its introduction in the West Riding half-a-dozen years before; but they had resisted by peaceful means, and only in the bitter conditions of the winter of 1812 did opposition take the form of open violence. In mid-January, rumors began to circulate of a pending outbreak. A sworn witness gave evidence before the Leeds magistrates of "a conspiracy to destroy the Machinery of certain Mills employed in the dressing of cloth." A few days later, the Oatlands mill of Messrs. Oates, Wood, and Smithson near Leeds was set on fire; and reports became rife of the sound of musket fire and marching feet across the moors. These reports assumed a more solid substance in early February, when small groups of men, armed and with blackened faces, went round the towns and villages, forcibly entering the homes of the master craftsmen, and breaking their shearing frames or dressing machines before their eyes: no less than nine such cases of machine breaking were reported in the area of Huddersfield between February 23 and March 11. Among the victims was William Hinchcliffe, cloth dresser of Golcar, who swore before witnesses

that, about the hour of One in the Morning of the 27th. of February Instant himself and family were alarmed by a Gun being fired through his window, when he saw a large number of people about his house— that soon afterwards the Door of his Shop was broken open and he heard a number of People rush in, and a great Noise of Hammers striking the frames and Shears there . . . That as soon as they were gone, this Examinant went out to see what they had done and found Five Dressing or Shearing frames and about Thirty pairs of Shears broke to pieces.

At Huddersfield a Mr. Smith, who had made himself unpopular by his liberal use of the new machine, received a threatening letter from "Ned Ludd, Clerk," who styled himself "the General of the Army of Redressers"; it was couched in the following terms:

Sir,
    Information has just been given in that you are a holder of those detestable Shearing Frames. . . . You will take notice that if they are not taken down by the end of next week I shall attach one of my Lieutenants to destroy them . . . and if you have the impudence to fire at any of my Men they have orders to Murder you and burn all your Housing. . . .[10]

Such threats were fairly common among the Yorkshire Luddites, who enjoyed a deservedly higher reputation for violence than their fellows in the other counties. A particular target of their animosity was William Cartwright of Rawfolds, one of the principal promoters of the new machine and active in the voluntary associations set up by the clothiers to protect their interests. On April 11, 150 armed men met at Coopers' Bridge to mount an assault on Cartwright's mill. But their intended victim, being forewarned, had taken the precaution to summon support and to barricade himself behind massive doors; so that, when the alarm was given, the assailants were met with a sharp volley of gunfire that killed two and put the rest to flight. A week later, an attempt was made on Cartwright's life. He escaped; but another manufacturer, John Horsfall, chairman of the Huddersfield Committee for the Suppression of the Outrages, was not so fortunate. Returning one night at the end of April from the Huddersfield Exchange, he was shot dead. It was, in fact, for all the threats and violent talk, the only outrage of its kind; and it may well have lost the Luddites as much support among the relatively uncommitted as it terrorized manufacturers into abstaining from using shearing frames. At any rate, from now on machine breaking virtually ceased; and after May, although there continued to be much talk of "Luddite" activity, it was not in terms of broken frames or assaults on factories and mills, but of raids for arms, collections of money and provisions, or, most often, common robbery. Once more, as in Lancashire and Cheshire, the deployment of the militia, the use of spies, and the disposition of mobile regular army units played a considerable part in bringing the movement to an end: by early September, there were 1,000 troops billeted in thirty public houses in Huddersfield alone.[11] So the Luddite bands were tracked down and broken up. As in other areas, informants were at first slow to come forward, but during the summer and autumn some one hundred prisoners were taken and lodged in York Castle. Of these, 64 came up for trial before a Special Commission in January 1813. Half were acquitted; 7 were transported for 7 years (for taking illegal oaths, and therefore not strictly for Luddite activity); 3 were hanged for the murder of Horsfall, and 14 more for a variety of misdemeanors.[12]

After the York trials and executions, Luddism collapsed in all the counties of the north. As we have seen, it had an occasional and short-lived revival in the midlands in the early months of 1813, in the summer and autumn of 1814, and again in 1816. But these were altogether minor outbreaks and added a mere couple of hundred broken frames to the 1,000 already destroyed.[13]

It now simply remains to discuss a few general questions. Had the Luddites achieved their objects? These objects, as we have seen, for all the uniformity of Luddite practice, varied from one group of counties to the other. The croppers of the West Riding, and the handloom weavers of Lancashire and Cheshire who attacked steam looms at Stockport, Middleton, and Westhoughton in 1812, were certainly hostile to the new machinery, and their main object (though not their only one) was to destroy it and to prevent its further use. But the midlands Luddites, who not only launched the movement but did the greatest damage to machines, had no such primary intention: they were merely using attacks upon machinery as a means of coercing their employers to make concessions in wages and in other matters concerning their employment. The point is aptly made in a proclamation claiming to have been issued from "Ned Lud's office, Sherwood Forest" in the winter of 1811-12, in which hosiers and lace manufacturers are warned that the Luddites would

break and destroy all manner of frames whatsoever that make the following spurious articles and all frames whatsoever that do not pay the regular price heretofore agreed to by the Masters and Workmen. . . .[14]

Of course, contemporaries confused by all the bustle, rumors, and commotion were inclined to read far deeper and more sinister designs into these activities; and the magistrates and government themselves, though better informed than the general public, could hardly fail to associate machine breaking with the political reform movements and minor conspiracies and "revolutions" that were also a feature of these years. Thus there was a disposition to believe that the Luddites were really out to overthrow the government by force. Dr. Darvall's careful examination of the evidence shows that there is little substance, in fact, in such a view. Yet we have seen that there were moments when Luddism might overlap with, or impinge upon, a movement whose object was to remove, though not to overthrow, the government. Such was the case at Manchester in April 1812, when an angry crowd—said to have been largely composed of weavers[15]—broke up a meeting of "loyal" merchants and endorsed the anti-ministerial resolutions of the City of London. Again, "Ned Ludd's" letter to Mr. Smith of Huddersfield, from which we have already quoted, added the intention to unseat by force "that damned set of rogues, Perceval and Co., to whom we attribute all the miseries of our Country." Nor is it surprising that such views should find occasional expression in Luddite literature (or what purported to be such), as the Perceval government's use of the Orders in Council was widely held responsible for the deep depression that had fallen on the export trade. Even if Luddism had such occasional political overtones, however, they were intrusive rather than intrinsic to a movement whose essential objects were to prevent the use of machinery or merely to coerce the employers.[16]

Within these limits, Luddism had successes though they proved short lived. The Nottingham hosiers gave up making "cut-ups," reopened negotiations with the stockingers, and offered higher wages. The Yorkshire woolen masters, under the first impact of the Luddite terror, laid up their shearing frames; only in the northwestern counties, where the factories using steam looms were few and large, no concessions, even temporary, were made. What successes the Luddites achieved were due to their remarkably flexible tactics, their highly developed organization, the nature of the country in which they generally operated, and, above all, to the widespread public sympathy that they undoubtedly enjoyed. It was this, even more than the terror they inspired, that made it so difficult for the authorities to secure early arrests and convictions. But such successes could not, in the nature of things, be lasting.

The militia, though in some places considered liable to disaffection, proved to be trustworthy and effective, particularly when buttressed by regular army units and supported by the pervasive activities of a host of government spies. Once the forces of law and order had mastered their opponents' tactics and were intelligently deployed, the Luddite bands stood little chance against the 12,000 troops that had been mustered to defeat them. And once their ringleaders, or those reputed to be such, had been brought to trial and thirty of them hanged, the hosiers and clothiers took fresh heart and withdrew their temporary concessions; even where the employers did not do so, their momentary gains were swallowed by the depression of the subsequent years.

Yet, for all this, Luddism was by no means a merely blind and futile gesture by ignorant and desperate men; still less, of course, a last-ditch attempt to arrest the course of technical progress. It was certainly, like the modern strike, an action not lightly undertaken but undertaken nonetheless when more peaceable and leisurely negotiations failed to bring redress. Machine breaking had a long—should we say time-honored?—tradition, and the northern and midlands Luddites were merely engaging on a wider scale in a form of action that miners, weavers, sawyers, and others had practiced over many generations. Such methods, as we have seen, were well suited to a time when industry was still widely scattered over villages and moorlands, or in the suburbs of small towns, before the new factory town had yet come into its own. This was still the case, though it would not last for long, in Regency England; and it is no coincidence that the next—and the last—great outbreak of machine wrecking would be the work not of industrial but of agricultural workers.° For, apart from minor survivals, after 1817† industrial machine breaking had already had its day. Luddism, like other forms of popular action appropriate to the pre-industrial age, had no future in the new industrial society.

° See Chapter 10.
† As, for example, the burning down in 1831 of Beck's factory at Coventry by weavers who feared for their employment (J. Prest, *The Industrial Revolution in Coventry* (London, 1960), pp. 30, 48). Stocking frames were broken at Leicester as late as 1833 (the convict record of David Bland, a house servant, Tasmanian State Archives, MSS. 2/135, 2/393).

REFERENCES

1. F. O. Darvall, *Popular Disturbances and Public Order in Regency England* (London, 1934), pp. 259-60, 209-10. I have depended largely on Dr. Darvall's book for my account of these riots. But see also E. P. Thompson, *The Making of the English Working Class* (London, 1963), pp. 494-602.
2. Darvall, pp. 18-21, 33, 54; *Monthly Magazine*, XXXIV, 272 (October 1, 1812).
3. Cited by Darvall, p. 72.
4. Cited by Darvall, p. 73.
5. *Ibid.*, pp. 49-58.
6. *Monthly Magazine*, XXXIII, 387 (May 1, 1812).
7. *Annual Register*, LIV, "Chronicle," 61-2 (April 26, 1812).
8. Darvall, *op. cit.*, p. 104, *Annual Register*, LIV, "Chronicle," 78-9, 84-5; *Gentleman's Magazine*, LXXXII(1), 582-3; Mitchell Library (Sydney), MS. 4/4004: Indents of Convict Ships, 1801-14.
9. Darvall, *op. cit.*, pp. 58-63.
10. *Gentleman's Magazine*, LXXXII(1), 285 (March 1812); Darvall *op. cit.*, pp. 106-13.
11. *Ibid.*, p. 124.
12. *Ibid.*, p. 130; *Annual Register*, LV, "General History," 98; *Gentleman's Magazine*, LXXXIII(1), 80-81.
13. Darvall, *op cit.*, p. 209.
14. *Ibid.*, p. 170.
15. *Gentleman's Magazine*, LXXXII(1), 381 (April 1812).
16. This view can no longer be sustained since E. P. Thompson devoted a long chapter to establishing a continuity between Luddism and the earlier political "conspiacies" in which workers were involved (*The Making of the English Working Class*, pp. 521-602). M. Thomis, however, arriving later on the scene discounts a great deal of his argument (*The Luddites*, Newton Abbot, 1970).

SIX

The French Revolution:

(1) The Political Riot

We have seen that it was through the *parlements* that the Parisian *menu peuple* learned their first political lessons and that under their influence city, unlike rural, riots tended to develop into political demonstrations. This was particularly so in the last two years of the Old Régime, when the *parlement* of Paris, locked in its final dispute with Louis XVI's ministers, provoked enthusiastic and noisy celebrations on the island of the Cité after returning to the capital from exile. Yet this was only a beginning. The crowds that assembled to greet the *parlement* were limited to students, lawyers' clerks, and journeymen of a number of districts. The lessons learned were still rudimentary and skin deep. Above all, they were restricted to the city and had not, as yet, aroused a response among the peasants in the countryside. The onset and course of the Revolution were to change all this. In challenging the "privileged" orders (including the *parlements*) for control of the Estates General of 1789, the *bourgeoisie*, or Third Estate, appealed to the whole nation; its ideas and slogans were seized upon by the rural as well as by the city population; and, under this impact, the food riot of the countryside and the occasional political demonstration of the city became converted into the great popular *jacqueries* and *journées* (or "days") of the summer and autumn of 1789. In turn, these early "spontaneous" demonstrations began to grow into more sophisticated political movements of the urban sans-culottes: these reflected both the intensity of the struggle of parties and the growing political experience and awareness of the sans-culottes themselves. This was a long-drawn-out process, and no detailed examination will be attempted here.[1] The purpose of this chapter is rather to illustrate the transition from one type of riot to the other and to indicate the main stages by which the political *journées*,° the most characteristic of all the forms of popular participation in the Revolution, originated and took shape.

After its first challenge to the Ministry in the "aristocratic revolt" of 1787, the Paris *parlement* won an early victory and, having spent a week or two in exile, was allowed to return to Paris. The returning magistrates received a tumultuous welcome on the island of the Cité, in the Place Dauphine, in the Rue du Harlay, and at the approaches to the Law Courts. The authorities had been prepared for disorder, and the courts were ringed with 500 Gardes de Paris, supported by a regiment of the Gardes Françaises. Crowds, composed of the clerks of the Palais de Justice and the apprentices and journeymen of the luxury trades of the Cité, filled the Pont Neuf and its approaches, let off squibs and fireworks, and pelted the troops with stones. On September 28, when the disturbances reached their climax, the troops were stung to open fire: there were no casualties, though a passing lawyer had his coat pierced by a stray bullet; and four young men were arrested. The disorders lasted for a week, during which bonfires were lit before the Law Courts, anti-royalist tracts were distributed, and Calonne, former Comptroller General, and the Comtesse de Polignac, governess of the royal children, were burned in effigy. On October 3, the *parlement* itself called a halt to the riots by proscribing all meetings and firework displays in the vicinity of the Law Courts. It had been a limited and localized affair. Its main support had been drawn from the lawyers' clerks

---

° The most important of these revolutionary *journées* were:

In *1789:* Réveillon riots (April 28-29), Paris revolution and capture of the
    Bastille (July 12-14), march to Versailles (October 5-6).

In *1791:* March to Vincennes (February 28), Champ de Mars demonstration and petition (July 17).

In *1792:* Invasion of Tuileries (June 20), overthrow of monarchy (August 10), September massacres (September 2-4).

In *1793:* Expulsion of "Girondin" deputies (May 31-June 2), insurrection of September 4-5.

In *1794:* Overthrow of Robespierre (9th Thermidor—July 27).

In *1795:* Popular riots of Germinal (April 1) and 1st-4th Prairial (May 20-23), royalist rising of 13th Vendémiaire (October 5).

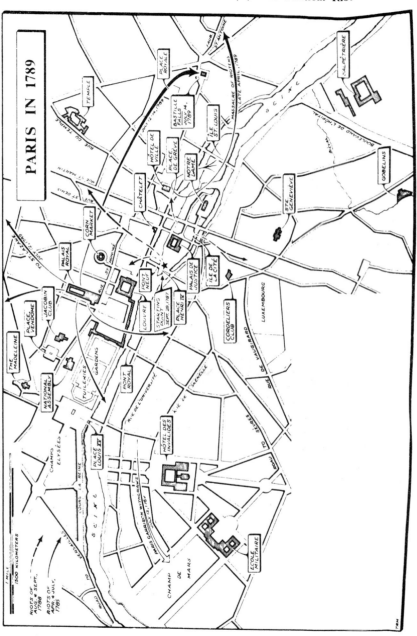

PARIS IN 1789

and journeymen of the Cité; and the faubourgs and markets had not yet become involved.

In the following months the crisis deepened, both because of the sharpening political tension and the rising price of bread. In May, the *parlement* courted further popularity by condemning the hated *lettres de cachet,* whereby the Ministry's opponents were incarcerated without trial, and the whole system of arbitrary government. The government riposted by surrounding the Law Courts with troops; an edict drafted by Lamoignon, Keeper of the Seals, vested a great part of the *parlement's* jurisdiction in other courts; and the rebellious magistrates were once more packed off to the provinces in exile. But such was the support for the *parlements*— in Paris and in other cities—that the ministers were compelled to bow before the storm: Brienne, the Chief Minister, was dismissed and replaced by Necker; the Estates General were promised for the following year; Lamoignon's edict was withdrawn; and the Paris *parlement* was recalled soon after. The victory was hailed by further celebrations in the Cité: fireworks were let off in profusion, bonfires were lit, and the occupants of coaches crossing the Pont Neuf were made to bow low to the statue of Henri IV, most popular of France's Kings, and to shout "A bas Lamoignon!" and "Vive Henri Quatre!"

This time, the disturbances assumed a new and more serious note: the price of the 4-pound loaf had risen in three weeks from 9 to 11 sous; and, at the end of August, the clerks of the Palais de Justice were joined by the *menu peuple* of the faubourgs and markets. The riots became more violent and spread into other districts; guard posts on both sides of the Pont Neuf, which spanned the Cité, were ransacked and burned to the ground. The Guards were ordered to meet force with force; and, in the Place de Grève on the north bank of the river, 600 demonstrators were fired on by troops, who killed seven or eight and put the rest to flight. After a fortnight's intermission, the riots resumed with further celebrations in the Cité and further bloody clashes between troops and journeymen and students at places as far apart as the Rue St. Martin in the north and the university quarter in the south. Over 50 persons were arrested, but the crowds won the day: both the unpopular Lamoignon and the Chevalier Dubois, commander of the Garde de Paris, were dismissed from office before the riots came to and end.[2]

The Paris *parlement* had therefore succeeded, in its duel with government, in harnessing to its cause the energies of a significant part of the capital's sans-culottes; and with their support it had won notable successes. But both the alliance and the achievement proved short lived. Even before the disturbances were over, the *parlement* had antagonized a large part of its supporters by insisting that the Estates General should be composed as it had been when it last met 175 years before—that is, that each "order" should meet separately and have equal representation. Thus the Third Estate would always be outvoted and the "privileged" orders would, as traditionally, call the tune. The Third Estate, seeing its hopes endangered, replied with a pamphlet war that in a remarkably short time turned the tables on the *parlements* and won nationwide support for its own aims, which included double representation for the Third Estate (a demand soon conceded by the government itself) and the merging of all three separate orders into one. The high hopes raised, even in country areas, by the prospect of an Estates General similarly constituted is illustrated in Arthur Young's encounter with a peasant woman of Champagne, who told him that

It was said at present that *something was to be done by some great folks for such poor ones, but she did not know who, nor how,* but God send us better, *car les tailles et les droits nous écrasent.*[3]

Young's entry in his journal of this conversation dates from July 12; but long before that the militant slogan of "tiers état"—the symbol of the popular challenge to privilege—had begun to circulate among the Parisian *menu peuple:* the earliest example that I have found in police records dates from early April.[4] Two to three weeks later, it was to be voiced in a popular riot; but one in which the *menu peuple* were largely rioting to promote their own ends and were not yet completely won for the aims of the *bourgeois* politicians of the Third Estate. This was the bloody fray that broke out in the Faubourg St. Antoine—soon to be distinguished as the most revolutionary of all the faubourgs—at the end of April, a week before the long-awaited Estates General met at Versailles. On April 23, two manufacturers, Réveillon and Henriot, both prominent members of the local Third Estate, had, in their respective assemblies of electors, regretted the high wages paid in industry. Whether or not they advocated a reduction in wages is not certain (and both were said to be good employers), but so it was interpreted by the wage earners of the faubourg; and their remarks, made at a time when the price of bread was phenomenally high,° provoked a violent outburst of disorder. Five or six hundred *ouvriers* gathered near the Bastille and, having hanged Réveillon (the most prominent of the culprits) in effigy, paraded dummy figures of both their intended victims round the various districts of the capital. Gathering reinforcements at the docks and in the manufactories and workshops, they arrived at the Hôtel de Ville in the Place de Grève some 2,000 strong. Finding Réveillon's house barred by troops of the Royal Cravate Regiment, they made for Henriot's house and, like the English Gordon rioters, destroyed his furniture and personal effects. Dispersed by the military, they re-formed the following morning, and while more troops were summoned bands of workers went round the districts recruiting fresh supporters by intimidation or persuasion. The climax came between 6 and 8 o'clock in the evening, when Réveillon's house was stormed, the Guards of the Royal Cravate were brushed aside, and the destruction of the previous night was repeated on a greater scale. The Duc du Châtelet, commanding the Gardes Françaises, gave the order to fire, and a massacre followed in the narrow congested streets, where thousands crowded the roofs and windows, while the crowd fought back with shouts of "Liberté . . . nous ne cèderons pas." Others shouted "Vive le tiers état!" and "Vive le Roi et vive M. Necker!" Thus the new "patriot" slogans of the day, strangely at variance with the rioters' behavior, were already being absorbed by the Paris *menu peuple* and turned, if need be, to their own advantage.[5]

As yet, then, the activities of the Parisian sans-culottes had not been fully harmonized with those of the revolutionary *bourgeoisie*. The latter hoped, no doubt, to realize their aims without resorting to the hazardous expedient of calling in the masses. These hopes, however, were frustrated by the obstinate refusal of the aristocracy to make concessions and by the feeble vacillations of the King. Persuaded by the Queen and his younger brother, the Comte d'Artois, Louis decided to call in troops, dismiss the newly formed

---

° The price of the 4-pound loaf had, since February, been 14½ sous.

National Assembly, overawe Paris, and replace Necker, considered too tender to the "patriot" cause, by Breteuil, a nominee of Marie Antoinette. It was the arrival of the news of Necker's dismissal at noon on July 12 that touched off the popular revolution in the capital. Crowds assembled in the gardens of the Palais Royal, the home of the popular Duc d'Orléans, heard Camille Desmoulins and other orators give the call to arms. Groups of marchers formed and paraded busts of Necker and Orléans, the heroes of the hour, along the boulevards. Theatres were closed as a sign of mourning. Besenval, commander of the Paris garrison, withdrew to the Champ de Mars and left the capital in the hands of the people. The first operation was to destroy the hated *barrières*, or customs posts, that ringed the city and whose tolls on food and wine were bitterly resented by the small consumers: in four days' rioting directed from the Palais Royal, 40 of the 54 posts were systematically destroyed. The monastery of the St. Lazare brotherhood was broken into, looted, searched for arms and grain, and its prisoners were released. Other religious houses and gunsmiths were raided for guns, swords, and pistols. All night long (as we learn from the eyewitness account of a tallow chandler's laborer[6]), milling throngs of civilians and disaffected troops surged through the streets, shouting the newly learned "patriot" slogans, sounding the tocsin, and searching for grain and arms. Meanwhile, the Paris electors of the Third Estate, who had formed themselves into a provisional city government at the Hôtel de Ville, thoroughly alarmed at the turn of events, began to enroll a citizen's militia, or National Guard, as much to guard the capital against the riotous poor as against the military threat from Versailles.

So the search for arms and ammunition continued. It was, in fact, to search for arms, far more than to release prisoners and even more than to settle old scores with a hated symbol of the past, that led Parisians on July 14 to assault the ancient fortress of the Bastille. The insurgents were short of powder, and it was known that stocks had recently been sent there from the arsenal. Besides, the air was thick with rumors of impending attacks from Versailles, while the Bastille's guns were ominously trained on the crowded tenements of the St. Antoine quarter. So, after 30,000 muskets had been removed from the Hôtel des Invalides across the river, the cry went up, "To the Bastille!" The siege—or rather

negotiations with the Bastille's governor, the Marquis de Launay
—was directed, with fumbling uncertainty, by the Committee of
Electors at the City Hall; but the initiative to take the fortress by
storm, when peaceful parley led to no result, was taken not by
them but by the armed citizens that crowded round its walls.
The Bastille's guns had already killed and wounded 150 of the
citizens' number when Hulin, a former noncommissioned officer,
marched two detachments of the Gardes Françaises, who had recently joined the insurrection, up to the main gate and, joined by
a few hundred armed civilians, prepared for a direct assault. Persuaded by his garrison, de Launay ordered the main drawbridge to
be lowered; and the fall of the Bastille marked the culmination of
the first great popular *journée* of the Revolution.

The Bastille's surrender, though by no means a military feat of
great importance, had remarkable political results. The National
Assembly was saved and received royal recognition. In the capital,
power passed to the Committee of Electors, who set up a City
Council (the Commune) with Bailly as mayor. On July 17, the
King himself came to Paris attended by fifty deputies and making
a virtue of necessity donned the red, white, and blue cockade of
the Revolution. For a great deal of this the Paris crowds, in which
the sans-culottes played the major part, had been responsible. Yet
the Revolution was not yet secure and the gains of July had to be
fought for again in October. As long as Court and King remained
at Versailles and an active minority of deputies could, in alliance
with the Court, frustrate the constitutional program of the Assembly (and this ability became all too evident in August and
September), effective power still remained divided between the
old Third Estate and its liberal aristocratic allies, and the adherents
of the Old Régime. Once more the King, succumbing to the pressure of what remained of the old Court party, tried to break the
deadlock by a further display of force, and summoned troops—
this time the Flanders Regiment—to Versailles. At a banquet given
in their honor, the national cockade (at least, so it was reported
in Paris) was trampled underfoot. To avenge the insult, the Paris
"patriots" called for a march to Versailles—either to deliver an
ultimatum or to fetch the royal family to Paris. Meanwhile, there
had been another crisis in the supply of bread; and on October 5
a food riot of angry market women developed into the great wom-

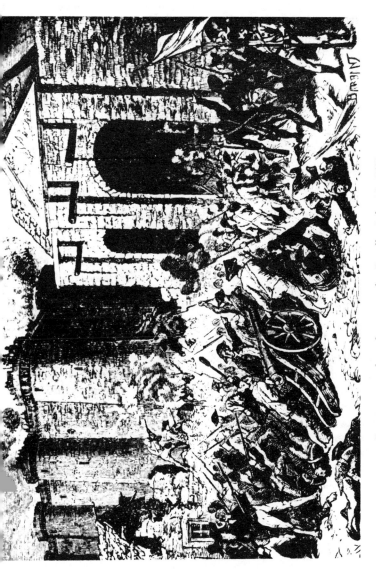

Parisians assault and capture the Bastille, July 14, 1789.

en's march which, supported by the battalions of the National Guard, brought the King, soon followed by the National Assembly, back in triumph to the capital. Thus, for the second time in a dozen weeks, the Parisian *menu peuple* had come to the Assembly's rescue and saved the Revolution.[7]

The year 1789 was not only a year of city riots and revolutions. The country also had its share; and here, too, the riot underwent a similar transformation. After the grain riots of 1775, the countryside had been relatively undisturbed. There had, of course, been the usual crop of bread riots: at Toulouse and Grenoble in 1778, at Bayeux in 1784, and at Rennes in 1785; but they had been scattered and sporadic. There was no further generalized movement of rural protest until the winter of 1788-9; and then it occurred in response to a dual crisis. On the one hand, there were the disastrous harvests of 1787 and 1788, which sent prices rocketing in nearly all the main grain-producing regions. On the other hand, the government had, under pressure of the "aristocratic revolt," summoned the provincial Estates to meet and was preparing to convene the electors, of whom the peasants formed the overwhelming majority, to draw up their *cahiers de doléances,* or notebooks of grievances, in every part of France. The peasants' response assumed, in the first place, the traditional form of a revolt against shortage and rising prices. Starting in December 1788, it expressed itself in attacks on grain boats and granaries; assaults on customs officials, merchants, and *laboureurs;* rioting at town halls and at bakers' shops and markets; *taxation populaire* of bread and wheat; and widespread destruction of property. Reports of such activities came in from nearly every province: in December and January, from Brittany and Touraine; in March and April, from Burgundy, the Ile de France, Languedoc, Nivernais, Orléanais, Picardy, Poitou, Provence, and Touraine; in July, from Normandy and Champagne. North of Paris, the fight against famine developed into a movement against the game laws and hunting right of the nobility, the first for many years. On the estates of the Prince de Conti at Pontoise and Beaumont (scenes of the riots of 1775), at Conflans Ste. Honorine and other villages, the peasants set traps for the rabbits infesting their fields, leading to clashes with the rural constabulary. In Artois, a dozen villages combined to exterminate the Comte d'Oisy's game and refused to

pay him traditional dues. South and west of Paris, near Fontainebleau and St. Germain, whole parishes were disarmed under
suspicion of poaching the game in the royal forests. In Lorraine
and Hainault, landless peasants and small proprietors joined
forces to oppose plans to clear the woodlands and enclose the
fields. Meanwhile, after lying dormant for nearly a century, peasant anger against royal taxes and seigneurial dues had broken out
in Provence in March, at Gap in April, and in the Cambrésis and
Picardy in May.[8]

Thus, under the impact of economic crisis and political events,
the peasant movement developed from early protests against
prices, through attacks on enclosure, gaming rights, and royal
forests, to a frontal assault on the feudal land system itself. This
was by no means a purely spontaneous development: in part, it
grew out of the strange phenomenon known as *la Grande Peur*,
the Great Fear, of the late summer of 1789. The Great Fear had its
origins in rural vagrancy, the product of the economic crisis; the
dispersal of royal troops after the popular victory in Paris; and in
the peasants' deep-grained belief, which they shared with many
townsmen, in the existence of an "aristocratic plot." The conviction grew that "brigands," be they village poor or disbanded
soldiers, were being armed to ravage the countryside and to destroy the peasants' property. As in the riots of 1775, the rumor
spread from market to market and along the course of rivers and
during July and August inflamed the rural population in every
province outside Brittany in the north and Alsace and Lorraine in
the east. So the peasants armed and awaited the invaders. But the
"brigands," the product of panic and excited imagination, failed to
materialize; and the peasants in many districts, cheated of one
quarry, turned against another, and directed their weapons against
the manors of the lords instead. For the châteaux housed not only
the seigneurs (who were largely left unscathed) but the hated
manorial rolls on which were inscribed the feudal rents and obligations, many of them recently invented or revived, that placed a
heavy burden on the small proprietor's land. Thus the peasants,
bitterly resentful of age-old seigneurial exactions, responded to
the appeal of the Third Estate by staging their own particular
kind of revolution. They left a trail of burning châteaux in every
part of France. The movement yielded quick results. Prodded into

action, the National Assembly issued its decrees of August 4 and 5, which abolished, or made redeemable, all seigneurial burdens on the land. Where such burdens were commuted to a money payment, the peasants refused to pay; and three years later the Jacobin government accepted the accomplished fact and annulled the peasants' debt.[9]

The peasant revolution simmered in the countryside throughout the revolutionary years; yet it generally relapsed into food riots or attacks on enclosure and never regained its early scope and vigor. In Paris, as in other cities, the situation was altogether different. The great riots of 1789, though rich in consequence, were only a beginning. The political indoctrination of the sans-culottes with the new ideas of the Revolution had barely yet begun. Clubs and "fraternal" societies were formed, which, after 1790, opened their doors to wage earners and craftsmen. By such means the ideas of the democrats and later of the republicans were transmitted to and absorbed by the people of the faubourgs and the markets. An early outcome of this new stage of political indoctrination was the great rally and petition in the Champ de Mars in July 1791, which called for the abdication of the King after his ill-fated flight to Varennes and for the substitution of a new "executive authority." The many thousands of signatories included a majority of sans-culottes; and we know from other evidence that a great number of them, at least, understood perfectly well what the petition was about. They, too, formed the bulk of the demonstrators who had gathered from every section in the capital, and of whom fifty were shot dead and another twelve wounded by Lafayette's National Guard.

This "massacre," like the war that followed nine months later, deepened the divisions among "patriots"; and the sans-culottes, who were admitted to the meetings of the Sections in July 1792, came more and more under the influence of the Jacobins, republicans, and democrats. It was they who planned and directed the armed attack of the Tuileries in August 1792, which ended the monarchy and ushered in the Republic; and it was carried through by the regular battalions of the National Guard, which were largely composed of the shopkeepers, tradesmen, and journeymen of Paris. The same force was used by the Jacobins in June 1793, this time under Hanriot, a sans-culotte general, to expel their

"Girondin" opponents from the National Convention.[10] And so, by stages of political indoctrination and experience, through attendance at meetings of sectional assemblies, societies, and committees and through service in the National Guard and the *armée révolutionnaire,* formed to assure the city's food supply,[11] trained militants and leaders were emerging from among the sans-culottes themselves. They were by no means docile agents of the Jacobins or any other ruling party: they had their own social aspirations, outlook, clubs, and slogans, and their own ideas on how the country should be governed.[12] This being so, it was inevitable that the political riot, when still resorted to, should undergo a further transformation.

This process reached its climax in the great popular insurrection of Prairial of the Year III (May 20-23, 1795). The sans-culottes, by this time divided among themselves and antagonized by the Jacobin government's policies, had offered no effective resistance to Robespierre's overthrow in July 1794. But the inflation that followed, accompanied by the closure of the remaining revolutionary clubs and the persecution of former "terrorists" and "patriots," gradually roused them to take action. A first skirmish took place on 12th Germinal (April 1, 1795), when the National Convention was invaded by an angry crowd of men and women, shouting for bread and wearing in their caps and bonnets the insurgent slogan, "Bread and the Constitution of 1793."* The intruders, having received some verbal support from the few Jacobin deputies that remained in the Assembly, were soon ejected by loyal detachments of the National Guard; and the movement temporarily subsided.

But, as the food situation went from bad to worse, the stirrings in the streets and markets and among the militants in the sections became more pronounced; and on 1st Prairial (May 20), there was a new outbreak, this time of a far more violent and dangerous character. On this occasion, as in October 1789, it was the women that took the lead and urged their menfolk to take action. Again, as in October, it started with riots at bakers' shops that developed

---

* This was the democratic Constitution of June 1793, which the Jacobins, who had drafted it, put into cold storage "for the duration" and their successors repealed in September 1795.

into a march on the Assembly. But this was a combined military
and political demonstration that reached a higher pitch of political
maturity than that of 1789. In October, the women chanted as
they marched to Versailles (or so tradition has it), "Let us fetch
the baker, the baker's wife and the little baker's boy": thus the
political intention, though evident in the outcome, was never
clearly underlined. In May 1795, however, the insurgents bore
political slogans in their caps and blouses and had clearly defined
political aims: these were to release the political prisoners, to re-
establish the Paris Commune (suppressed after Robespierre's
fall), to implement the Constitution of 1793, and to reimpose the
abandoned controls on the price and supply of food. And, unlike
the participants in the *journées* from 1789 to 1793, they received
no marching orders from revolutionary leaders or outside political
groups: they acted on their own account under their own banners
and slogans. It was, in fact, the first, and the last, great political
demonstration both initiated and carried through by the sans-
culottes themselves.

Yet they failed completely, and were ignominiously defeated
and savagely repressed. Once more, as in April, they were ejected
from the Assembly; but they regrouped their forces in the Faubourg St. Antoine, the center of rebellion, and the following afternoon marched on the Convention with a force of 20,000 National
Guards. For the first time in the Revolution, however, a regular
army, loyal to the government, was drawn up to meet them; and
to avoid a massacre both sides agreed to negotiate rather than to
fight it out. So lulled by false promises the insurgents retired to
their sections. The Faubourg St. Antoine was invested next day,
and on the fourth day of the rebellion the insurgents surrendered
without having fired a shot. Defeat was followed by a heavy toll
of reprisals and proscriptions: 36 rebels were condemned to death
and 37 to prison or deportation by a military court; some 1,200
alleged "terrorists" (not all of them insurgents) were arrested and
1,700 disarmed in a single week; and many followed later.[13]

Thus beheaded, the sans-culotte movement died a sudden
death; and, having, like the cactus, burst into full bloom at the
very point of its extinction, it never rose again. There was a final
insurrection in October; but this time the sans-culottes were passive spectators and the participants were civil servants, lawyers,

clerks, shopkeepers, and army officers of the royalist or near-royalist sections.[14] After this the army, called in by the Convention, remained in occupation, and the days of revolutionary crowds and riots, whatever their complexion, were over for thirty-five years.

REFERENCES

1. For a fuller treatment, see my *The Crowd in the French Revolution* (Oxford, 1959).
2. *Ibid.,* pp. 28-33.
3. Arthur Young, *Travels in France and Italy* (Everyman Library, London, 1915), p. 159.
4. Archives Nationales, Y 18762 (April 12, 1789).
5. See *The Crowd in the French Revolution,* pp. 34-44.
6. Archives Nationales, Z^2 4691.
7. For these two episodes, see *The Crowd in the French Revolution,* pp. 47-79.
8. See my article, "The Outbreak of the French Revolution," *Past and Present,* November 1955, pp. 28-42.
9. G. Lefebvre, *The Great Fear of 1789* (London, 1973) and "La Révolution française et les paysans," in *Etudes sur la Révolution française* (Paris, 1954), pp. 246-68.
10. See *The Crowd in the French Revolution,* pp. 80-94, 101-8, 121-6.
11. R. C. Cobb, *Les armées révolutionaires* (2 vols. Paris and The Hague, 1961-3).
12. A. Soboul, *Les sans-culottes parisiens en l'an II* (Paris, 1958).
13. For the events of Germinal–Prairial, see K. Tönnesson, *La défaite des sans-culottes* (Oslo and Paris, 1959).
14. See *The Crowd in the French Revolution,* pp. 160-77.

SEVEN

The French Revolution:
(2) The Food Riot

One of the great issues of the French Revolution was the supply of cheap and plentiful food. This was, as throughout the eighteenth century, a constant preoccupation of the small consumers of town and countryside, many of whom, as we saw in the last chapter, played a conspicuous part in the political riots and demonstrations. It is therefore hardly surprising that even in the most ostensibly *political* of these episodes the food problem should so frequently obtrude. We have seen that, in September 1788, when Parisians were celebrating the *parlement's* second return, a sharp increase in the price of bread transformed the scope and nature of the riots. In the following April, the Réveillon riots in the Faubourg St. Antoine were probably due as much to the high price of bread as to the manufacturers' attacks on wages: in fact, food shops (but no others) were broken into, and the lieutenant of police himself believed that the insurgents had the twofold aim of settling accounts with Réveillon and of compelling the authorities to reduce the price of bread. The food problem also played a part in the events leading up to the capture of the Bastille. Among those raiding the St. Lazare monastery on the night of July 12 were some who said they were "looking for bread"; and, at the *barrières*, a locksmith who was busy destroying a customs post was heard to say, *nous allons boire le vin à trois sols* ("we shall drink wine at 3 sous a liter").

In October this problem was even more in evidence. The women's march tor Versailles developed from bread riots at bakers' shops and at the Hôtel de Ville; and Barnave, one of the most observant of the revolutionary leaders, in reporting the event to his constituents, stressed the dual nature of these riots: *bourgeoisie* and "people" (he wrote) acted in a common cause; but whereas the former acted solely to defeat the plots of the aristocracy, the latter were equally concerned with the price of bread (*y mêlant l'intérêt du pain*). And so we could go on up to the last popular outbreaks of 1795, when insurgents wore in their caps the dual device, "Bread and the Constitution of 1793." In fact, of all the major *journées* of the Revolution in the capital, there was only one in which the price or supply of food or bread appears to have played no part at all; and that was the demonstration of July 17, 1791, when Parisians gathered in the Champ de Mars to sign a petition calling for the abdication of the King.[1]

If, then, the food riot was latent in so many political demonstrations, it needs scarcely surprise us that it should, on occasion, break out on its own account. This would happen for much the same reasons as before the Revolution—when supplies were short and prices were unusually high. For reasons that we have already noted, 1789 was precisely such a year; and we have observed the growing volume of food riots reported from different parts of the country before the peasants transferred their attention in late July to the châteaux and manorial rolls. Provincial towns were equally affected, and we read of food riots, often accompanied by popular price control, in cities as widely scattered as Amiens, Bordeaux, Caen, Chartres, Grenoble, Marseilles, Orleans, Nantes, and Rheims.[2] In Paris, too, where the daily loaf in 1789 swallowed up an increasingly high proportion of the laborer's and craftsman's wage,[3] the experience might have been no different if popular anger had not so frequently been diverted into political channels: October 1789 is evidently a case in point.

The revolutionary authorities had, by November of that year, weathered the bread crisis inherited from the Old Régime: and the eighteen months that followed were a period of comparative social calm. But this was more by luck than judgment, as they had no policies for dealing with such problems, and the problems were bound to recur. When they did, they were due in part to failing harvests, in part to the falling value of paper money (the *assignat*), and even more, after April 1792, to the headlong wartime inflation which the prevailing doctrine of economic liberalism was powerless to arrest. It was a combination of these factors that led to the next great shortage, and the next great wave of riots, in 1792. In August 1791, a shortage of flour in Paris had brought a rapid rise in the price of bread; and in November several of the grain-producing regions of the north and west were convulsed by disturbances which took the form of stopping the export of grain to other parts. As wheat prices rose more steeply (in Paris by a little over a quarter, but in the provinces by an average of 40 percent), riots broke out all over the country. In scope and intensity, they rivaled those of 1789.[4]

Of these disturbances, none were so widespread and protracted as those in the great grain-producing plain of the Beauce, which, with Chartres at its center, lay enclosed between the Seine and the Loire.[5] The cause of distress was not so much the failure of the harvest as the depletion of the markets by the large producers, who either sold direct to Paris dealers and those supplying the

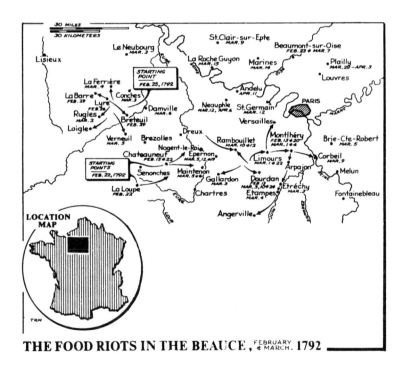

THE FOOD RIOTS IN THE BEAUCE, FEBRUARY & MARCH, 1792

hard-hit areas of the south, or hoarded their stocks in the expectation of a higher price. The movement began among the poor woodcutters, nailers, and blacksmiths of the forest of Conches and Breteuil in the valley of the Eure. It was a snowball movement, launched in the first place by a handful of nailers of Les Baux-de-Breteuil, who, in marching on the neighboring market of Lyre, were joined by the whole of the local population whom their mayor, though forewarned, did nothing to stop. Leaving Lyre with 400 supporters, they made for the market of La Barre and in the following days for Le Neubourg, Conches, Verneuil, Breteuil, and Rugles, all markets lying within easy reach of the forest. They marched in orderly procession, with flags flying and drums rolling, and gathered reinforcements as they went: at Le Neubourg, people from twenty-five parishes were said to have taken part. The local National Guard, themselves often poor peasants, made no effort to arrest their progress; and at Conches, the Guard and the municipal officers came out to meet them and obligingly imposed a ceiling on the price of wheat and oats. A similar pattern was followed at Breteuil and other markets; by now the original band had been duplicated by others; and soon price fixing was no longer limited to bread or grain but extended to eggs and butter and even to wood, coal, and iron. For many of these villagers were also rural craftsmen; and in early March no less than 5,000 in the one case and 8,000 in the other arrived at the forges at Baudouin and La Louche to compel the masters to sell their iron at a cut-down price. In reporting the event, the authorities of Evreux, the local capital, noted that such measures being beyond the capacity of "a multitude of coarse and ignorant people," it was evident that they had been guided by "an invisible hand"; and rioters (they added), having imposed a price control on food, aimed to scale down rural leases and abolish taxes. "Everywhere they raise the summons to anarchy and civil war." But the movement, even if it had such wider social objectives, was strictly based on the forest parishes around Conches and Breteuil; and at the very moment when it prepared to extend northwards to Evreux, ten to fifteen miles away, it began to lose support and fell an easy victim to the *gendarmerie* and militia sent to suppress it. By mid-March it had collapsed, and 63 prisoners lay awaiting trial in Evreux jail.

Meanwhile, another center of agitation had opened to the south, in the neighboring department of Eure-et-Loire. Starting near Chartres in February, at La Loupe and Châteauneuf, riots spread to the neighboring parishes and market towns and reached eastwards into Seine-et-Oise. On March 8, the authorities at Chartres informed the National Assembly that

the enemies of law and order have appeared in the markets of Maintenon and Epernon and are preparing to incite disorder in those of Châteauneuf, Brezolles, La Loupe, Senonches and Nogent-le-Roi.

Once more, itinerant bands summoned villagers to action by ringing the church bells and imposed their price controls on dealers in the markets; but this time they entered farms as well to check the farmers' stocks and even, on occasion, forced them to raise their wages. The market towns of Seine-et-Oise, many of them centers for the provisioning of Paris and scenes of the riots of 1775, were soon involved: Dourdan (on February 19 and again on March 3, 10, and 24), Limours, Montlhéry, Etampes, St. Arnould, and Rambouillet. From Limours a first attempt to reach Versailles proved unsuccessful. At Etampes on March 4, the mayor (Simoneau, a wealthy tanner of the district) summoned troops to halt the invasion and was shot dead in the market. A week later, at the great market town of Melun, across the border of Seine-et-Marne, 10,000 villagers assembled, armed with pitchforks and accompanied by drums and banners. The townsmen, too, were under arms; but by agreement both sides laid down their arms and the price of the *setier* of wheat was reduced from 30 to 20 francs.

Though largely spent by April, this first great movement in the *beauceron* plain simmered down until autumn. Versailles was now affected; further outbreaks occurred at Dourdan and Limours; and Orléans, like Etampes, was the scene of a bloody clash when a dealer was massacred and several rioters were shot. After this, the National Assembly half-heartedly restored the partial regulations of the Old Régime; but they did little to stock the markets in the Beauce. So a new and more extensive movement opened in November and spread, within three weeks, to eight departments. This time, it started east of Le Mans, in Sarthe, in the wooded

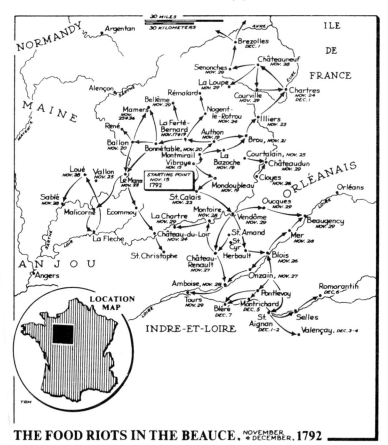

THE FOOD RIOTS IN THE BEAUCE. NOVEMBER & DECEMBER, 1792

country round Vibraye and Montmirail. Once more foresters and rural craftsmen and glass workers from the manufactory of Le Plessis-Dorin took the initial lead and, in the third and fourth weeks of November, raided the local markets under arms. From this focal point bands of villagers—sometimes in groups of 5,000 to 10,000 men—fanned out in all directions. Eastwards, they marched to Châteaudun, whose National Guard, though called to arms, was powerless to resist them. Northwards, they made for Chartres, passing through Brou on November 21. At Chartres, however, the authorities won a reprieve by making (and faithfully discharging) a promise to intervene on their behalf with the

Assembly. Northwestwards from Chartres, they once more roused the villagers of the forest country from which the earlier movement had started, and reimposed price controls that had lapsed since March in the markets of La Loupe, Senonches, Châteauneuf-en-Thymerais, Verneuil, and Brezolles. Again turning eastwards, through the market town of Courville, a second expedition, 10,000 strong, appeared at Chartres on December 1. This time the rioters were disarmed and dispersed; for the municipal officers, being forewarned, had mobilized the National Guard and brought in troops.

Elsewhere, however, the volunteers and National Guard, far from acting as a force of law and order, joined the rioters, rounded up support and spread their message. At La Ferté-Bernard, north of Vibraye, 200 national volunteers were among those who welcomed the invading villagers and helped them to reduce the prices in the market. From here bands spread westwards into Sarthe, where they were joined by the battalions of the National Guard of Le Mans and Nogent-le-Rotrou. At Nogent, the rioters wore oak leaves in their hats and danced around a "tree of liberty" to shouts of "Long Live the Nation! The price of wheat is coming down!" With their new allies, they were able to terrorize more than one local authority into submission: that of Château-du-Loir was even persuaded to reduce the price of grain in a neighboring market! The movement spread further: northwards into Orne and southwards into Loir-et-Cher and Indre-et-Loire, where, having passed through Vendôme, it fanned out along the northern bank of the river. Blois and Amboise, where the National Guard defected, accepted the rioters' terms; but they were driven back from Tours; as also, further north, from Sablé and La Flèche. At Sablé, they left 200 prisoners in the hands of the troops; and from now on (it was late November), the local authorities, drawing National Guards from other departments, began to have their measure. Minor outbreaks persisted for some weeks to come; but the movement had spent its force and, by early December, the crisis was past and peace and order were restored.

Meanwhile, Paris had experienced another type of crisis and another type of food riot. As in the provinces, the background to the crisis was the depreciation of the *assignat;* its value had, by January 1792, fallen to 65 percent of that of 1790. But here the immediate cause of disturbance was not the price of bread or flour, but the shortage of sugar and other colonial products, a shortage arising from the civil war that had broken out in the West Indies between the planters and the natives. In January, the price of sugar nearly trebled by rising in a few days from 22-25 sous to 3 livres or 3½ livres a pound; and riots broke out in the Faubourgs St. Antoine, St. Marcel, and St. Denis and in the central commercial districts. The rioters, believing—with some justice —that the real reason for the shortage was the withholding of supplies by the merchants in the expectations of higher prices, and that colonial disturbance was as much a pretext as a cause, broke into the shops and warehouses of some of the large wholesalers and dealers, and demanded that sugar be sold at its former price; in some districts, they extended their operations to bread, meat, wine, and other wares. The disturbance began in the Beaubourg Section on January 20 with a riot of market women and spread, a few days later, to the Faubourg St. Antoine, where half-a-dozen grocers were forced to sell their sugar at a lower price. Another wave of rioting broke out in February; on the fourteenth, over twenty grocers in the Rue du Faubourg St. Antoine alone were threatened with invasion, and several were forced to sell sugar at 20 sous a pound before order could be restored. The same day, in the Faubourg St. Marcel it was rumored that large stocks of sugar, long accumulating in a warehouse, were going to be distributed all over Paris. Crowds seized the first loads of sugar as they left under military escort and sold them in the street at 25 or 30 sous a pound. The next day, women rang the bell in the church of St. Marcel and attempts were made to force the warehouse doors. Pétion, the mayor, arrived on the scene with a large military force which scattered the rioters and committed fourteen prisoners to the Conciergerie. They commanded considerable public sympathy: a petition for their release addressed to the Assembly was signed by 150 local residents, all of them voters and two of them clergy.[6]

It was the first substantial movement of *taxation populaire* in the capital since the riots of 1775. It was far surpassed, however, by the disturbances that broke out for a similar cause in February 1793.[7] Prices, which had fallen in the summer and autumn, had risen again since the New Year. By February, the price of sugar

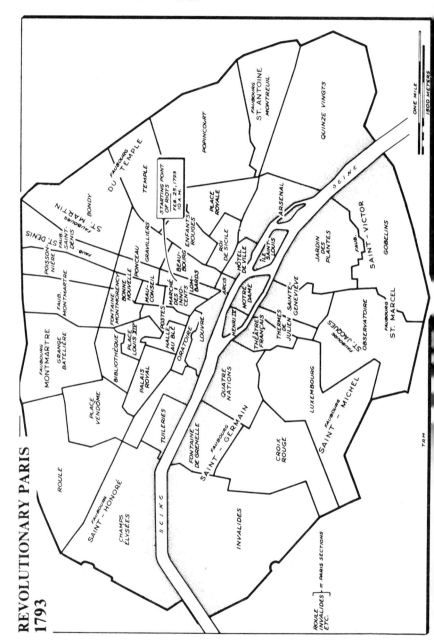

had once more doubled, while coffee had risen from 34 to 40 sous, soap from 12 to 23-28 sous, and tallow candles from 15 to 18½-20 sous. The consequence was a popular outburst, far more extensive and persistent than the sugar riots of the previous year, in which all, or nearly all, the 48 Parisian sections were involved and which, perhaps more clearly than any other incident in the Revolution, underlined the basic conflict of interest between the *menu peuple* and the possessing classes, including the democrats who spoke or applauded at the Jacobin Club or sat with the "Mountain" on the upper benches of the Chamber. There had been two deputations of women to the Convention on February 23, one of which (headed by laundresses) complained of the price of soap. Two days later, the riots broke out. They took the form of a mass invasion of grocers' and chandlers' shops and the forcible reduction of prices to a level dictated by the insurgents: most commonly, refined sugar was sold at 18-25 sous, unrefined sugar at 10-12 sous, tallow candles at 12 sous, soap at 10-12 sous, and coffee at 20 sous. Starting in the central commercial quarter at 10 o'clock in the morning, the movement spread with remarkable speed to every part of the city. Moving eastwards, it reached the Hôtel de Ville soon after 10, the former Place Royale at midday, the Arsenal at 2, the Droits de l'Homme section at 3, the Quinze Vingts in the Faubourg St. Antoine between 3 and 4, and Montreuil and the Marais at 4. Meanwhile, extending northwards, it reached the section of the Amis de la Patrie at 2:30 and those of Bondy and Mont Blanc at 5 o'clock. In the west, it reached the Gardes Françaises at 2:20, the Louvre at 4, the Palais Royal at 7, the Tuileries at 8, and République (the former, and present, Roule) at 10. From the Tuileries it appears to have crossed over to the other side of the river, for there were disturbances between 8 and 9 that night in the Left-Bank Section of the Fontaine de Grenelle. The next day minor outbreaks followed in a number of Sections; the market women of the center and laundresses of the Rue de Bièvre in the Faubourg St. Marcel played a part. But Santerre, the commander of the National Guard, absent at Versailles on the twenty-fifth, mobilized his forces at an early hour and brought the movement to a close.

This was by no means the last great wave of food riots in the Revolution. Similar disturbances occurred, though on a smaller scale, in Paris and elsewhere, in the autumn, and again in 1794; and in 1795, the great year of near-famine in the provinces, food riots and social conflicts reached a pitch barely reached in 1789 itself.[8] But these incidents in 1792 and 1793 will serve as well as any others to illustrate the scope and nature of the food riots of the Revolutionary period. Were they merely a repetition in changed circumstances of the earlier riots of the eighteenth century, such as those of 1775, or did they mark a new departure? And, if so, in what respects?

It is evident that the form and pattern of these riots, and the selection of their victims, were much the same as twenty years before. The progression of disturbance in the Beauce, though not identical, was broadly similar to that of 1775. The composition of the rioters again conforms to a familar pattern: among the 62 prisoners charged in Seine-et-Oise and 117 in Eure, there is the same mixture of small peasants, daily laborers, and rural craftsmen, with a sprinkling of farmers, curés, and rural proprietors.[9] Above all, the systematic enforcement of price control by riot, both in Paris and the Beauce, was in the tradition of the *taxation populaire* of the Old Régime in France. In this sense, the food riot of the Revolution was a conservative and traditional device that, with its appeal to ancient usage, looked backwards rather than forwards and marked no radical departure from the riots of the past. There is even the same belief expressed that the cause promoted is not only just but sanctioned by authority: at Vibraye, in November 1792, rioters insisted that they were enforcing a decree of the Convention[10] in much the same way as, in 1775, it was believed that the King had intervened in person to reduce the price of wheat and bread.

Nevertheless, although the element of continuity of form and pattern and behavior is striking, it is obvious enough that the political climate and popular mentality had greatly changed since 1789. In the riots of 1775, we noted no particular animosity towards Court and nobility: the King, in fact, was held in reverence; and the seigneur only took his place among the victims if he happened to have an accessible surplus of grain. In the Beauce in 1792, the main targets were still the large farmers, merchants, and *laboureurs,* as familiar there as in the Ile de France, the Beauvaisis and Brie: indeed, the Revolution had sharpened rather than weakened the antagonism between large producers and small consumers. There is little evidence of any particular hostility to the rural *noblesse:* only one château was destroyed, and the term "aristocrat," so liberally voiced in the riots, applied above all to the new rich in the peasant and urban community. Yet there are political, "patriotic," and antiroyalist undercurrents and accompaniments (particularly in the riots of November 1792) that are completely absent from the riots of the past. Itinerant bands parade to cries of "Vive la Nation!" and announce themselves to villagers and townsmen as "brothers and liberators." At Blois, they lacerate the standards of the National Guard that have a background of *fleurs de lys:* and, at the nearby château of Ménars, they pull down a statue of Louis XV. At Amboise, they chant the slogan: "Down with moderates, royalists and administrators that are enemies of the People, and up with the sans-culottes!" [11] Thus echoes of 1789, and even more of the patriotic war and sans-culotte movement of 1792, give a particular edge to riots whose basic aims are still those of the urban and rural poor of the Old Régime.

In Paris, too, the grocery riots of 1793, at least, had political undertones. It is not that their origins, any more than of those in the Beauce, owed anything to the "hidden hand" of clerical or aristocratic intrigue. In both cases, the rioters' critics, whether of the Paris City Council, the Jacobin Club, or among the parties in the Convention, were quick to ascribe their activities to a counter-revolutionary plot. Robespierre, though he refused to condemn Simoneau's assassins at Etampes, expressed surprise that Parisians could have been misguided enough to riot for *de chétives marchandises* ("paltry grocer's goods"). Barère spoke darkly of "the perfidious incitement of aristocrats in disguise" and, to prove his point, insisted that such "luxuries" as sugar and coffee were unlikely subjects of popular passion. Such strictures clearly fell wide of the mark, though they seemed sensible enough to men reared on "aristocratic plots" and to whom any interference with the free circulation of supplies seemed a negation of the "liberties" that the Revolution had proclaimed. But some of the critics were nearer the mark when they blamed the Paris disturbances on Jacques Roux, the "red priest" of the Gravilliers Section, and his fellow *Enragés*, the only political group in the capital that openly favored the regulation of prices and supplies. Roux was a member of the City Council and on the morning of February 25 had made a speech defending the rioters' conduct. Moreover, the disturbances had actually started in Roux's own section. From this it was easily inferred that he had not only inspired but instigated the riots and played an active part in their direction. Mathiez, the French historian, is inclined to share this view. In fact, it is difficult to establish from the records any direct link between Jacques Roux and the grocery rioters. Yet it seems highly likely that the views that he and his associates had persistently expressed should have aroused an active response among the market workers, craftsmen, and shopkeepers of the sections in which he lived and worked.[12]

What is perhaps even more important is that these movements were remarkably successful and, for all their connections with the past, contributed to something new. This was the law of the General Maximum of September 29, 1793. By imposing a ceiling on the prices of most articles of prime necessity (including wages), it went much further than the piecemeal regulations of the Old Régime. The Maximum, which survived in a diluted form for fifteen months, had a long preparatory history. It was the outcome of the ideas of a handful of pamphleteers, popular pressure, and wartime emergency; and of these the last two were incomparably more important than the first. In 1789 several *cahiers de doléances* had suggested that municipal granaries should be built and that wages should be geared to the price of bread. In 1790, two Parisian pamphleteers, Rutledge and de Chaillon, published proposals for the state regulation of grain and flour. A Lyons municipal officer, L'Ange, urged that the state should buy up the entire harvest at fixed prices and build 30,00 granaries to house it; while at Orléans, Taboureau called for a *maximum* and Vergnaud favored a system of public bakeries, a rigorous control of prices based on a sliding scale, and supervision of all bakers and millers. Something of the kind emerged at Lyons when its short-lived radical Commune, in the Spring of 1793, municipalized the city's bread supply.[13] Under the impact of the riots of 1792, some local authorities, including those of Orléans and Tours, urged that a ceiling be placed on the price of grain; most, however, clung to the notion that prosperity could only revive in a free market. This was generally, too, the opinion of the Assembly. The Constituent

Assembly had, by its decrees of August 29 and September 18, 1789, abolished the old regulations and restored (even more fully than Turgot in 1774) freedom of trade in grain and flour. In September 1792, following the first wave of riots of that year, the Convention had consented to revive the old regulations, while refusing to envisage a general price control.

Meanwhile, however, the needs of war, as well as the clamor of the small consumer, were gradually compelling the Jacobins, even before they came into office, to modify their views. On May 4, the Assembly, following the example of the Paris Commune, imposed a ceiling on the prices of bread and flour. But this was only a first step: it neither satisfied the small consumers and their spokesmen nor helped to solve the increasingly urgent problems of military supplies. The rioters of 1792 and 1793 had already—unlike those of 1775—extended their "taxing" operations far beyond the primary necessities of wheat, bread, and flour: in Paris they had imposed controls on sugar, soap, coffee, candles, meat, and wine; and in the provinces, on oats, soap, butter, eggs, and even on clogs, timber, coal, and iron. Meanwhile, prices continued to rise and the value of the *assignat* to fall: 36 percent of its nominal value in June, it slumped further to 22 percent in August. The same month, the Convention decreed the *levée en masse*, which called nearly three-quarters of a million men to arms. Jacques Roux and his *Enragés* had since January been campaigning for a general Maximum on prices, and by early September the cry was taken up by nearly every Paris section. It was voiced by a massive demonstration of sans-culottes who, on September 5, accompanied Hébert and other municipal leaders to the Convention to present their demands. At last, three weeks later, under the triple stimulus of argument, emergency, and riot, the Convention yielded, temporarily abandoned its liberal principles, and, through the General Maximum, embarked on a far-reaching program of economic controls.

Though comparatively short-lived the Maximum marked an important stage between the limited regulations of the Old Régime and the comprehensive state-directed economy of the future. To this the sans-culottes, both through instinct and experience and through the adoption of new political precepts, had made their contribution. In this sense the food riots of the Revolution, although based on traditional models and voicing traditional demands, had, by looking forwards as well as backwards, a degree of sophistication and a historical importance far exceeding those of the past.

REFERENCES

1. See my *The Crowd in the French Revolution*, pp. 31, 42-3, 63, 200-209.
2. R. B. Rose, "18th-Century Price-Riots, the French Revolution and the Jacobin Maximum," *International Review of Social History*, III (1959), 432-45.
3. For food prices and wages in Paris in 1789, see my article, "Prices, Wages and Popular Movements in Paris during the French Revolution," *Economic History Review*, VI, no. 3 (1954), 246-67.
4. See A. Mathiez, *La vie chère et le mouvement social sous la Terreur* (Paris, 1927), pp. 50-109.
5. For this episode, see A. Mathiez, *ibid.*, pp. 62-6, 103-106; and above all, M. Vovelle, "Les taxations populaires de février-mars et novembre-décembre 1792 dans la Beauce et sur ses confins, "*Mémoirs et documents*, no. XIII (Paris, 1958), 107-59.
6. See *The Crowd in the French Revolution*, pp. 95-8.
7. *Ibid.*, pp. 114-8. For a fuller account, see my "Les émeutes des 25, 26 février 1793 à Paris," *Annales historiques de la Révolution française*, Jan.- March 1953, pp. 33-57.
8. For famine, food problems, and disturbances in 1795 and early 1796, see various articles by Richard Cobb, including: "Les disettes de l'an II et de l'an III dans le district de Mantes et la vallée de la Basse Seine," *Mémoires de la Fédération des sociétés historiques et archéologiques de Paris et de l'Ile de France*, vol. III, Paris, 1954, pp. 227-51; "Problèmes de subsistances de l'an II et de l'an III. L'example d'un petit port normand: Honfleur," *Actes du 81ᵉ congrès des sociétés savantes, Rouen-Caen, 1956* (Paris, 1956), pp. 295-335; "Les journées de germinal an II dans la zone de ravitaillement de Paris," *Annales de Normandie*, nos. 3-4, Oct.-Dec. 1955, pp. 233-60; "Une émeute de la faim dans la banlieue rouennaise: les journées des 13, 14, et 15 germinal an II à Sotteville-les-Rouen," *ibid.*, no. 2, May 1956, pp. 151-7; "Disette et mortalité: la crise de l'an III et de l'an IV a Rouen," *ibid.*, nos. 3-4, Oct.-Dec. 1956, pp. 267-91.
9. Vovelle, *op. cit.*, pp. 139-40.
10. *Ibid.*, p. 137.
11. *Ibid.*, pp. 153, 157-8.
12. See Mathiez, *op. cit.*, pp. 139-61; and my article cited in reference 7, pp. 53-4.
13. R. B. Rose, "The French Revolution and the Grain Supply," *Bulletin of the John Rylands Library*, XXXIX, i (Sept. 1956), 171-87.

EIGHT

The French Revolution:
(3) The Labor Dispute

On the eve of the Revolution, France was second only to England as an industrial country. Since Colbert's day, large manufactories promoted by the state had made their appearance. The Le Creusot foundries, recently built on an English model, had a share capital of 10 million livres. The Anzin Mining Company employed 4,000 workers and by 1791 was equipped with twelve steam engines supplied by Boulton and Watt. French textiles rivaled those of England: 60,000 workers were employed at Rouen and Lille, 20,000 at Elbeuf, and 14,000 at Sedan; Van Robais' mills at Abbeville alone employed 12,000; while at Lyons, the great silk-weaving city of the south, there lived and worked 58,000 silk merchants, master workmen (*maîtres ouvriers*), and their journeymen. Even Paris, though primarily a city of small crafts, could, in 1791, count as many as fifty manufactories employing 100 to 800 workers apiece.

With all this, however, the industrial revolution had not yet begun in France as it had in England. Mechanization was still in its earliest infancy; there were no factory towns, and no modern factory population. Outside the forges, mines, building sites, and urban manufactories (themselves an extension of the domestic system), industry was largely carried on by weavers and spinners in their cottages, or by master craftsmen and their journeymen in the small medieval city workshops. In these, except for certain "free" or "open" areas (like Lyons and parts of Paris), numbers were strictly regulated by the guilds. The journeyman still frequently slept in his master's house, ate at his table, and even (though rarely by 1789) married his daughter or widow. Thus, there was often no clear distinction between master and workman. There were seasonal building workers and miners who, off season, returned to the farm; there were the *maitres ouvriers* of Lyons and the "piece masters" of Orléans, and there were journeymen who aspired to be masters or who, even while remaining journeymen, employed their own labor. In consequence, the wage earners had little conception of themselves as a separate social class, and we find that the few *cahiers de doléances* drafted on the eve of the Revolution by wage earners rarely voice demands that are not those of their masters.[1]

And yet the workman was acutely, and increasingly, aware of his economic position. The old medieval guild, once designed to protect all members of the craft, had declined. It had ceased to protect the journeymen, who became progressively reduced to the status of a wage earner with only the slenderest chance of ever becoming a master. Many small masters, in turn, found their material interests increasingly divorced from those of the merchant manufacturers, who subcontracted work and paid them piece rates for themselves and their employees. Abandoned by the guilds, the journeymen sought refuge in their own protective associations, the *compagnonnages.* The best known of these, the *Devoir de Liberté* and *Compagnons du Devoir* (more commonly called simply *Gavots* and *Dévorants*), organized carpenters and building workers on the *Tour de France,* negotiated wages, found jobs, and on occasion conducted strikes. Strikes were, in fact, becoming more frequent as prices tended progressively, throughout the century, to outstrip wages; yet they rarely assumed the magnitude of food riots. To cite a few examples, in 1724, a wage strike of stocking-frame weavers was broken by the arrest of their leaders. In 1737, the Paris journeymen weavers struck in protest against new regulations restricting entry to the *maîtrise.* In 1750, the Angoulême paper workers struck for four months for higher wages. In Paris, the hatters were in dispute in 1749, 1765, and again in June 1789: on the last occasion over rival journeymen's associations. In 1776, the Paris bookbinders conducted a general strike for a fourteen-hour day. The biggest dispute of all in the capital before the Revolution was that of 1786, which simultaneously involved carpenters, farriers, locksmiths, bakers, and stonemasons. In the same year, porters and carriers, striking in protest against a rival monopoly set up by Court favorites, marched to Versailles to petition the King. Of all these disputes, however, the most militant and violent were not those of laborers or journeymen but those conducted by the *maîtres ouvriers* of Lyons against the silk merchants in 1744, 1779, and 1788. The last two of these assumed insurrectional proportions, and the last had the remarkable result of virtually driving out the merchants from the electoral meetings of the guild in 1789, and leaving the field clear for the *maîtres ouvriers* to dictate the *cahier* of the silk industry.[2]

Apart from the Lyons strikes, which developed into riots, these disputes were conducted with little violence or bloodshed: this is the more remarkable when we compare them with those going on among miners, coal heavers, and weavers in England at this time.°
Some Frenchmen, it is true, like the English, violently resisted technical innovations that seemed to threaten their livelihood. In the *cahiers* and petitions of 1789, there are numerous demands by masters and journeymen—and even occasional merchants—for the "total destruction" of new mechanical devices, many of which (like the spinning jenny) had been imported from England. In Normandy, where English competition since the "Free Trade" treaty of 1786 caused heavy unemployment, the workers passed from words to deeds. In November 1788, cotton machinery was wrecked by the spinners of Falaise; machines were destroyed at Rouen in July 1789 (on the very day the Bastille fell); and six months later, Arthur Young laments in an eloquent passage the wholesale destruction of spinning jennies by the cotton operatives of Louviers, "under the idea that such machines were contrary to their interests."[3] There were threats of such disturbances under Napoleon; they were frequent under the Restoration and in the early years of Louis Philippe, and were reported as late as 1848.[4] It is therefore perhaps all the more surprising that the other (and in England the more common) type of "Luddism"—Dr. Hobsbawm's "collective bargaining by riot"—should appear to be so conspicuously absent from such disputes.† The point is underlined by the bookseller-diarist Hardy's description of the Réveillon riots (ad-

---

° See Chapter 4.

† Manuel, however, quotes an early example from Bordeaux, where in 1511 trench diggers, on strike for higher wages, wrecked a pump (F. E. Manuel, "The Luddite Movement in France," *Journal of Modern History*, X (1938), 180, n. 3).

mittedly not primarily a labor dispute) in April 1789. After noting
the damage done to Réveillon's house and property, he adds the
comment: "The whole building was gutted, *with the exception of
the workshop and the warehouse.*⁵ If this was not mere chance, it
was an omission of some significance. But why this should be so
is a mystery that I am not competent to clarify.

During the Revolution, labor disputes were not so prominent
a feature of social life as food riots, but they were by no means
unknown. In Paris, there were three wage or labor movements of
some importance: those of 1789, 1791, and 1794. The first, that of
August-September 1789, was strictly more than a mere wage
movement, as it arose over a number of issues directly springing
from the Revolutionary crisis of that summer. Many shops had
been forced to close down. The luxury trades, in particular, had
suffered from the first great wave of emigration: Necker issued
20,000 passports in the first two months after the fall of the Bastille.
Among the workers affected were bakers, wigmakers, shoemakers,
apothecaries, and domestic servants. It started on August 14,
when unemployed bakers' assistants marched in orderly procession
to the Hôtel de Ville to ask for work; they were promised redress
and quickly dispersed. On the eighteenth, 1,000 journeymen tailors met at the Louvre to demand an increase of 10 sous in their
wages; they sent a deputation to the Hôtel de Ville and succeeded
later in persuading the masters to meet their claim. The wigmakers,
who like the servants were among the more obvious victims of the
crisis, sought a remedy through the reorganization of their labor
exchanges. Four thousand assembled in the Champs Elysées,
where they had a scuffle with the National Guard; but they were
received at the Hôtel de Ville, a meeting was arranged with the
masters, and a new code was eventually drawn up.

The other workers were less successful. Both the shoemakers
and apothecaries, who were asking for higher wages, were curtly
refused permission to hold meetings and were forced to withdraw their claims. The servants' demands were partly political
and partly economic and were provoked by the events of 1789.
Four hundred of them met at the Palais Royal and sent a deputation of forty to request the municipal authorities to grant them
full citizen rights and the right to attend the district assemblies
and enroll in the National Guard (from both of which, as servile

dependents, they were barred), and, in view of unemployment, to exclude all Savoyards from their calling. They were persuaded to disperse quietly and did not carry out a threat to assemble 40,000-strong in the Champs Elysées next day. But the Commune rejected each one of their demands. It had, in fact, shown little sympathy for any of these movements: having passed a decree on August 7 forbidding all "seditious" meetings, it was inclined to apply it rigorously to all such situations. The first wave of disputes had no important repercussions; but some workers, at least, must have learned that in matters of wages and working conditions they must expect no greater consideration from the new authorities than from the old.[6]

The matter was put to the test again, and under circumstances affecting far wider groups of workers, in the spring and summer of 1791. This time, it was a wage movement pure and simple, and as it occurred in a period of comparatively low and stable prices the issue of the supply or price of food did not arise. But wages had barely risen since the outbreak of the Revolution; and although unemployment persisted in the luxury trades, in others there was a shortage of labor and the moment was opportune for seeking an advance. The journeymen carpenters were the first in the field: in April, they presented their employers with a demand for a minimum daily wage of 50 sous. It was a concerted movement and not one limited to Paris: in early April, we read, the *Campagnons du Devoir* of Arnay-le-Duc in the Côte d'Or were on their way to attend a carpenters' meeting in the capital; and a few weeks later the Paris carpenters were urging those of Orléans to follow their example.[7] They also received some support from the democrats of the Cordeliers Club: they met in the club's hall, and the carpenters' *Union Fraternelle* (unlike the *Compagnons du Devoir*, a perfectly legal body), which directed their campaign, actually linked with the club through an intermediate organization called the Comité Central. Marat, too, had opened his paper, *L'Ami du Peuple*, to workers' correspondence, and in early June he published a letter purporting to come from 560 building workers engaged on the construction of the church of Ste. Geneviève (the future Panthéon), in which the master builders were castigated as "ignorant, rapacious and insatiable oppressors." With such support, the carpenters were able, at an early stage in the campaign, to persuade the main body of contractors to agree to their terms. Yet an active minority refused and protested to the Assembly; and the City Council was called upon to arbitrate. The Council, far from favoring the workers, condemned the carpenters' association as illegal, rejected their proposal for a minimum wage as being contrary to liberal principles, and even threatened to prosecute their leaders as disturbers of the peace. Their meetings, however, were allowed to continue; though Bailly, the mayor, ordered that they should be closely watched, as he feared that the carpenters' example might be followed by workers in other trades.

He was not mistaken. The carpenters' movement was quickly followed by movements of hatters, typographers, and others. By early June, a wider movement had developed, and the master farriers, in a petition to the Assembly, warned of the existence of a "general coalition" of 80,000 Paris workers, which they said included joiners, cobblers, and locksmiths as well as their own journeymen. Though these numbers may well have been exaggerated, the Assembly took fright. Quite apart from the threat to public order, it was argued that the workers, through their "coalitions," were illegally reviving the guilds and similar "corporate" bodies that had recently been dissolved. And so the Assembly responded to the petitions of the master farriers and carpenters by adopting the famous Loi Le Chapelier, which declared all *coalitions ouvrières*, combinations or trade unions, to be illegal and threatened the striking workers with prosecution. It is a remarkable fact that no one other than Marat (and he on quite particular grounds) protested: the workers accepted the verdict and the democrats raised no objection. Even at the height of Jacobin democracy no attempt was made to repeal the law; and it remained on the statute book for nearly a hundred years to come. This was no doubt the most important of the consequences that flowed from the carpenters' movement; though the support that they received from the Cordeliers Club was also of considerable significance. Such alliances were rare, even during the Revolution.[8]

The workers' movement of 1794 had even more remarkable results, as it played an important part in the events that led to Robespierre's overthrow in Thermidor.[9] To understand the nature of the conflict that then developed we must go back to September 1793. It was then, as we noted in the last chapter, that the Jacobin-dominated Convention, under pressure of the Paris Sections and streets, adopted the law of the General Maximum. This, it may be remembered, provided for ceilings on both prices and wages: the former were to be allowed to rise by one-third over those of June 1790, the latter by one-half. In theory, therefore, the law was favorable to the workers, as "real" as well as money wages would be raised; but much, of course, depended on the degree to which wages had already risen and on who was due to implement and operate the law. In some parts of the country (up to June 1793, at least, when the government began to conduct an enquiry), wages had lagged far behind prices; in others, it was wages that had risen the higher; and this, although the evidence is slight, was probably the case in Paris: in fact Thirion, a leading Jacobin, told the Convention in early September that Parisians' wages had risen "well above the prices of consumer goods." Even if this were not strictly so, the wage earners certainly gained substantially from the operation of the law for several months to come. At first, the provisions relating to the prices of commodities were generally enforced, though more rigorously in some regions than in others. Producers, wholesalers, and shopkeepers who were not eager to cooperate were sternly reminded of the penalties for breaches of the law by local "revolutionary" and anti-hoarding committees, and the "revolutionary army" sent round the grain-producing areas to ensure the capital's supplies. Consequently, the prices of controlled goods tended to come down to the legal maximum and inflation was arrested: in fact, between August and December, the value of the *assignat* rose (in terms of 1790) from 22 to 48 percent.

At this stage the Paris wage earners, who benefited like all small consumers from the control on prices, gained a double advantage in that the Commune, which was responsible for implementing the clause of the law relating to wages, seemed in no hurry to put it into execution. This was by no means universally the case. In many parts of France, particularly in agricultural districts, the authorities quickly and strictly applied the law to the workers' wages and often showed far more determination to control wages than prices: so much so that the government had, on occasion, to intervene to protect the workers against the "excessive egoism" of the large producers and the committees on which they served.

In Paris, however, the position was rather the reverse. Paris was the largest center of radical popular democracy with a militant tradition all its own; the sans-culottes were strongly entrenched in the Commune and the Sections; and among the sans-culottes the wage earners, though politically less prominent than the shop-keepers and workshop masters, were by far the largest social group. Besides, until March 1794, the Paris Commune was dominated by Hébert and his associates, who although not conspicuously well disposed towards wage movements° looked to the sans-culottes for their political support. So the provisions relating to wages re-mained unenforced. In consequence, this being a period of war mobilization and labor shortage, wages rose higher and by early 1794 were in many cases treble those of 1790. There was, how-ever, an important exception. In the case of workers on govern-ment contracts, it was the Committee of Public Safety and not the City Council that was responsible for implementing the law; and the numbers of these workers, particularly in the newly created workshops for the manufacture of arms and ammunition, was ris-ing rapidly from month to month. At first the Committee, anxious to set an example, drew up rates for these workers that corres-ponded fairly closely to the provisions of the law; in addition, stringent measures were taken to keep the workers tied to their jobs and to control any "seditious" wage agitation in the shops. Yet, as labor continued scarce, the government was compelled to infringe its own regulations; and in May 1794, new contracts were signed allowing workers engaged in the production of small arms to earn four times the amount they had earned in 1790.[10]

However, this state of affairs was not intended to last. Apart from its own dilemmas, the government was under considerable pressure from moderates and large producers; and, having armed itself with extensive powers by a law of December 4, 1793, it pro-ceeded gradually to redress the balance in favor of the producer, to curb the activities of the sans-culottes, and to destroy the "Hébertist" opposition on its Left. The Maximum on prices was relaxed in March, so that the prices of most essential goods rose

---

° To quote an instance: During the popular "insurrection" of September 4, 1793, the National Guard was ordered to disperse building workers who were demonstrating for bread and higher wages.

higher and disturbances recurred in the Paris markets. Hébert and his associates were arrested and executed in April, the Commune was "purged" of opposition elements, and many of the "popular" societies, formed in the Sections by the sans-culottes, were closed down. The stage was now set for taking sterner measures to check the rise in wages before drastically reducing them in accordance with the law. On April 21, when a deputation of tobacco workers attended at the City Hall to ask for higher wages, the Le Chapelier law was invoked against them and five workers arrested. Other wage claims and strikes followed, involving plasterers, bakers, pork butchers, and port workers. The Commune made further arrests and threatened to prosecute workers leaving their jobs without permission. May was quiet, but in June the arms workers began to press their claims again. And not only they; at this time we find Barère instructing the public prosecutor of the Revolutionary Tribunal to take proceedings against the "counter-revolutionaries" (Barère was much given to using such terms) who were stirring up the workers engaged in the manufacture of *assignats,* arms, gunpowder, and saltpeter. Other trades joined in, and in June and July building workers, potters, and workers engaged on a variety of public contracts were voicing demands for higher wages. On July 7, even the Committee's own printing workers struck work, leading to the arrest of three of their number.

In the middle of all this agitation, the Paris Commune decided, at long last, to publish the new rates of wages to operate in the capital. This disastrous document followed the provisions of the General Maximum law to the letter, took no account of subsequent increases in both wages and prices, and faced many workers with the prospect of having their wages reduced by half while prices were rising further.[11] The moment was badly chosen, as a political crisis was already tearing the governing committees apart; and four days after the wages proclamation Robespierre and his closest lieutenants were expelled from the Convention, arrested and proscribed, and, having temporarily eluded their captors, compelled to take refuge among their friends in the Hôtel de Ville. The same day, the Hôtel de Ville was besieged by angry workers protesting against the Maximum on wages; and the rumor spread that the workers had risen "because of the Maximum," that they were marching on the Convention, and even that Robespierre had been killed in the course of the disturbance. The Commune attempted a diversion by blaming Barère, who after some hesitation had joined Robespierre's opponents, for the new scales of wages. The manoeuver failed; and the workers' hostility, added to the confusion and indifference of the Sections to their cause, contributed to the ease with which the fallen leaders were disarmed and hustled to the guillotine. When, the next day, the councilors of the Commune were in turn being driven to the place of execution, workers, to show their approval, are said to have shouted as they passed: "Foutu maximum!" [12]

We know from other evidence that the Paris wage earners believed that the removal of Robespierre and his associates would mean the end of the hated *maximum des salaires* and clear the way for higher wages. For a while, this proved to be the case: the new authorities repudiated the rates published on July 23 and in a further proclamation allowed for a more generous and elastic interpretation of the law. The workers responded by returning to their workshops. But the new rulers were also concerned to restore the freedom of the market; and as prices rose higher the value of the workers' wages rapidly declined. In November, the arms workers were pressing their claims again; and this time the Convention, far from being willing to make concessions, ordered the government workshops to be closed. Soon after, inflation took over; and the arms workers called off their wages movement and joined with other sans-culottes in resisting the calamitous rise in prices. And so, once more, the food riot rather than the strike became the order of the day.

The wage movement of the spring and summer of 1794 was certainly remarkable. It was more extensive and protracted than any other in the Revolution; for several months, it absorbed the workers' attention far more than food riots or other forms of social protest; and, far from merely lying on the periphery of political events (as the earlier movements had), it contributed to the overthrow of the government in power. But does this mean that it marks a new and important stage in the relations between capital and labor? Daniel Guérin, a French historian, thinks that it does. "The mass movement," he writes, "took on a modern form. Even before the *bourgeoisie* had finished crushing the last traces of the Old Régime, the class struggle between employers and wage earners passed to the front of the stage." [13] At first sight, this may seem a reasonable point of view. If we look at the events of 1794 in isolation, we must agree that the workers were now more interested in settling accounts with employers than with merchants and producers, that wages rather than prices were the issue of prime concern, and that the strike, and no longer the food riot, was at the forefront of the social struggle. And yet such a view is based on an optical illusion. It fails to take proper account of the exceptional circumstances of the spring and summer of that year, a period exceptionally favorable for putting forward claims for higher wages: labor was scarce, there was little or no unemployment; though prices were rising, there was no runaway inflation; and large numbers of small workshop workers—among the most militant of the Paris sans-culottes—had been drafted into larger units of 200 men and more. Not one of these factors continued after December 1794; and as inflation and unemployment took over, the workers abandoned the strike and resorted to the traditional and more familiar type of social protest.

In fact, the labor disputes and wage movements of the Revolution followed the general pattern of those of the Old Régime. They might be more widespread and more protracted; they were sometimes touched, like those of 1791 and 1794, by the struggle of contending parties; they might, like those of 1794, have important political results; but they tended, as earlier movements, to occur in periods of stable prices and when prices rose steeply to give way to food riots; they were certainly not more violent; and the relations between capital and labor remained substantially unchanged. Yet this is not to say that nothing had changed and no important new lessons had been learned for the future. The wage earners, like others, had been steeped in and fired by the new explosive ideas of the Revolution. For all their occasional lawyers' tricks and reservations, the revolutionaries (and none more insistently than the Jacobins) had proclaimed the common rights of man, equality, and the dignity of human labor. Such ideas once learned were not easily forgotten, and would have a future harvest in the more insistent claims that labor would make on capital. In England, less touched by the new ideas but already undergoing an industrial revolution, such a development in employer-worker relations was already taking place. France would have a similar experience, and at a considerably higher pitch, in the 1830's and '40's.

REFERENCES

1. See my "The Parisian Wage-Earning Population and the Insurrectionary Movements of 1789-91" (unpublished Ph.D. thesis in 2 vols., London University, 1950), I, 11-33.
2. *Ibid.*, I, 16-20. See also my article, "Les ouvriers parisiens dans la Révolution française," *La Pensée,* June-Sept. 1953, pp. 108 ff.
3. "The Parisian Wage-Earning Population," I, 26-7; C. Schmidt, "La crise industrielle de 1788 en France," *Revue historique,* XCVII (1908), 86; F. E. Manuel, "The Luddite Movement in France," *Journal of Modern History,* X (1938), 183; Arthur Young, *Travels in France and Italy* (Everyman Library, London, 1915), p. 134.
4. Manuel, *op. cit.,* pp. 183-211; P. Amann, "The Changing Outlines of 1848," *American Historical Review,* LXVIII (1963), 941.
5. Quoted by Sophie A. Lotté in her contribution to "I sansculotti; una discussione tra storici marxisti", in *Critica Storica,* I (1962), 387-91 (author's italics; my translation).
6. S. Hardy, *Mes loisirs, ou journal d'événements tels qu'ils parviennent à ma connoissance* (MS. in 8 vols. Paris 1764-89. Bibliothèque Nationale, fonds français, nos. 6680-7), VIII, 434, 438-9, 455; Grace M. Jaffé, *Le mouvement ouvrier à Paris pendant la Révolution française (1789-1791)* (Paris, 1927), pp. 65-73.
7. S. Lacroix, *Actes de la Commune de Paris pendant le Révolution française,* 2nd series (8 vols. Paris, 1900-1914), III, 700; G. Lefebvre, "Urban Society in the Orléanais in the late Eighteenth Century," *Past and Present,* April 1961, p. 68.
8. Jaffé, *op. cit.,* Part II; Lacroix, *loc. cit.;* "The Parisian Wage-Earning Population," I, 179-85.
9. For much of what follows, see my paper, "Die Arbeiter und die Revolutionsregierung," in W. Markov (ed.), *Maximilien Robespierre 1758-1794* (Berlin, 1958), pp. 301-22.
10. C. Richard, *Le Comité de Salut public et les fabrications de guerre sous la Terreur* (Paris, 1922), pp. 699-709, 720.
11. G. Rudé and A. Soboul, "Le maximum des salaires parisiens et le 9 thermidor," *Annales historiques de la Révolution française,* Jan.-March 1954, pp. 1-22.
12. A. Aulard, *Paris pendant la réaction thermidorienne* (5 vols. Paris, 1898-1902), I, 11.
13. D. Guerin, *La lutte de classes sous la première République (1793-1797)* (2 vols. Paris, 1946), II, 155 (my translation).

NINE

"Church and King" Riots

So far, we have been mainly concerned with popular movements that were either nonpolitical, like strikes and rural food riots, or imbued with the political ideas of radicals, democrats and republicans, or other reformist or revolutionary groups and parties. This, admittedly, was not entirely so in the case of certain city riots, such as the Gordon Riots in London and the disturbances provoked by the *parlement* in pre-revolutionary Paris. The first, in spite of radical undertones, injured rather than advanced the radical cause; and the second were certainly intended by their promoters to further the interest of the privileged classes against both monarchy and Third Estate. Yet neither, though enlisted in the service of a cause that might be termed "reactionary" rather than "progressive," was conservative in the sense that it promoted established or traditional institutions. The *parlement* was deliberately challenging the "despotism" of Louis XVI and his ministers; and the Gordon rioters, while overtly championing the Protestant Church, were not demonstrating their loyalty to George III—far from it; they charged him with breaking his Coronation Oath by relaxing the disabilities of Roman Catholics.

In contrast with all these other movements, a distinctive feature of "Church and King" riots and demonstrations is their political conservatism.[1] Where other movements, inspired by liberal, democratic, republican, or anticlerical ideas, are concerned to destroy privilege or absolute monarchy, or to enlarge the frontiers of religious toleration, these rioters proclaim their attachment to the established order and traditional way of life against their disruption by "Jacobins," "unbelievers," "foreigners," or other alien elements. Such movements have a long history from the Paris anti-

135

Huguenot Commune of 1588 to the Tsarist Russian "Black Hundreds," if not beyond; but above all, they flourished during the French Revolution; for the French, once they left France and exported their revolutionary ideas elsewhere, could be shown to be not only infidels and republicans, but "foreigners" as well. This was by no means a universal experience, as the French found powerful support and valuable allies in the Netherlands, Switzerland, Germany, and Northern Italy—countries with a considerable middle class and which, even before the French arrived, had absorbed many of the ideas of the Enlightenment and the Declaration of the Rights of Man.

In certain countries, however, particularly those in which the middle class was weak and the influence of the Catholic Church was strong, there were urban and peasant communities that showed themselves to be not only remarkably resistant but positively hostile to the new ideas from France. For quite particular reasons this was not the case with Catholic Ireland or Poland, but it was demonstrably so in southern Italy, Spain, and the Tyrol. In Southern Italy, as soon as Bonaparte's back was safely turned in 1798, bandits and peasant bands launched a guerrilla war to drive out the French. In 1809, Tyrolese peasants under Andreas Hofer waged a long and bitter campaign against Napoleon's Bavarian allies, to whom their country had been ceded, not for national independence but for Austria and Holy Church. In France itself, the peasants of the Vendée and *chouans* of Brittany and Normandy rallied to their priests and former manorial lords against the Revolution and for nearly ten years fought a desparate and bloody civil war against the Jacobins, the Directory, and Napoleon. And of all the loyalist peasant movements the most remarkable was that in Spain. When Napoleon installed his brother Joseph on the Spanish throne, the peasants rebelled and, led by priests and nobles, fought a five-year guerrilla war that played a significant part in driving the French out of the Peninsula. Some, like Sheridan in England, saw it as a first example of an occupied country turning the principles of the French Revolution against the French themselves. It was hardly that, as no people in Europe had shown itself so impervious as the Spanish to French revolutionary ideas. Even so, it was more than a purely "Church and King" rebellion on the Vendéan or Tyrolese pattern, because the Spanish peasants, while staunch defenders of their ancient faith and Bourbon dynasty, were also fighting what amounted to a national and patriotic war.

Such protracted rebellions in the name of "Church and King" were more characteristic of the countryside than of cities, both because peasants were more stable recruits for loyalist causes and because the country lent itself more readily to guerrilla warfare than the town. Yet the "Church and King" riot, as distinct from the conservative guerrilla movement, was essentially an urban manifestation. The first outbreak of this kind at the time of the French Revolution occurred in Brussels in March 1790, when the houses of wealthy "Vonckists" (members of the pro-French democratic, or "patriot," party) were pillaged and destroyed, and a "patriot" leader was forced to his knees and made to declare: "I recognise, by order of the Brussels people, that the Patriotic Society of which I am a member is nothing but a band of rogues." [2] Again, the Viennese poorer classes(with the exception, it appears, of the cobblers) were staunchly "Church and King" and anti-Jacobin in the 1790's and, in 1793, rioted against the execution of Louis XVI; and the *lazzaroni*, or "lower orders," of Naples staged a bloody *jacquerie* against the French and their own liberal, French-collaborating officials in 1799.[3] In Rome, perhaps the least submissive to the French of all Italian cities, the common people responded to the call of their priests (in this case, the Pope himself was "King") and rioted against the French to cries of "Viva Maria!"

Yet, in France itself there was no urban equivalent to the Vendée. The nearest perhaps was Nantes, in the west, the scene of Carrier's gruesome *noyades* of 1793; but the anti-Jacobin outbreak here was more in the nature of a spill-over from the Vendée than a "Church and King" movement in its own right. Several French cities rebelled against Jacobin rule: Caen, Bordeaux, Toulon, Lyons, and Marseilles were among them; but these revolts were anti-Jacobin rather than royalist; and even the White Terror in the south that followed Robespierre's execution, though certainly "counter-revolutionary" in both form and intent, took the form of savage reprisals for wrongs suffered or imagined rather than of a demonstration for "Church and King." Even the royalist-promoted insurrection in Paris in October 1795 (the 13th Vendémiaire) does not really qualify. The National Convention had decreed (as much to ward off the royalist danger as to perpetuate its own existence) that in the elections to the new legislature set up under the Constitution of that year, only one-third of the deputies should be freely elected and two-thirds should be hand-picked by the outgoing Assembly. The fury that this provoked among the Parisian Sections (now solidly *bourgeois* and moderate after being purged of all Jacobins and sans-culottes) was ably exploited by the royalist Lepeletier Section and led to an armed rebellion in which some 7,000 to 8,000 citizens took part. But for most of the insurgents, it was far more of a demonstration in de-fence of property, which they believed to be endangered, than a conscious attempt to overthrow the Republic; and above all, they failed to enlist the support of the common people of the city. The sans-culottes, though badly hit by inflation and deeply suspicious of the Convention's policies, preferred a *bourgeois* Republic to none at all, and refused to join the rebels.[4]

This last point is crucial; for the second common feature of the "Church and King" movement or riot is its dependence on solid popular support. Moreover, beneath its borrowed slogans (and this is particularly true of cities), there is always an element of social protest: we have already seen something of the kind in the London Gordon Riots. Whereas in radical or Jacobin-type dis-turbances popular anger is directed, if not against hoarders and speculators (or those reputed to be such), against aristocrats, Court, clergy, or privileged corporations, the target of "Church and King" is nearly always "the rich" or the wealthy middle class, and the ideas and institutions that they sponsor. This was evidently so in the case of the Brussels and Neopolitan riots of which we have spoken; and it has been suggested that the Vendéan peasants were all the more willing to follow their priests and nobles be-cause the latter had commonly employed middle-class lawyers and agents to represent them in their dealings with their tenants; and it was they rather than their masters that had incurred the peasants' odium.[5] The "Church and King" movement was there-fore a two-edged weapon which, because of its popular social bias, might lead to curious and ambivalent situations, highly embar-rassing to those whose interests it was overtly promoting. Thus, as Dr. Hobsbawm tells us:

The Viennese who rioted against the execution of the French King in 1793 directed their fury against the French emigrant nobles. The *lazzeroni* of Naples . . . were passionate defenders of Church and King, and even more savage anti-Jacobins in 1799. Yet they sang songs against all the upper classes who, in their view, had "betrayed the king," notably "knights and monks," sacked the houses of royalists impartially, and defined as Jacobins and enemies of the king any owners of property, or more simply, anyone with a carriage.

This element in "Church and King" might lead even otherwise politically conservative peasants into strange associations; and Dr. Hobsbawm quotes the manifesto of an Italian "Church and King" brigand of 1863, who thus proclaimed his common devotion to Pope, King, and Garibaldi:

Out with the traitors, out with the beggars, long live the fair kingdom of Naples with its most religious sovereign, long live the vicar of Christ Pius IX, and long live our ardent republican brothers! [6]

It is a little like the southern Irishman who cheered Sir Edward Carson, the determined enemy of Irish Home Rule, because, like himself, he was "agin the Government."

To return, after this slight digression, to the period of the French Revolution; and this time to England. "Church and King" riots and movements were certainly more typical of agrarian than industrial countries and of those of absolute rather than of limited monarchy. Yet, owing to the peculiar circumstances of the time, England's manufacturing cities also had, in the 1790's, disturbances that may properly be labeled "Church and King." The circumstances were briefly these. Religious dissenters (Quakers, Baptists, Presbyterians, and Unitarians), driven out from England's corporate towns by the Anglican restoration of Charles II's day, had taken refuge in the growing industrial cities of the midlands and the north. Here new opportunities had arisen both for holding civic office and for accumulating wealth. Wealthy middle-class dissenters set up Dissenting Academies and joined with others in discussing and promoting the ideas of the Enlightenment through such bodies as the Lunar Society in Birmingham and the Literary and Philosophical Society in Manchester. Some, though not others, took part in the parliamentary reform movements of the 1760's-1780's; but the outbreak of the French Revolution tended to associate religious dissent and political reform more closely. This was due partly to the sharpening of political controversy that the Revolution provoked, in England as elsewhere; but, more particularly, it came about because the dissenters had launched a campaign in 1787 for the repeal of the Test and Corporation Acts, and the news from Paris gave them fresh encouragement and tended, in their own and others' eyes, to identify their hopes of reform with those of the French. Tories and Anglicans, on the other hand, as custodians of the monarchical constitution and Established Church, saw both threatened by a double danger that they were inclined to see as one; and to meet it they formed King and Church clubs and similar bodies, of which the first appeared in Manchester in March 1790.[7] The popular contingents were provided by the "lower orders" of the rapidly expanding manufacturing cities, not yet organized in labor movements, continually provoked by poor wages and rising food prices,[*] and resentful of magistrates and wealthy industrialists and merchants, whether Presbyterian, Quaker, Unitarian, or other.

From this combination of elements (though their proportions varied widely) sprang the "Church and King" riots of 1791-4 in Birmingham, Manchester, and Nottingham. The Nottingham disturbances were of a different kind from the others: for one thing, they occurred after England had entered the war against France, which branded the reforming party as anti-patriotic as well as Jacobin. Here the religious element played little or no part, and both loyalists and reformers had popular support. The Nottingham Constitutional Society had collected 2,500 signatures to a petition for parliamentary reform, which had been discussed and rejected by the Commons in February 1793; and in the street battles, between reformers and loyalists that followed in June that year and in July 1794, the reformers gave as good as they received: there were several wounded on either side.[8] In the Manchester disturbances of June and December 1792, as was more usual in such cases,

---

[*] There were food riots in Birmingham in1782; wage movements in Nottingham in 1783, 1790, and 1793; and further food riots in Birmingham, Nottingham, and Leicester in 1792 (R. W. Wearmouth, *Methodism and the Common People of England of the Eighteenth Century* (London, 1945), Chapters 1-3; *Gentleman's Magazine,* LXII (Jan.-June 1792), 471-2).

the reformist defenders were heavily outnumbered. The "Church and King" party had, as we have seen, formed a club in 1790; and, a few months later, the reformers, whose leading spirit was Thomas Walker, a prosperous cotton manufacturer, formed themselves into a Constitutional Society. The society, like those in London and Birmingham, celebrated the anniversary of the fall of the Bastille in July 1791; but Manchester, unlike these other cities, was on this occasion saved from loyalist-provoked disturbance—possibly because Walker was Borough Reeve that year. In the following June, however, crowds assembled in St. Anne's Square and using trees as battering rams attacked the Cross Street Chapel (the original home of the Literary and Philosophical Society) and a new Unitarian chapel in Moseley Street. In September, Thomas Walker's name appeared on an address to the French National Convention jointly sponsored by the Manchester Constitutional and Reformation Societies, the London Corresponding Society, and other militant reforming bodies; so he was a natural target for the hostility of "Church and King." A boycott of all radical clubs had been declared by the city's innkeepers; the press and loyalist clubs joined in the hue and cry; and something like an anti-Jacobin terror and panic had been whipped up before the crowd stepped in again. On December 10, *the Gentleman's Magazine* reported:

A great crowd assembled around the Herald-office [the local radical newspaper], some of the windows of which they broke, and dispersed; the next night they met stronger, and paraded the streets, singing and shouting—*God save the King!* they then proceeded to the object of their late resentment, and again broke the windows. They afterwards went to the house of Mr. Walker, where they also demolished some of the windows; here, however, they were resisted by Mr. W. who firing upon them, they dispersed; two men in this affair are said to be wounded.

The next day some friends of Mr. Walker waited upon the Committee established for protection of property, &c. who sent a deputation to promise him support, if he desisted from the use of fire arms; advising him at the same time, as the most prudent step, to leave town in a few days, as the mob were seriously clamorous for his person. No other violence however, than the breaking of the windows of the house of Messrs. Falkner and Walker has yet been committed.—When this account came away, a reassemblage of the mob was apprehended, and the magistrates and military were accordingly waiting. But, fortunately, their exertions were not wanted.

The "exertions" of magistrates were certainly not much in evidence, and Walker had been largely left to fend for himself.[9]

This reluctance of magistrates to intervene had been more strikingly evident in the far wilder orgies that rocked Birmingham in July 1791.[10] The central figure in this affair was Joseph Priestley, the distinguished scientist and Unitarian minister. The Unitarians were more strongly entrenched in Birmingham than in any other city; and Priestley, together with William Russell, a Unitarian merchant, had played the leading part in the local campaign to win full toleration for dissenters. In November 1789, one of Priestley's sermons had provoked a violent sectarian dispute, in the course of which Anglicans charged dissenters with attempting to disrupt both monarchy and Church. The charge was made to appear the more plausible as Priestley, and many of his associates, had warmly welcomed the French Revolution and renewed their efforts to promote parliamentary reform in England. In June 1791, Priestley lent his name to an appeal for support for a newly planned Warwickshire Constitutional Society, pledged to male adult suffrage and shorter parliaments. And to crown his misdeeds in the eyes of the loyalists, this "arch-priest of Pandaemonian liberty" (as a contributor to the *Gentleman's Magazine* termed him) and his friends gave public notice of a dinner to be held at the Birmingham Hotel to celebrate the second anniversary of the fall of the Bastille.

This was the occasion that provoked the Birmingham riots. Yet the dinner itself was sedate and unprovocative enough. Some 80 to 90 gentlemen assembled, chose an Anglican as their chairman, solemnly drank eighteen toasts, including toasts to the King, the Constitution, and the prosperity of Birmingham as well as to the French Assembly and the Majesty of the People; and, anxious not to cause public offense, quickly concluded their business and dispersed. Priestley was not there, probably because he had read warning signs that same morning, when slogans appeared on the walls proclaiming "destruction to the Presbyterians" and "Church and King for ever!" On arrival at the dinner, guests were greeted (such was the confusion as to its purpose) with shouts of "no popery" and, when they departed, were pelted with mud and stones; but they got away safely before the hotel was invaded and looted. The rioters now started on their work in earnest and continued, without serious interruption, for the next three days. Having threatened a Quaker meeting house, they went on to the Unitarian New Meeting (of which Priestley was minister) and burned it to the ground. But they showed discrimination: the Old Meeting, being enclosed by other buildings, was "pulled down" and not fired, after the pews and pulpits had been wrenched out to make a bonfire in the burial ground next door. Priestley's house at Fair Field, Sparkbrook, one and a half miles away, was next on the list. The victim, warned of the crowd's approach, had already made his escape; but his house was ransacked and burned down, and his books, priceless notes, and scientific instruments were all smashed and destroyed. One rioter was killed by a falling cornice stone; most slept the night in the field adjoining the ruins, from which they were only prised the next day by the Earl of Orford who, no doubt with the best of intentions, marched them into Birmingham; but in the event (as the magistrates were half-hearted or powerless to intervene) they were left free to roam the streets to shouts of "Church and King!" and to release prisoners from the lock-up and city jail.

Further attacks followed on the properties of prominent Unitarians and Quakers, most of them wealthy, some suspect for their "philosophical-radical" associations, others tarnished (in the eyes of the crowd) for their connection with law and justice. An early victim was John Ryland, a merchant banker, whose elegant mansion, Baskerville House at Easy Hill, was set on fire after the rioters had absorbed £300 worth of liquor in his cellars. "Many of the rioters," reported the *Annual Register*, "who were drunk, perished in the cellars, either by the flames, or suffocation by the falling of the roof." Later, newly enrolled constables, armed with half mop-sticks, arrived on the scene, but were disarmed and put to flight, leaving one dead and several injured behind them. Other victims that day included William Hutton, local historian and commissioner of the Birmingham Court of Requests (the court specialized in the collection of petty debts); and John Taylor, former High Sheriff, a justice of the peace, and a wealthy manu-

facturer and banker. Hutton's house and stationer's shop in the
High Street were looted and demolished: once more, to avoid a
general conflagration, arson was deliberately rejected; but his
country house at Washwood Heath, three miles out of the city,
was burned to the ground. The same fate befell John Taylor's
residence, Bordesley Hall, which, after the furniture had been
stripped and demolished and the out-offices, stables, and ricks
had been set alight, "exhibited a most tremendous scene of de-
vestation." The next day a Baptist meeting hall was looted, and
further victims of plunder or arson included Joseph Jukes and
John Coates of Ladywood; John Hobson, dissenting minister of
Bordesley Heath; Thomas Hawkes of Moseley Wake Green; John
Harewood, a blind Baptist preacher; William Humphreys of
Sparkbrook; and William Russell, justice of the peace, merchant,
and Unitarian leader, of Showell Green. The military had not yet
arrived, and in the city (reported the *Annual Register*), "small
parties of three or five levied contributions of meat, liquor, and
money, with the same indifference that they would levy parish
taxes."

By Sunday night, July 17 (the fourth day of the riots), the
Dragoons began to ride in from Nottingham, and the riots in the
city ended. But they continued for a few more days in the neighboring countryside. The afternoon before, the main body of rioters
had begun to move south from Birmingham, via Ladywood,
Edgbaston, King's Heath, and Moseley, in the direction of King's
Norton and the dissenters' meeting house there, seven miles away,
which they reduced to ashes. At Warstock, Mr. Cox, a Unitarian
farmer, had his cellar emptied and his house destroyed. Returning
from the Kinkswood chapel, a small group of rioters attacked the
property of Dr. William Withering at Edgaston Hall: Withering,
though an Anglican, was a friend of Priestley's and a fellow member of the Lunar Society. Being forewarned of trouble, he had
hired a body of stout defenders, who drove away the assailants
and took a prisoner. This was virtually the last of the riots, though
there were rumors the next two days of skirmishes and minor
"depredations" at Alcester, Bromsgrove, Hagley, and Halesowen.
On the morning of the twentieth, it was reported that "the country
round for ten miles was scoured by the light horse; but not one
rioter was met with, and all the manufactories are at work, as if

no interruption had taken place." The riots had lasted five days, three of them without effective challenge by the law. Four dissenters' meeting houses (three Unitarian and one Baptist) had been severely damaged or destroyed; and the houses of at least twenty-seven persons had been looted, demolished, fired, or simply threatened. Losses were estimated at £100,000, about a quarter of which was later paid in compensation. Considering the scale of the damage and the duration of the riots, judicial retribution was not severe: seventeen rioters were brought to trial at the Worcester and Warwick assizes; only four were found guilty, and two were hanged.[11]

Who were the rioters, and who and what provoked them? Though the evidence is slight on both accounts, the first question appears to be more easily answered than the second. From the few arrests and indictments and contemporary accounts, Mr. Rose concludes that those taking part were largely drawn from the city's industrial artisans and laborers.[12] There seems little reason to doubt it; and the definition is certainly more exact than the label given them in a French revolutionary document of 1793: "the aristocrats of Birmingham"![13] But why should they engage in such orgies of destruction? Were they paid to do so? There is no evidence to support it: in fact, we are told that when a Captain Carver tried to save John Taylor's house by offering a reward of 100 guineas, "he was hustled amidst the crowd, with a cry of 'No Bribery!' and narrowly escaped their fury."[14] Was it for loot? Loot certainly played a part: we read that Black Country colliers, who descended on the city after the riots were all but over, returned home "laden with spoils." But such an explanation would fail to take account of the crowd's discrimination and the pin-pointing of its attacks on selected targets, with every effort made to avoid damaging adjoining property. The men whose names were on the riot captains' "lists" (again, we must add, either mythical or real) were a highly selected group of persons: political reformers, admirers of the French, members of the Lunar Society, dissenters (Quakers, Baptists, and Unitarians); many of them prominent in civic life, and nearly all men of wealth and substance. The "hard and black hands" seem, in fact, to have been all the more willing to get to grips with the dissenters and philosophical radicals—the declared enemies of Church and King—

because they were also leading figures among the city's wealthy middle class.[15] Nor need this surprise us: we saw a similar social bias in the attacks on Catholic houses in Londen eleven years before.

For those in authority, the nature of this social bias created its particular problems and presented a dilemma. To give the crowd its head to teach the enemies of Church and King a lesson was one thing; but what was the guarantee that it would stop at that and not engage in a general assault on property? In London, in 1780, the magistrates and City Corporation had shown remarkable complacency as long as the "No Popery" crowds confined their activities to attacks on Roman Catholic chapels, schools, and houses; but when they began to burn down prisons, to collect the toll money on Blackfriars Bridge and threaten the Bank of England, it was quite another matter. Of course, then as now, there were dedicated hotheads who were prepared to take the risk; and it seems well established that certain of the justices in Birmingham, staunch supporters of Church and King and declared opponents of dissent and political reform, acted with criminal negligence or even directly incited the rioters to act.[16] Some highly placed persons—outside Birmingham, they included the Marquess of Buckingham and the Lord Advocate of Scotland—were openly jubilant at the turn of events and thought them a suitable example for others to follow. To some of the victims, the King himself did not appear entirely blameless; and Priestley wrote that "the friends of the court, if not the prime ministers themselves, were the favorers of that riot; having, no doubt, thought to intimidate the friends of liberty by the measure." Priestley had certainly the right to feel bitter: he had lost his laboratory and library, had been hounded from Birmingham, and eventually sought refuge in the United States; and George III appeared to lend credence to the charge by expressing his pleasure, in a letter to Dundas, that "Priestley is the sufferer for the doctrine he and his party have instilled." Yet, whatever the King's private feelings in the matter, Dundas perfectly well understood that the riots had wider, and more dangerous, social implications. He acted with energy in dispatching troops to Birmingham (the request was only sent on July 15) and pointedly warned the magistrates that "in the present temper of the people" it was "difficult to foresee what turn affairs might be likely to take." He saw the prime cause of the riots as the "levelling principle" infecting "the lower classes of the people"; and he ordered one military unit intended for Birmingham to be sent through Coventry and Wolverhampton, where similar disturbances were feared.[17]

In short, to those in authority, anxious as they might be to curb the activities of radicals and reformers, the "Church and King" riot was nearly always more of a liability than an asset. The Birmingham riots, as we have seen, had their sequel in Manchester and Nottingham; but these were half-hearted imitations, as responsible persons, however firm their attachment to Church and monarchy, saw them more as a warning than as an example to be prescribed to others. The Emperor Francis I of Austria probably spoke for other rulers as well as for himself when he said of his own "popular legitimists": "Now they are patriots for me; but one day they may be patriots against me."[18]

It was not only that the crowd, with its social aspirations, might be fickle in its political loyalties and that its behavior could not be predicted. Times were rapidly changing as well. As industrialization spread and the factory system began to take root, the "hard and black hands" found other causes to lure them and targets other than "Jacobins," Protestant and Catholic dissenters, or even just "the rich," against which to vent their anger when wages were low or prices high. "Church and King" had, in France, as we have seen, been no answer to the permeation of radical ideas among the common people; and in England, too, there were already industrial city populations who were turning to radical political solutions. In London, this had begun to happen at the time of Wilkes, if not before; in the early 1790's, Sheffield's "lower orders" celebrated the victories of France's revolutionary armies, and its Constitutional Society of 2,000 members was mainly composed of "the lower sort of workmen."[19] By 1815, this shift from loyalism to radicalism had become general among the English industrial population, and it would soon be so in France and other countries, too. In fact, the "Church and King" riot, even more decidedly than Luddism and other pre-industrial popular manifestations, had little place in the emerging society of the future.

REFERENCES

1. See E. J. Hobsbawm, *Primitive Rebels* (Manchester, 1959), pp. 7, 28, 81, 112, 118, 120-123, 175. I am indebted to Professor Hobsbawm for several of the ideas expressed in this chapter.
2. *Relation véritable du soulèvement général du Peuple de Bruxelles* (Paris, 1790).
3. Hobsbawm, *op. cit.*, pp. 112, 120.
4. See my *The Crowd in the French Revolution* (Oxford, 1959), pp. 160-77.
5. J. Godechot, *Les Révolutions (1770-1799)* (Paris, 1963), pp. 323-4.
6. Hobsbawm, *op. cit.*, pp. 112, 119.
7. See P. A. Brown, *The French Revolution in English History* (London, 1923), pp. 51-74.
8. *Gentleman's Magazine*, LXIII (July-Dec. 1793), 630; Wearmouth, *loc. cit.*
9. Brown, *op. cit.*, pp. 61, 69, 90, 124; *Annual Register*, XXXIV (1792), 70-72; *Gentleman's Magazine*, LXII (June-Dec. 1792), 1144-5. See also Frida Knight, *The Strange Case of Thomas Walker* (London, 1957).
10. For a scholarly study of this affair, see R. B. Rose, "The Priestley Riots of 1791," *Past and Present*, Nov. 1960, pp. 68-88. What follows is largely taken from Mr. Rose's paper, supplemented by the accounts in the *Annual Register* and *Gentleman's Magazine*.
11. Rose, *op. cit.*, pp. 68-76, 78, 82; Brown, *op. cit.*, pp. 78-81; *Gentleman's Magazine*, LXI (July-Dec. 1791), 674-6, 772; *Annual Register*, XXXIII (1791), 25-9, 34-5.
12. Rose, *op. cit.*, p. 83.
13. W. Markov and A. Soboul (eds.), *Die Sanskulotten von Paris: Dokumente zur Geschichte der Volksbewegung 1793-1794* (Berlin, 1957), p. 2.
14. *Annual Register*, XXXIII, 127.
15. Rose, *op. cit.*, pp. 75, 83.
16. *Ibid.*, pp. 80-82.
17. *Ibid.*, pp. 77-8; Brown, *op. cit.*, 80-81.
18. Hobsbawm, *op. cit.*, p. 119.
19. B. Simon, *Studies in the History of Education 1780-1870* (London, 1960), p. 182; E. P. Thompson, *The Making of the English Working Class*, p. 104.

TEN

"Captain Swing"
and "Rebecca's Daughters"

The 1790's in England saw virtually the end of the older type of city riot: the radical demonstrations in London and Manchester in the years following the Napoleonic Wars were political outbreaks of quite a different kind.* But the countryside was, as might be expected, slower to change in this respect as in so many others. The old English village, though long undermined by enclosure, improving landlords and migration to the towns, took longer to die than the factory town to come to birth; and the early years of the nineteenth century were marked by a series of social protests denoting the stubbornness with which the old English (and Welsh) peasantry resisted the new and clung to the old ways of life. Of these, none perhaps was more remarkable than the strange affair of Bossenden Wood in Kent, where seven villagers, the devoted followers of Sir William Courtenay (the alias of John Tom), lost their lives in a last-ditch battle with the military. This was a millenarial movement of Kentish peasants, who believed implicitly, and were prepared to die for, the "great news" that their leader appeared to bring them.[1] It took place in 1838—in the very year that the People's Charter, the first great popular manifesto of the new industrial age, was drafted and issued in London. But it was

---

* There was still, however, a hangover from the past in the anti-Corn Law riots in London in 1815, and, even more, in the Bristol riots of 1831, when the Mansion House and Bishop's Palace were sacked, prisoners' were released from the jails, and houses and shops were looted and burned down (E. P. Thompson. *The Making of the English Working Class*, pp. 74-5).

only a localized movement, confined to a handful of villages within a single county. On a far larger scale were the "Swing" riots of 1830 in the English southern counties and the "Rebecca" riots of 1839 and 1842-3 in Wales. *

The disturbances in the southern counties broke out in one of the most troubled years in the whole of English history: it marks the highest point in Professor Rostow's "social tension chart" for 1790-1850, and ushered in a two-year period that has been described as being of "a sustained intensity of excitement unknown since 1641." [2] This "last laborers' revolt" (as the Hammonds termed it) arose from a complex of social and political causes that will not be analyzed here. Suffice it to say that such factors as tithe, rents, wages, pauperism and poverty, agricultural depression, poaching and the game laws, and radical agitation may all have played a part. [3] Gibbon Wakefield, at this time himself a radical, was inclined to see the squire and parson, rather than the tenant farmer, as the supposed villain of the piece; and he and the French historian, Halévy, have both stressed the influence exerted on the laborers by the revolution that, in July, broke out in France and quickly spread to Switzerland, Germany, and Belgium. The English rural poor, Wakefield insisted, identified themselves with the "heroes of the barricades," the news of whose exploits inflamed them "against those whom they most justly consider as their oppressors." [4]

However this may be, there were other, more immediate, issues that roused the laborers' anger and resentment: in the first place, that of wages, which in Kent (a county of relatively high earnings) ranged from 10s. to 13s.6d. a week, in Berkshire and Hampshire from 7 to 9s., and in Wiltshire from as little as 6 to 7s. But, if wages were the underlying cause that generalized disturbance, the spark that set the movement off was not so much the refusal of farmers to pay higher earnings as the introduction of threshing machines. This happened near Canterbury in Kent at the end of

---

* The name "Swing" appears to derive from the swinging stick of the flail used in threshing (E. Halévy, *The Triumph of Reform 1830-1841* (London, 1950), p. 7); "Rebecca" and her "daughters" derive from *Genesis*, XXIV, 60: "And they blessed Rebekah and said unto her, let thy seed possess the gates of those which hate them."

August—preceded, Halévy tells us, by the farmers' employment of cheaper Irish labor. The machines were smashed by the laborers. A lull followed, during which further machines were introduced, both in Kent and other southern counties. On the night of October 5, the *Gentleman's Magazine* reported, laborers "set fire to and burnt the barns and cornstacks belonging to the Rev. Mr. Price of Lyminge." Elsewhere in the county, "a body of men, amounting to upwards of 200 in number, lately assembled at the respective residences of Sir Henry Oxenden, Sir Henry Tucker Montresor, Mr. Kelsey, Mr. Holtum, and Mr. Sankey, farmers, and violently broke into their barns, where they destroyed the thrashing-machines they found in them respectively." [5]

This was only a beginning. As machines were brought in to other districts and as laborers took courage from the Kentishmen's example, the riots spread to further counties. The means of propagation varied: it might be by alehouse gossip, by traveling bands who, in some cases, crossed from one county to another; or, as the riots got under way, they might follow the pattern of the French peasant disturbances of 1775 and 1789 and spread by a simple spontaneous "contagion," from village to village or pub to pub. With rare exceptions, the organization was on a purely local scale; and bands led by "foremen" or "captains" operated over a number of adjoining villages, at most. A problem was to muster men: "this [runs a press report] they do openly by forcing the farm laborers to join them; we mean that a few of the more determined insist on the company of others, and their demands increase with their numbers." By such means the disturbances spread with remarkable speed, rarely lingering in any one county for more than a few days. In the next two to three weeks, the "diabolical spirit" reached further westwards into West Sussex, Hampshire, Wiltshire, Dorset and Gloucester. In Berkshire there were two separate focal points: one in the centre around Thatcham, where a new movement (over wages at first) reached west to Newbury and southwards back into Hampshire; the other started in the wooded country near Windsor and followed an uneven northern course into Buckingham, Oxford and Northampton. In Norfolk a new focal point appeared at North Walsham near the coast and spread south to Norwich and into both parts of Suffolk (where Church of England

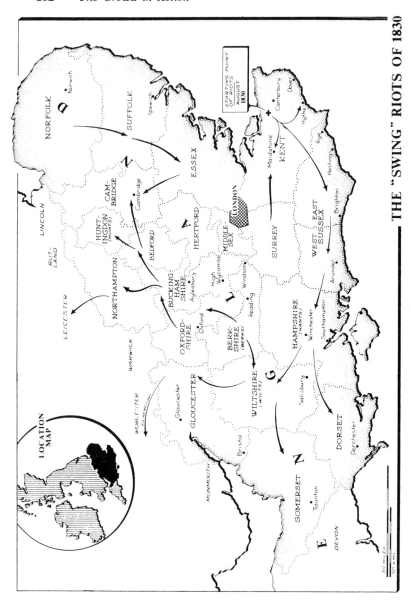

THE "SWING" RIOTS OF 1830

parsons were a major target) and into Essex, where wages movements and machine-breaking went on side by side. From Essex
riots reached into Cambridgeshire, Leicester and Lincoln; and,
in Cumberland, there were threatening letters signed "Swing";
but no action followed.

In all, before the riots subsided in early December, sixteen counties had been more or less seriously affected, while incidents may
have occurred in a dozen others as far north as Leicester and as
far west as Hereford.

Though machine wrecking and arson played the major role in
the disturbances, there were important local variations: at High
Wycombe, in Buckinghamshire, it was the machinery in the paper
mills (several of the arrested rioters were paper workers) and not
the threshing machines that were destroyed. In many parishes,
the rioters' first place of call was the vicarage, where the incumbent
was politely but firmly asked to promise a reduction of the tithes.
"In the case of the Rev. Mr. Kirby, of Mayfield, Sussex [runs a
report], the tithes were brought down from 1,400 l. to 400 l. and
the remaining sum divided among the farmers for the payment of
the laborer." Similar visits were paid to lay tithe impropriators,
overseers of the poor, tithe collectors, and land bailiffs; and from
such reports it appears that the laborers, though often well disposed towards the farmers (and this was Wakefield's view), were
primarily concerned with wages and with making it easier for the
farmers to raise them. "From the farmers they demand 2s 6d. per
day in summer, and 2s. in winter, as their wages for work and
constant employment." While most farmers were treated civilly
and often offered food, drink, or money to the rioters, those who
refused to sign new contracts for higher wages might be mishand-
led: such as the Sussex farmer to whom "a rope was brought out,
and he was assured that he must accept either the one or the other."
On the other hand, farmers might be inclined, from hostility to
squire and parson and even to larger farmers, not only to sympath-
ize but actually to incite their laborers to action: in Essex, for example, farmers were reported to have told the laborers that "tithes,
government taxes, rent and machinery were the causes which produced low wages."

The other constant demand was that all threshing machines should be destroyed; and many small farmers, to whom the machine appeared to give no great advantage, were only too willing to oblige. But where farmers refused, the rioters would do it for them; in some cases charging a fee of 5, 10 or even as much as 40s. for the performance; and if the owners resisted, they would pay an additional price in terms of fired hay ricks, an occasional man-handling, or a ducking in the pond. Yet there was no loss of life among the victims, and such a violent incident as that related of John Bennett of Pit House, Member of Parliament for Wiltshire, was the exception rather than the rule. When Bennett rode out to meet the rioters,

they began to pelt him with flint-stones and brickbats; just at this moment, the Hindon troop, under the command of Capt. Wyndham, came up, and saved Mr. Bennett, who was very much wounded on the head, as well as Capt. Wyndham. The cavalry attempted to charge upon them, but the mob rushed into the plantations which surround the house, where they continued pelting the cavalry, who at last affected the charge, when several were wounded, and some mortally; one man was shot dead on the spot.

But, generally, proceedings were orderly and conducted with due solemnity, as though the laborers felt a moral obligation to carry out such duties: in fact, there were occasions, reminiscent once more of the French in 1775 and 1789, when they claimed official authority for acting as they did. And so successful were they in persuading or intimidating farmers that the Home Secretary felt obliged, on December 8, to address a circular to magistrates, "dictating a discontinuance of all yielding to threat or intimidation, either as respects the recommendation of an uniform rate of wages or the non-employment of the thrashing machines which, it is justly observed, are as much under the protection of the law as any other machinery." [7]

At all events, the authorities were considerably alarmed; and once the rioters were brought to heel by a concentration of dragoons and special constables in the disaffected areas, the reprisals meted out to them were savage and severe. Nearly 2,000 rioters or suspects were brought to trial between November 1830 and March 1831 before Special Commissions or county quarter sessions at

Winchester, Salisbury, Southampton, Reading, Aylesbury, Oxford, Dorchester, Canterbury, Dover, and Maidstone. Nine were sentenced to hang, 644 were sent to prison, and 481 were transported to the Australian colonies for terms of 7 to 14 years or life. It was the largest batch of prisoners ever transported from England for a common crime, thus underlining the enormity of the laborers' offence in the eyes of government and magistrates.

Other remarkable features of these disturbances were the nature of the rioters and the sympathy that they elicited in other quarters. Farmers, as we have seen, had urged them on, seeing their activities as a useful means of reducing tithes and rents; and even the burning of their stacks did not necessarily cause them serious loss, as they were generally insured, whereas tithe stacks (so Wakefield tells us) were often not. Reports also suggest that radicals and dissenting ministers played some part, either in instigating riots or in acting as intermediaries between the laborers and their victims: there were certainly Protestant nonconformists among those transported to Australia. Nor were the rioters themselves confined to village laborers. Local reports speak of "men in good employment" and of "persons above the common laborers"; and Mr. Justice Parke, who tried upwards of 270 indicted prisoners in Wiltshire, commented sourly on the frequent participation of those "whose wages were such as to place them far above want": in particular, he instanced "blacksmiths, carpenters and artisans, and men in a superior condition of life." [8] The point is borne out by the Australian convict records, which show that between one in four and one in five of those· transported were employed in rural crafts. Similar evidence suggests that most were settled family men, that their standard of literacy was relatively high, and that comparatively few from certain counties—for example, Buckinghamshire and Wiltshire—appear to have left their wives and families "on the parish." Above all, they were for the most part men of high moral character, whose "crime" rate, both in England before and in Australia after their sentence, was considerably lower than that of the usual run of convicts. The superintendent of convicts in London, who visited them in the docks before they sailed, said "he never saw a finer set of men"; and Governor Arthur of Van Diemen's Land—to which the majority were sent—bore repeated witness to their "exemplary" conduct and good behavior.[9] In brief, these "village Hampdens" (the Hammonds use the term) were respectable working men whose sense of justice had been outraged by the displacement of human labor by machinery as deeply as their illustrious forbear, John Hampden of Buckinghamshire, had been incensed against Charles I over Ship Money two hundred years before.

The Rebecca riots in Wales, like the southern counties' riots in England, owed their origins to a variety of causes, but all were associated with the dissolution of old village ties. In Wales, far more than in the English rural areas, nonconformity had made rapid strides in the last fifty years: by the time of the religious census of 1851, in the three disaffected shires of West Wales—Pembrokeshire, Carmarthenshire, and Cardiganshire—there were four Protestant dissenters to every member of the Church of England. Nonconformity lay at the heart of the Rebecca movement, as it expressed the deep malaise of the farming and laboring population at a time when the old social structure was breaking down in backward and isolated regions, while old and antiquated forms of government survived. While nonconformity gave the movement its peculiar ideology, its social pattern derived from a disintegrating peasant community, in which farmers and laborers still had much in common: their poverty, their tenacity to maintain the old ways against the mounting tide of progress, and a tradition of resistance and hostility to alien English landlords, magistrates, and stewards. The farmers' grievances were many: the exactions of the tithe owner, the tyranny of magistrates, church rates, county rates, fees paid to magistrates' clerks, high rents, and the operation and financing of the New Poor Law. And, to inflame dissatisfaction, came a succession of bad harvests and in 1838 the first Chartist emissaries from England. Yet the spark that touched off and gave its own hallmark to the Rebecca movement was none of these accumulated grievances, but the recent extension of the system of toll gates on the country roads operated by the Turnpike Trusts. The Trusts had been in existence for over a century and had on occasion, as in England, provoked earlier disturbance. But previously they had been inefficiently run and although a standing grievance had not aroused intense dissatisfaction. Now a professional toll farmer, Thomas Bullin, an Englishman, took charge of all gates belonging to eight of the Trusts, including those of Cardigan, Carmarthen, Newcastle, and Whitland. They were run as a business proposition, higher tolls were charged, and more gates were built, many along side roads where there had been none before. To all they were a nuisance, but to none so much as to the farmer carting lime from a nearby kiln, who might be called upon to pay toll three or four times along a single short stretch of road. In was, in fact, not so much the amount of the toll charged as the multiplication of gates that was the main bone of contention and caused resentment to flare into conspiracy and violence.[10]

In January 1839, the trustees of the Whitland Trust decided to build four new gates between Narberth and Haverfordwest on the Carmarthen-Pembrokeshire border. Almost as soon as they had been erected, two of the gates were destroyed at night by men with blackened faces, several of whom were dressed in women's clothes. Rebecca and her "daughters," in fact if not yet in name, had made their first appearance. The yeomanry was sent for and a number of suspects arrested; but they could not be prosecuted for lack of witnesses. Meanwhile, a third riot had taken place. This time, the rioters' leader was addressed as "Becca" by his followers, and from this time on the name "Rebecca riots" came into use. Surprisingly, the trustees' decision to erect new gates was rescinded, on the motion of the county Member of Parliament, when a public meeting was called. So the first brief phase of rioting ended in an unexpected victory for the popular cause.

The next and far more protracted phase of the riots started in the winter of 1842, a year of labor unrest and one that marked the high point of Chartist activity in England. In South Cardiganshire, in October, cornstacks belonging to local gentry were fired. It was the work of tenant farmers; and it was they, too, and not their laborers, that reopened Rebecca's campaign against the toll gates in November. This time the movement lasted, with minor intermissions, throughout 1843; and isolated incidents were recorded as late as September 1844. The main area of disturbance was still Carmarthenshire and Pembrokeshire, and the southern part of Cardiganshire; and there were even incursions, though they were scattered and sporadic, into the Wye Valley in Radnorshire, into Brecknockshire and Glamorgan almost as far south as Cardiff. The general pattern, as before, was the smashing or re-

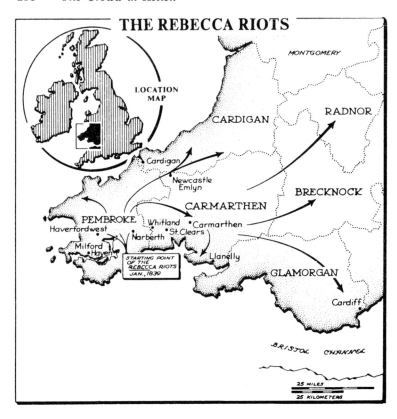

THE REBECCA RIOTS

moval of toll gates by night, occasionally accompanied by the burning of the toll house or the keeper's cottage. Rebecca (as her historian reminds us) was strictly Sabbatarian: she never worked on Sundays and even studiously avoided late night sessions on Saturdays and Monday early mornings. She was remarkably discriminating: only toll gates considered to be "unjust" were dealt with, particularly those studding the side roads, which, through their proliferation, placed a heavy extra cost on the carting of lime. Turnpikes on main roads, however, might be respected; and in one of her threatening letters, this one addressed to special constables, "Becca" makes the point:

You depend that all the Gates that are on these small roads shall be destroyed; I am willing for gates on the Queens Road to stand.

She was also profoundly nationalist and in the same letter blasts the "sons of Hengist" and insists that "it will be no hard matter for Bowlin and Comp. to finish the job they started." [11] She had flashes of whimsy humor: special constables sent to defend the gates were forced to pull them down; and, at the Pwll-trap gate near Haverfordwest, she called on the onlookers to record their verdict ("My children, this gate has no business here, has it?") before ordering it to be leveled to the ground. She and her "daughters" operated in groups of 40 to 100 and sometimes as many as 250. They wore disguise or simply blackened faces; at times several, at other times only the leader, rode on a horse. Many were armed, and one eyewitness, who sent a detailed account of one of their operations to the Home Office in London, commented on the military precision with which Rebecca disposed her forces: an advance guard of twenty men armed with guns; a main body of 200 men, most carrying axes and hammers, though some carrying arms; and a rear guard, also armed. But these paraphernalia of violence, though terrifying to many observers, were not in practice as sinister as they appeared. The rioters used powder and rarely ball, and over the whole period of Rebecca's activities she claimed only one certain victim: an old woman who was shot down at her turnpike on the Glamorgan-Carmarthenshire border.°

Yet, as the campaign progressed, the riots both lost their early easy-going nature and began to fasten on other targets. Farmers were summoned to make contributions and to attend the nocturnal meetings; and failing compliance were threatened with reprisals. The vicar of Penbryn, who had impounded a dissenter's Bible in lieu of tithe, was ordered to return it or face mutilation. The master of the Newcastle Emlyn workhouse was warned in a letter headed "the Vengeance of Blood" that he "would be taken care of" if he did not vacate the building. Church of England parsons were

---

° It was a clear case of murder; yet the investigating jury brought in a verdict "that the deceased died from suffusion of blood which produced suffocation, but from what cause is to the jurors unknown" (*Annual Register*, LXXXV, 262).

warned to give up their tithes, landlords to lower rents, and even farmers to stop hoarding corn or to confine their tenure to single farms. Occasionally, Rebecca passed from words to deeds; and obstructive magistrates, landowners, parsons, and farmers were beaten up, fired on, or had their homes and stacks destroyed by fire.

Throughout, toll gates remained the main objects of attack; but Rebecca was beginning to extend her operations into other fields. Salmon weirs were destroyed on the rivers; ricks were burned (often acts of personal vengeance rather than of public justice); fences were pulled down, though (such was Rebecca's sense of propriety) never those that had been authorized by act of Parliament; and several workhouses were threatened. In fact, the attack on the workhouse at Carmarthen was one of the most sensational episodes of the riots. Yet it appears not to have been intended by the organizers of the great procession that marched into Carmarthen on June 10. Those summoned to attend were told that the object was to lay before the magistrates a list of grievances regarding tolls, tithes, the Poor Law, and church rates: they included an Englishman who was warned that "non-compliance will bring vengeance on your head." From the early hours, small groups of farmers and laborers began to emerge from the surrounding hills and valleys and, formed into orderly ranks and headed by a band, they entered Carmarthen by the Water Street gate (recently demolished). An eyewitness judged that 2,000 men and women came on foot, followed by 300 mounted farmers, among them one dressed in women's clothes and wearing long ringlets of horsehair, who symbolized Rebecca. Yet arms had been left behind and the procession was peaceable enough until it had made a complete tour of the town and left its resolutions at the Guildhall. At this point, things got out of hand and the local "rabble of the town," fishermen among them, appear to have diverted the marchers to the workhouse, forced the master to give up his keys, let the paupers out, and smashed the furniture and tossed the bedding out of windows, before being driven out by the 4th Light Dragoons. Sixty prisoners were taken; but magistrates proved lenient, and only six were later sentenced to terms of hard labor varying from eight months to a year.

The summer of 1843 saw both the peak and the gradual decline of the Rebecca movement. The Carmarthen tenant farmers had launched a means of protest that had yielded good results; but, as it gained momentum and absorbed new social elements, it was inclined to lose its original purpose and fall into other hands. As the riots spread eastwards and southwards to the coast, coal miners and copper and iron workers, depressed by falling wages and unemployment, began to play a part. Unemployed workers from Merthyr in Glamorgan were drifting back to their homes in the villages of West Wales; some sought employment in Carmarthenshire; many were prepared to earn a few extra shillings by smashing gates or firing ricks. Laborers began to meet and to demand higher wages or to call on the farmers to reduce the price of corn; some resorted to their own means of "natural justice" by firing the farmers' stacks. Toll gates continued to be smashed right through the autumn, but even here the movement tended to fall into the hands of professionals who charged a price for their services—men like Dai'r Cantwr and Shoni Sgubor Fawr, who were later transported to Tasmania. So, where the troops had failed to crush them (1,800 men under Colonel Love had long been stationed in the counties), the farmers began to seek redress by other means. Great public meetings, convened to draft petitions to the Queen or to the Parliament at Westminster, became more frequent, and Rebecca's nocturnal antics correspondingly began to wane. The turning point came at the end of September, when a toll gate, removed one night on the outskirts of Llanelly, was the next morning replaced by forty local farmers. At Llanelly, too, in early November, 300 farmers were sworn in as special constables to stop disorder, whereas at Carmarthen, three months before, of 190 summoned all but two had refused to take the oath. Meanwhile, police had been drafted in force from London and the troops, under direct War Office supervision, had been reorganized and scattered round the riot-infested districts in smaller mobile units. This made gate smashing a more hazardous occupation; but it was, above all, the farmers' change of heart that brought the riots to an end.

Rebecca had already scored notable successes and a government Commission of Enquiry, promoted by a liberal Home Secretary, would lead to more. In June, the Newcastle trustees, prompted by Lloyd Hall, a lawyer sympathetic to the farmers, had agreed to reduce tolls to their pre-1837 level, to reduce the tally holders' interest from 5 to 3½ percent, and not to rebuild three of their demolished gates. In August, the Cardigan trustees made similar concessions, and in the autumn the Main Trust followed suit. In any case, by this time half the gates in Carmarthen, the main center of disturbance, had been destroyed and tolls went often uncollected. The government inquiry echoed many of Rebecca's grievances, declared the Trusts to have been mismanaged and proposed that they should be consolidated and administered by county Road Boards. Parliament endorsed the measure and also made tolls uniform and reduced their number. In addition, the farmers and their laborers benefited from the General Enclosure Act of 1845, and the repeal of the Corn Laws and the General Enclosure Act of the two following years. Above all, the railways built through England's western counties eased the over-population of the villages by carrying growing numbers of Welshmen to work in the new industrial areas.

Who was Rebecca? She had many faces and was variously described as "a man with a drawn sword," "a person of most gentlemanly address and voice," as being mounted on "a splendid horse," as speaking "excellent English like an Englishman," as being "clad in white," and as having a hand "as soft as a female's and entirely that of one unused to work." Several Rebeccas were identified: among them, Stephen Evans, a farmer and local historian; Michael Bower, a young farmer who led the procession into Carmarthen; John Hughes, a farmer's son of Llan-non, who was transported to Tasmania; and the two leaders of Rebecca's most violent and "lunatic" phase, Shoni and Dai'r Cantwr. Was there a super-Rebecca or mastermind that inspired the operation as a whole? A favorite contender for the title has been Hugh Williams, the farmers' advocate, radical reformer, Chartist, and brother-in-law of the Anti-Corn Law Leaguer, Richard Cobden; but Rebecca's historian, having sifted all the evidence, rejects the suggestion as having no validity.[12]

In Wales, as in England, the rural riots of the 1830's and 1840's had been the final upsurge of a dying social class: in the one case the laborers, in the other the farmers, had taken the lead; but the problem in both cases was much the same. As capitalist industry and agriculture developed, the peasant, like the handloom weaver, was inevitably doomed. The names of the legendary heroes, Rebecca, Ned Ludd, and even Captain Swing, would, like Robin Hood, live on and become magnified in folklore; but their exploits would not be repeated and would have no more future than the classes whose protests they briefly voiced.

REFERENCES

1. P. G. Rogers, *Battle in Bossenden Wood. The Strange Story of Sir William Courtenay* (London, 1961).
2. W. W. Rostow, *British Economy of the Nineteenth Century* (Oxford, 1948), p. 124; G. M. Young, *Victorian England. Portrait of an Age* (London, 1961), p. 27.
3. For the riots, see J. L. and B. Hammond, *The Village Labourer* (2 vols, London, 1948) and E. J. Hobsbawm and G. Rudé, *Captain Swing* (London, 1969).
4. E. Gibbon Wakefield, *Swing Unmasked, or the Causes of Rural Incendiarism* (London, 1831); Halévy, *op. cit.*, pp. 6-9.
5. *Gentleman's Magazine*, C (July-Dec. 1830), 362,
6. *Ibid.*, C, 459 (Nov. 1830).
7. *Gentleman's Magazine*, C, 459, 555.
8. *Ibid.*, C, 639.
9. *Captain Swing*, p. 248.
10. D. Williams, *The Rebecca Riots: A Study in Agrarian Discontent* (Cardiff, 1953), pp. 1-184. I have drawn largely on Professor Williams' work for what follows. See also *Annual Register*, LXXXV (1843), 257-63.
11. Reproduced in full by D. Williams, *op. cit.*, facing p. 212.
12. For the foregoing, see D. Williams, *op. cit.*, pp. 185-293.

ELEVEN

The French Revolution of 1848

Two factors, perhaps more than any others, ensured that the crowds in the French revolution of 1848 would not be identical with those of 1789. One was the beginning (but only the beginning) of modern industry; the other the spread of socialist, or near-socialist, ideas among the industrial and working population. The factory system and mechanization had taken root in the textiles of the north and east, in mines, chemicals, silk, soap, sugar refineries, and parts of metallurgy: in 1847, 5,000 steam engines were in use where, seven year before, there had been only 2,000. The railways had also made their appearance in the 1840's: by 1850, 2,000 miles of track had been laid, and Paris had new rail repair workshops at St. Denis and the village of La Chapelle. Yet, outside these industries, the "revolution" had made little progress: three-quarters of France's population still worked on the land and her industrial workers continued, for the most part, to be employed in the workshops and cottages of sixty years before. The population of Paris had grown to a little over a million; but apart from her railways and engineering shops she was still a city of manufactories, homeworkers, and petty crafts; and the small workshop, far from disappearing, had increased its hold. There were still only five workers to every employer; and the main centers of the working population were still the old faubourgs and markets of 1789, though now extending north, south, and east into industrial suburbs that were villages half a century before.[1] The age of the great industrial employer, like that of the factory worker, was yet to come. It was the banker, the merchant manufacturer, the speculator and owner of real estate, and not the industrialist, that ruled the roost and formed the backbone of what Marx termed "the Joint Stock Company for the exploitation of France's national

164

wealth" (and Tocqueville said much the same), and to whom
Guizot gave his comforting cure for social ills: "Enrichissez-vous!"

Though social and industrial change was slow, ideas were
breeding fast; and the 1830's saw a remarkable development in
the political education of the French industrial population. In
the revolution of 1830, workers had left their workshops to take
up arms and overthrow the monarchy of Charles X; and as far as
can be told from the records there were many workers and craftsmen among those decorated for their part in these events and
among those killed and buried beneath the "column of July."[2] Yet
this was only a repetition, though on a larger scale, of what had
happened in 1789 and 1792; and the workers were in no position,
once the revolution had been made, to affect its course.

What was new in the 1830's, following the July experience, was
that workers were beginning to associate in organized groups—
not merely on a workshop basis under their masters—to take
part in political affairs. The first workers' newspapers, the
Journal des Ouvriers, the *Artisan*, and *Le Peuple*, appeared in
September 1830; and, the first of the two great insurrections of
Lyons silk weavers broke out in November 1831, under the slogan
Vivre en travaillant ou mourir en combattant. It had far deeper
social aims than a mere rise in wages or the provision of work,
and although a joint outbreak of small masters and journeymen,
it is generally held to mark the birth of the modern labor movement. It came at a time of wretched housing, low wages, and depression and was followed, in Paris, by a series of riots and armed
insurrections, aimed not primarily at merchants and manufacturers but at the government itself. Among those arrested in the
most violent of them all—that of of June 5–6, 1832, in the cloisters
of St. Méry, where 70 troops and 80 rioters were killed—we find
several craftsmen, and journeymen whose names reappear in later
riots: and one—a journeyman baker—who was rearrested shortly
after for taking part in a *coalition ouvrière*, or wage movement.[3]
It may seem trivial, but the point is of great significance: here for
the first time we find the same workers being engaged in successive political demonstrations, wage demands being put forward at
a time of economic depression, and wage earners participating as
readily in political as in economic movements. This had not been
seen in earlier revolutions and represents a landmark in the history
of working-class action and ideas.

The early working-class movement: Lyons silk-weavers' insurrection of November 1831.

Soon after the second Lyons outbreak in April 1834, this phase of political rioting ended, but the fermentation of political ideas continued. In the same year, the word "socialism" was first used by Pierre Leroux, and the ideas of Babeuf (via his old disciple Buonarotti), Blanqui, Barbès, Blanc, Cabet, Proudhon and the Saint-Simonians began to circulate among the workers. Their remedies ranged from mild reformist measures to the class war and popular insurrection preached by Auguste Blanqui; they stressed the need for equality of distribution rather than the public ownership of the nation's wealth; but they all addressed their remedies to one specific class, the workers; and this in itself was new.[4] Under the impact of these ideas secret societies and clubs sprang up, such as Blanqui's Societies of the Families and of the Seasons and the Society of the Rights of Man, themselves the forbears of the far larger and more influential clubs, sometimes attracting attendances of 5,000 and more, that played so important a part in and after the February Revolution. Alexis de Tocqueville sensed the new spirit that these clubs engendered. In a speech to the Chamber in January 1848, he warned, the "working classes . . . are gradually forming opinions and ideas which are destined not only to upset this or that law, ministry, or even form of government, but society itself."[5]

How far Tocqueville was right or wrong in his prognostication the revolution that broke out in Paris four weeks later would reveal. The outbreak, as is common on such occasions, developed in successive stages, from a demand for mild reform into a popular revolution. It started with a campaign, supported by the liberal opposition, to hold banquets in favor of an extension of the suffrage. When Guizot banned the banquets, the opposition leaders withdrew; and the radical and republican journalists of *Le National* and *La Réforme* took them over and organized great popular demonstrations in support. At this point the *bourgeois* National Guard, instead of dispersing the crowds, sided with the reformers; and the King, bowing to public opinion, dismissed the Guizot Ministry. But the demonstrations, far from subsiding, grew in strength and drew their main support from the popular quarters in the east and center of the city. In the Boulevard des Capucines, several demonstrators (some accounts say 50, others 100) were killed and wounded in a bloody encounter with the troops. This gave a new purpose and direction to the riots: gunsmiths' shops were raided for arms; and on the morning of February 24, Paris was in open revolt.

A succession of opposition leaders now tried to form a government, but it was too late; and when the armed insurgents bore down on the Tuileries, the King abdicated and fled to England. An attempt was made to form a Regency for the child Comte de Paris; but crowds invaded the Chamber, brushed the old constitution makers aside, and received with acclamation a new "provisional" government, drawn up from lists of names submitted by the liberal and radical journalists, including those of the radical leader, Ledru-Rollin, and the poet Lamartine. But the crowds, mindful of the "betrayal" of 1830, were determined to reap their own share of the common victory; and the government when publicly proclaimed at the Hôtel de Ville bore two added names : those of the socialist leader Louis Blanc and the metal worker Albert. Yet this was by no means all. During the next days, massive demonstrations at the Hôtel de Ville, backed by the socialists and clubs, wrung from the Provisional Government a number of concessions : the promise of "the right to work"; "national" workshops for the unemployed (a distortion of Blanc's demand for state-run "social" workshops, but a concession nonetheless); the right to organize in unions; the 10-hour day; the abolition of debtors' prisons; male adult suffrage; and the immediate proclamation of the Republic.

Thus the wage earners had not only, as in 1789 and 1830, helped to make a revolution; once the initial victory had been won, they had continued to leave their mark upon it. In earlier revolutions, they had taken their ideas and slogans from the *bourgeoisie*, even if occasionally adapted to their own use; this time, they were organized in their own political clubs and trade associations, marched under their own banners and leaders, and were deeply imbued with the new ideas of socialism. Nevertheless, the revolution, still less its fruits, was not entirely theirs. As on similiar occasions in the past, they had left their workshops with their masters and, with them, jointly manned the barricades; radical journalists, students, *polytechniciens* and National Guards had also played their part; and on the lists of those decorated for their part in the February events the names of wage earners appear alongside those of shopkeepers, master craftsmen, and members of the liberal professions.* Tocqueville, in fact, saw only one side of the picture (though admittedly to persons like himself the most alarming) when he wrote that the workers were the sole victors of the revolution and the *bourgeoisie* its principal victims; and that socialism had been its "essential characteristic."[6] The workers had indeed won important concessions, but they were only temporary, and the government to all intents and purposes remained in *bourgeois* hands; a fact that would become the more apparent as the weeks went by. Moreover, if in Paris the wage earners had been able to give a new form and content to a popular revolution, in the provinces the older forms prevailed. In Alsace, Jewish homes and synagogues were wrecked (as in 1789), at Bourg a monastery, at Besançon the *mairie*, in Allier the customs, and in the Pyrenées and the Paris region the châteaux of the aristocracy. The state forests were ravaged in Ariège and Var; peasants rose in defense of ancient communal rights; and in an orgy of "Luddite" fury railways were torn up and bridges destroyed on the Paris–Rouen and Paris–Brussels lines and power looms and textile mills destroyed in Champagne, the Nord, and Normandy. Even in Paris, mechanical presses were wrecked by printing workers, so that the workers' paper, the *Atelier*, felt constrained to call on its readers to "respect the machines."†

February 1848, then, despite its important innovations, only marks a half-way stage between the older type of popular movement and disturbance and the new. The Paris insurrection that in June ranged *ouvriers* and *bourgeois* on opposing sides of the barricades would carry the transition to a higher point. The June "days" had their remoter origins in the breakdown of the alliance between *bourgeois* democrats and workers that followed soon

---

* Based on a hasty, incomplete study of lists in Arch. Préf. de Police, Aa 370. There appears to be no occupational record of the 340 insurgents killed in the fighting on February 22-24.

† C. Seignobos, *La Révolution de 1848* (Paris, 1921), pp. 19-20. In addition, there had been a wave of old-style grain riots (including *taxation populaire*) on the eve of the revolution in 1846-7; though spread over wide areas of France, they were mainly concentrated in the traditionalist west (see R. Gossez' "carte des troubles," in E. Labrousse (ed.), *Aspects de la crise et de la dépression de l'économie française au milieu du XIX* *siecle, 1846-1851* (La Roche-sur-Yon, 1956)).

after their common victory in February. The sight of workers in their *blouses*, or peasant smocks, mounting guard over public buildings and flocking to air their grievances and dictate their terms at the Luxembourg Palace, where Louis Blanc had set up his "workers Parliament," had begun to alarm many who, though revolutionaries and republicans in February, shared Tocqueville's concern that "property" might now be threatened. Further apprehension had been roused by the great workers' rally organized by Blanqui on March 17. A month later, the clubs and Blanc's Luxembourg Commission combined to stage a vast workers' demonstration, whose objects were to postpone elections to the new Assembly (the provincials were rightly suspected of not sharing the Parisians' revolutionary spirit), and to press the government to create a "democratic Republic" based on the "abolition of the exploitation of man by man" and the "organization of labor by association." The nonsocialist members of the government took fright, and Ledru-Rollin, in alliance with Lamartine, called on the National Guard to counter-demonstrate. At the Hôtel de Ville, it was the delegates of the National Guard who were received with honors; the workers' deputation was cold-shouldered and greeted with shouts of "down with the Communists!" The breach between the government and socialists was now complete.

The national elections followed a fortnight later and were a triumph for Lamartine's republican moderates, who won over 500 seats; even the combined monarchists –Orléanists and Legitimists —won 300 seats; while the socialists and their allies returned less than 100 members. The result was hailed by *Le National*, Lamartine's paper; and its radical rival, *La Réforme*, frankly saw it as "the defeat of the democratic and social Republic." In an attempt to redress the balance, the club leaders decided on another "insurrection." On May 15, their unarmed followers, supported by 14,000 unemployed workers from the government's national workshops, invaded the Assembly, ostensibly to present a petition in favor of war with Russia in defense of Poland. In the confusion that followed, some of their spokesmen declared the Assembly to be dissolved and read out, as in February, a list of new members of a provisional government, including Ledru-Rollin, the socialists, and leaders of the clubs. This may have been the intention all along, though it seems unlikely, as the demonstrators were un-

Government troops storm the barricade at the Place de la Bastille during the final phase of the Paris workers' insurrection of June 1848. (See pp. 172–4.)

armed and once the National Guard was brought onto the scene were easily rounded up and dispersed. The Assembly and the Executive Council, however, decided to treat the incident as a projected *coup d'état* and to teach the workers and socialists a lesson. *Il faut en finir!* Blanqui, Raspail, Barbès, and Albert, and about 400 others, were arrested. Blanc's Luxembourg Commission was closed down; and five weeks later the national workshops, whose 115,000 inmates were both a drain on the public purse and no longer immune to socialist agitation, were ordered to be dissolved.

The Executive Council's decree ordering the closure of the workshops was issued under the signature of Marie, the Minister of Public Works, on June 21. The workers were faced with the alternative of enlisting for the army (if 18 to 25 years of age), of being sent to drain the insalubrious marshes of Sologne, or of remaining in Paris without work or pay. It was an act of considerable provocation and to some, at least, it appeared that its consequences had been intended. Though deeper resentments, fed by weeks of frustrated hopes and disappointments, lay at the back of the civil war that followed, this was the spark that touched it off. The most vigorous of the workers' leaders were in prison; others, like Blanc, who had escaped arrest in May, urged caution; so, for lack of better, it was a strange mystic (a self-styled "prophet of misfortune" and "days of blood") and workshop foreman, Louis Pujol, who became their spokesman. On June 22, 1,200 to 1,500 workers, with banners flying, assembled at the Panthéon and sent a deputation of fifty-six delegates to parley with the government at the Luxembourg Palace. Marie, who received Pujol and five others, treated them with scant courtesy and replied to Pujol's threats with counter-threats. The same night a torchlight meeting, addressed by Pujol, was held at the Bastille; and another, early the next morning, took the familiar pledge "Liberty or Death!" As the marchers returned along the boulevards, the cry went up "to arms!" and the first barricade, made of overturned buses, mattresses, and paving stones, was erected near the Porte St. Denis on the Boulevard Bonne-Nouvelle.

The insurrection lasted three days and spread far beyond the ranks of the workshop workers. Its main centers were the old popular districts of earlier revolutions: the Faubourgs St. Martin, du Temple, and Poissonnière to the north; the Place de la Bastille and the Faubourg St. Antoine to the east; the Cité (though not the Hôtel de Ville) in the center; and the Place du Panthéon, the Faubourg St. Jacques, and Latin Quarter to the south. Beyond the old city limits of 1789, the centers extended into Montmartre in the north and Gentilly in the south. Thirty-eight barricades appeared in the Rue St. Jacques alone, 68 between the Hôtel de Ville and the Bastille, and 29 more along the great popular highway of the Rue du Faubourg St. Antoine. The insurgents had little trouble in finding arms: many were old soldiers, more were National Guards (including officers) from the eastern legions. They may have numbered as many as 100,000. This, as least, was the number of muskets later seized in the insurgent districts. And their aims? The immediate demand was twofold: to restore the national workshops and to dissolve the Assembly that had closed them down. As other workers joined the insurgents, other aims were added. Banners fluttering from the barricades bore such slogans as "Organization of labor by association," "Abolition of the exploitation of man by man," "Respect private property, death to looters," and "Bread and work, or Death"; and the few proclamations issued voiced the familiar demand for "the Democratic and Social Republic."

To deal with the rebels, the government could muster 30,000 troops of the line, 16,000 *gardes mobiles* (mainly recruited from young laborers and unemployed), 2,000 Republican Guards; and, theoretically, the National Guard. But only the Guards of the western districts could be relied on: the eastern battalions had joined the insurgents; and, of those in the center, only 4,000 out of 60,000 responded to the government's call. In the event, General Eugène Cavaignac, who was given the supreme command of the government's forces, pushed forward the *gardes mobiles* and the National Guards of the *bourgeois* districts, while holding the bulk of the regular troops in reserve. As the fighting developed, however, the railways brought powerful support in the form of volunteers from all parts of the country. "Among them [wrote Tocqueville] were many peasants, many shopkeepers, many landlords and nobles, all mingled together in the same ranks. . . . It was evident from that moment that we should end by gaining the day, for the insurgents received no reinforcements, whereas we had all France for reserves."[7]

After the first shock and confusion, the outcome was, in fact, hardly ever in doubt. The insurgents had touched a deep chord of response among the Paris working population, but they had no leaders other than those thrown up by the occasion; many socialists refused to join in, others joined only after the fighting had started. Above all, as far as the rest of France was concerned, the Parisian workers were out on a limb. On the first day, a triple attack by government forces failed to dislodge the insurgents from any but minor points of resistance; but the next day they lost the northern Faubourgs of St. Denis, Poissonnière, and du Temple and, on the Left Bank, the Place du Panthéon and the Montagne Ste. Geneviève. On the twenty-fifth, the forces of order succeeded in mopping up the last centers of resistance in the north and south of the city; and the rebels aroused indignation by the shooting (in the second case, by a stray bullet) of General Bréa and the Archbishop of Paris, both of whom had come to offer mediation. Only the old revolutionary stronghold of the Faubourg St. Antoine (as in May 1795) still held out. On the morning of the twenty-sixth, a deputation offered to lay down arms in return for an amnesty; but Cavaignac insisted on an unconditional surrender and soon after the battle resumed was able to enforce it. The insurrection was over.

The Assembly and propertied classes had been thoroughly alarmed, and the repression was correspondingly severe. Many had been killed in the course of the fighting, or massacred by the Mobile Guard: the police return of 2,000 killed and wounded is probably an underestimate. 15,000 persons were arrested; but, since many had been rounded up as suspects for the mere fact of wearing the worker's *blouse*, 6,374 were, after cross examination, released without trial or sentence. Over 4,000 were sentenced to prison, fortresses, or transportation to Algeria; only the assassins of General Bréa were guillotined. A commission met to inquire into the remoter causes of the disturbance. Ledru-Rollin, though attacked in the Assembly for complicity in the affair, escaped prosecution; but Blanc, innocent as he was of even the remotest connection with the outbreak, had to seek refuge in England to avoid trial. The clubs and revolutionary journals were closed down. Rid of the socialists and the fear of further workers' demonstrations, the Assembly settled down to dismantle what remained of the "social" Republic and to erect one that corresponded better to the interests of the victors.

Who were the insurgents and what had the insurrection been about? Marx and Tocqueville, though belonging to opposing camps and differing as to details, were both firmly agreed that it had been a struggle of class against class and marked a turning point in France's history. "What distinguished it," wrote Tocqueville, "among all the events of this kind which have succeeded one another in France for sixty years, is that it did not aim at changing the form of government, but at altering the order of society. It was . . . a struggle of class against class, a sort of Servile War." [8] To Marx it was, more precisely, a struggle of "proletariat" and "bourgeoisie"; and he added, in words almost identical with those of Tocqueville, that from now on revolution (and not only in France) meant "overthrow of bourgeois society, whereas, before February, it had meant overthrow of the form of state." [9] To contemporaries, who had no squeamish feelings about terms like "class war," neither statement would have appeared extreme: it was generally accepted (and there would be no point in picking out evidence to prove it) that the June revolt was an armed protest of the Paris workers, if not against the capitalists, at least against the property owners or "the rich."

Is the point equally acceptable to us, or does it require revision? The conflict was certainly not one between factory workers and their employers: this would have been impossible in the circumstances of the time. Paris, as we have seen, was still a city of small workshops and crafts that had little changed, in this respect, since the first great revolution of 1789. If we examine the occupations of the 11,693 persons who were charged in the affair, we find a remarkable similarity to the trades of those who stormed the Bastille and captured the Tuileries sixty years before. We find among them no fewer than 554 stonemasons, 510 joiners, 416 shoemakers, 321 cabinet makers, 286 tailors, 285 locksmiths, 283 painters, 140 carpenters, 187 turners, 119 jewelers, and 191 wine merchants; and most of these occupations are among the dozen largest categories to which the prisoners belonged. It is even likely—though here the evidence is not precise enough to be conclusive—that among these prisoners, small masters, shop-keepers, and independent craftsmen outnumbered wage earners, possibly by as much as two to one.[10] Rémi Gossez, a French historian who has studied the question far more deeply than any other, adds the point that, because of the government's pre-disposition to consider all *hommes en blouse* as potential rebels, the proportion of workers among those arrested and released was considerably higher than among the smaller number of those actually convicted. Moreover, he goes on to show that there was no clear-cut class division between the two opposing forces: workers served in the National Guard alongside property owners, shopkeepers, clerks, and professional men; the Mobile Guard was largely composed of young workers, many of whom had fought on the barricades in February; and, of industrial employers, most remained neutral in the fighting in order to guard their factories and shops, while several fought with their employees in the insurgents' ranks. From this he concludes that, while the social conflict was genuine enough, it was one that ranged small producers, lodgers, and sub-tenants (and not only wage earners) against shopkeepers and merchants, and against landlords and "principal" tenants (often shopkeepers), rather than against factory owners, masters, and industrial employers.[11]

Such points are worthy of attention, and they suggest that in some respects at least the June insurrection looks back to older forms of social protest by small consumers and producers that we have noted in earlier chapters. Striking as certain of the similarities between the crowds in 1789 and June 1848 are, however, the differences are equally great. In the first place, in the earlier revolution, the initiative was generally taken by the workshop masters, who were more literate and more highly politically educated than their apprentices and journeymen, and the tradi-tional crafts played the major role in popular insurrection. This time the case was somewhat different. The initial impetus, as we have seen, came from the workers in the national workshops: this in itself was something new, as when similar workshops were closed down in Paris in 1789 and again in 1791 it hardly caused a ripple in the struggle of the political parties. Yet, in June, it was only a minority of the workshop workers that took part: a fact due, no doubt, to the government's decision to continue paying wages even after the fighting had begun. The backbone of the insurrection came from other groups. Thus building workers account for the largest category of those arrested; and it was noted that each of the main centers of resistance was held by its own distinctive trade association: carters at La Villette, coal heavers and dockers along the St. Martin canal, bronze workers on the Boulevard du Temple, and joiners and cabinet makers in the Faubourg St. Antoine. But even more significant: industrial development, though slow and thinly spread, had brought in railways and the beginnings of mechanized industry; and among the arrested insurgents, alongside the joiners, cabinet makers and locksmiths of the older crafts and shops, we find the names of some 80 railwaymen and 257 *mécaniciens*.[12] It was the workers in the railway workshops of La Chapelle, already a thriving industrial suburb to the north of the old city, who built some of the first barricades in the Faubourg Poissonnière; and we find railwaymen also joining port and riverside workers in manning the barricades on the Island of the Cité. These workers had since February been among the most highly organized and militant in the capital; Gossez describes them as forming "the vanguard of the insurrection."[13]

The railways therefore played an ambivalent role. On the one hand, by bringing in trainloads of troops and provincial volunteers to swell the forces of order, they played a substantial part in crushing the insurrection; on the other hand, by creating a new type of industrial worker, they set a new stamp on the workers' movement that would have important consequences for the future. Marx (who, like Tocqueville, had not the advantage of studying police and military records) may have looked too far ahead when he wrote as though the Parisian proletariat was already fully formed; but he was certainly right to stress the new relations developing between the classes and their significance not only for France but for the rest of Europe. The Second Empire of Napoleon III saw another forward leap in industrial growth, in workers' organization, and in the relations between capital and labor; and soon such manifestations as *taxation populaire* and "Luddite" attacks on machinery, which still survived in 1848, would be almost as dead as the proverbial dodo.

REFERENCES

1. L. Chevalier, *La formation de la population parisienne au XIXe siècle* (Paris, 1950); C. H. Pouthas, *La population française pendant la première moitié du XIXe siècle* (Paris, 1956); C. Seignobos, *La Révolution de 1848* (Paris, 1921), pp. 358 ff.

2. See D. Pinkney, "The Crowd in the French Revolution of 1830", *Am.Hist.* LXX (1964), 1-19.

3. Arch. Préf. de Police, Aa 421.

4. See L. A. Loubère, "The Intellectual Origins of French Jacobin Socialism," *International Review of Social History*, IV (1959), 415-31.

5. *Recollections of Alexis de Tocqueville*, ed. J. P. Mayer (Meridian Books, New York, 1959), pp. 11-12.

6. *Ibid.*, pp. 78 ff.

7. *Ibid.*, pp. 169-70.

8. *Ibid.*, p. 150.

9. K. Marx, *Class Struggles in France, 1848-1850* (London, n.d.), pp. 56-60.

10. *Liste générale en ordre alphabétique des inculpés de juin 1848,* Archives Nationales, F7^e 2585-6.

11. R. Gossez, "Diversité des antagonismes sociaux vers le milieu du XIXe siècle," *Revue économique*, I (1956), 439-58.

12. G. Duveau, *La vie ouvrière en France sous le Second Empire* (Paris, 1946), pp. 42-3; *Liste générale . . . des inculpés de juin 1848.*

13. R. Gossez, "L'organisation ouvrière à Paris sous la Seconde République," in *1848. Revue des révolutions contemporaines*, XLI (1949), 31-45; "Diversité des antagonismes sociaux . . . ," p. 451.

TWELVE

Chartism

As 1848 was a watershed in France, so Chartism in Britain marked a similar transition from the older forms of popular movement to the new. Chartism was the first independent movement of the British working class, and it dominated all political thinking and government domestic policies in the first ten years of Queen Victoria's reign. It was, in short, a movement of the greatest possible significance; yet it was riddled with diversity and contradictions. On the one hand, it drew its political program not (like the Paris craftsmen) from a new stock of socialist ideas, but from the radical parliamentary reformers of the past. When William Lovett and the London Workingmen's Association, aided by Francis Place, drew up the Six Points of the People's Charter in 1838, including manhood suffrage, payment of members, secret ballot, and annual parliaments, they were repeating almost in every detail what a Reform Committee in Westminster, of which Charles Fox had been a member, had drafted fifty-eight years before; and in cities like London and Birmingham, cities of ancient crafts and petty workshops, much of the enthusiasm for the Charter sprang from the disappointment of radical craftsmen with the failure of the Whigs to give them the vote by the Reform Bill of 1832. To such men, the campaign for the Charter was a new stage in a long and protracted struggle not to win something new but to reclaim ancient and "natural" rights.

Chartism was far more than an appeal to tradition, however: it was also the product of the new industrial Britain, of the "fustian jackets, unshorn chins and blistered hands" of which the Irishman, Feargus O'Connor, more than any other, became the acknowledged leader and champion. To these men, the Charter was a means rather than an end: the means to fill hungry bellies and

179

right social ills, such as the New Poor Law, low wages, long
working hours, unemployment, and the high cost of food. It was
a "knife-and-fork" as much as a political question: a panacea that,
through the workingman's vote and the radical transformation of
Parliament, would (to quote a Wiltshire Chartist) bring the
worker "plenty of roast beef, plum pudding and strong beer by
working three hours a day."[1] But even among the "fustian jackets,"
who provided Chartism with its main body of support, there were
divergent social elements, of which some looked longingly to the
past and others, gropingly, towards the future. Of the first, there
were the domestic outworkers, the handloom weavers, wool
combers, and framework knitters of the western and midlands
counties and the Yorkshire West Riding, who were being squeezed,
uprooted, and impoverished by the new industrial system and for
whom the future appeared as one of unrelieved menace and disaster. On the other hand, there were the factory hands of the new
industrial areas, the cotton workers of Lancashire and Scotland,
and the miners of Northumberland, Durham, and the Black
Country of the midlands, for whom machinery, though by no
means an unmitigated blessing, had come to stay, and who were
increasingly seeking their remedies through trade unions, cooperation, and working-class association, and less and less through the
old "natural-justice" methods of the past.

Reflecting this diversity of social elements in the Chartist rank
and file was the diversity among its leaders: old-style radicals like
William Lovett in London and Thomas Attwood in Birmingham;
anti-Poor Law agitators like the Tory Richard Oastler and the
Methodist minister J. R. Stephens in the North; champions of trade
unionism like Dr. Peter McDouall; Jacobins or Jacobin socialists
like Julian Harney and James Bronterre O'Brien; new-type socialists like Ernest Jones, who corresponded with Marx; and, above
all, the strangely unpredictable Feargus O'Connor, who, perhaps
because he offered no particular solution and could respond to
every mood, evoked a wider and deeper response than any other.
It was through the association of such men that Chartism, for all
its centrifugal tendencies, became a national movement. Yet it was
always deeply rooted in local tradition and local grievance and
therefore inclined to resort to its own local forms of action.[2] This
was both its weakness and its strength.

Chartism, then, meant different things to different men: to some, the right to vote; to others, the end of the hated workhouses of the New Poor Law, the ten-hour day, "a fair day's wage for a fair day's work," or simply more food to fill a hungry belly. It was natural, therefore, that it should operate at different levels, having both national and regional or parochial manifestations. These might merge and overlap, or they might be separate in both time and space, or they might run along parallel lines and, while owing a common allegiance to the Charter, seem not to be connected in any way with each other. At the center of operations there was always an underlying unity of purpose: leaders might be divided as to "physical" and "moral force" or in their attitude to the Anti-Corn Law League, O'Connor's Land Plan, or the middle classes; but the single common denominator, the campaign for the People's Charter, never remained long out of sight. In one sense, in fact, the story of Chartism is that of the various attempts made to impose the Six Points of the Charter on a reluctant, and generally bitterly hostile, Parliament. The core of the campaign was the collection of signatures, canvassed in workshops, factories, mines, and public meetings, to a series of National Petitions addressed to the House of Commons. The first Petition, launched at Birmingham in 1838, had, by July 1839, attracted 1,280,000 signatures; but it was curtly rejected by the Commons after they had heard Lord John Russell condemn the Charter as a threat to property. The experience was repeated in 1842 and again in 1848. Before the second Petition was launched, the Chartists hit on the novel device of forming a National Charter Association. By 1842 it had enrolled 48,000 members. This time the Petition was signed by 3,317,702 persons—a far larger number than that of the country's voters; but Parliament was unimpressed and rejected it as it had the first. For some years the bitter divisions among the Chartist leaders made it seem that Chartism was dead; but in 1848, under the stimulus of economic depression and the events in France, the movement once more revived. This time six million signatures were claimed (though there may have been only half that number) and a great demonstration was called on Kennington Common in London to give the Petition a send-off. The demonstrators were peaceable enough; but the government, fearing French agents and Irish rebels even more than English rioters, mustered 170,000 special

constables and a large military force under the aged Duke of
Wellington to disperse them. It was, wrote Lord Palmerston, "a
glorious day, the Waterloo of peace and order." It was also, to all
intents and purposes, the end of Chartism as a national political
movement.[3]

But the campaign for the Charter in terms of National Petitions
to Parliament was only one aspect of Chartism; and for our purposes not the most significant. It would certainly not in itself have
given substance to Charles Kingsley's claim that, in those years,
"young men believed (and not so wrongly) that the masses were
their natural enemies, and that they might have to fight, any year
or any day, for the safety of their property and the honour of their
sisters."[4] The intense hostility between classes, similar to that in
France in June 1848, of which Chartism was both a symptom and a
cause, was due not so much to the Charter itself as to the great
series of strikes, riots, insurrections, and popular demonstrations
that developed in its wake and that drew its supporters—particularly those among the "fustian jackets"—together. These outbreaks,
which sometimes preceded and sometimes continued beyond the
Chartist petitioning movements, but more generally served as a
kind of continuous backcloth to them, also occurred in three main
cycles, each roughly corresponding to a period of trade depression:
the spring of 1837 to January 1840; mid-July to end-September
1842; and February to August 1848.[5] The issues varied widely and
though support for the Charter was generally a common factor
this was not always so.

The first outbreak began in 1837 with a great protest movement
in the northern manufacturing districts against the operation of
the Poor Law of 1834. It preceded the publication of the People's
Charter by several months and only gradually, through such
leaders as J. R. Stephens and Feargus O'Connor, became
harnessed to the Chartist movement. Between August 1838 and
July 1839 the accent was strictly on political campaigning for the
Charter; but once the Petition had been presented to Parliament,
the movement changed its form. Even before the Petition had been
presented, 30,000 Tyneside pitmen struck work in support of the
Charter and encouraged the Chartist Convention in Birmingham,
when Parliament proved obdurate, to call for a "Sacred Month,"
or general strike, to coerce Parliament to change its mind. Within

a week, the Chartist leaders had had second thoughts and called for token strikes instead, and there were "turn-outs" and demonstrations of Bolton spinners and Durham and Northumberland miners, and riots in Birmingham, Manchester, and Macclesfield in July and August; but the movement failed both from lack of response and from the divisions among the leaders. After this followed John Frost's armed march on Newport in Monmouthshire in November 1839 and a brief, equally abortive, rising in Sheffield and the West Riding in the winter of 1839–40. The second phase of the Chartist social movement broke out in the summer of 1842. Like the first, it began quite independently of the national Chartist leaders: the "Plug-Plot Riots," as they were called, were primarily concerned in their opening stages with such economic issues as higher wages and the abolition of truck (payment in goods in lieu of wages), and spread rapidly through all the principal manufacturing areas. It was only after several days' delay that a Chartist conference, assembled at Manchester, decided to give them its blessing. Meanwhile, too, the strikers themselves had linked their economic demands with the political aims of the Charter; but by this time the movement was already more than half spent. It ended, soon after, in a massive toll of arrests and sentences to prison and transportation.° The last phase, a far less widespread and less significant affair, was that of 1848. By this time, after a further depression in 1847, economic conditions were already on the mend; and only minor disturbances, including a food riot in Glasgow, preceded the presentation of the third National Petition to Parliament on April 10. After this followed a number of armed "insurrections," in a minor key and on a minor scale, in Manchester and London; but these were not so much local social outbursts, fed by local grievances, as the last flick of the tail of a dying political movement.

Chartism, in fact, was a rich and many-sided popular movement, the heir of a radical political tradition but equally the child of poor harvests and the poverty, bad housing, ill health, and unemployment that attended the growth of a new industrial society. As such, it looked to the past as well as to present realities for its solutions, and its forms of action and expression, like its leaders

° See pp. 184-9.

and the divergent social elements that composed it, blended the old and the new. To illustrate the point, let us look more closely at perhaps the most significant of all its manifestations, the social movement of 1842. It was the year that, more than any other of a cycle of lean years, justifies the term, "the Hungry Forties." In March, the Home Secretary, Sir James Graham, reported that in a population of 16 million there were 1,427,187 persons on poor relief. There had been a succession of bad harvests, and the average price of the quarter of wheat in 1841–2 ranged between 64s. 4d. and 57s. 3d. at a time when wages were falling: cotton operatives in Lancashire and Cheshire mills were earning 9s. 7d. a week; handloom weavers' wages were down to 1d. an hour; and in Leeds it was claimed that 20,000 people (one in seven or eight of the city's population) were compelled to live on an average income of 11¼d. a week. At Stockport there had been so many evictions for failure to pay rent that wags had chalked on the walls "Stockport to let." Commenting on the state of affairs in January of that year, the Chartist *Northern Star* concluded, in terms that might almost have been Jacobin-inspired; that the vast increase in the nation's wealth had been largely appropriated by a small number of great capitalists and "buyers," while "both masters' capital and workmen's wages are gone." [6]

On July 22, the price of the quarter of wheat rose (from 60s. 5d. in May and 62s. 3d. in June) to a seasonal peak of 64s. 5d.;[7] and a few days later Messrs. Bailey, textile manufacturers of Stalybridge, by Ashton-under-Lyne, announced their intention to reduce their weavers' and spinners' wages. Local Chartists had been active before the strike started, but it appears to have begun as a purely industrial dispute, into which the issue of the People's Charter was only injected later. It was called the Plug-Plot Riots because it took the form of a snowball movement in which the "turn-outs" marched from town to town, stopping work by pulling out the plugs from the factory boilers. It spread quickly from Ashton to Oldham and Manchester; almost simultaneously it broke out on the Tyneside and in Scotland; and from Manchester it radiated over Lancashire, Yorkshire, Staffordshire, Cheshire, the Potteries, Warwickshire, and South Wales.[8] It was fully reported in the press; and the *Annual Register's* account of the events in Manchester will give some of its flavor.

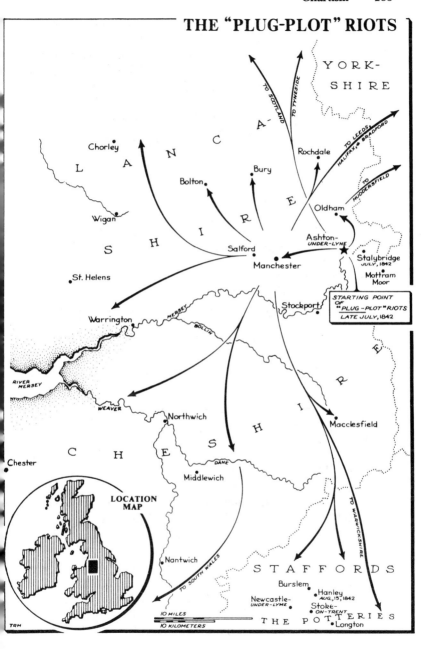

THE "PLUG-PLOT" RIOTS

Y O R K-
S H I R E

Chorley

L A N C A-

Bolton

Bury

Rochdale

TO SCOTLAND

TO TYNESIDE

TO LEEDS

HALIFAX & BRADFORD

TO HUDDERSFIELD

Oldham

Wigan

S H I R E

St. Helens

Salford

Manchester

Ashton-
UNDER-LYNE

Stalybridge
JULY, 1842

Mottram
Moor

STARTING POINT
OF
"PLUG-PLOT" RIOTS
LATE JULY, 1842

Warrington

MERSEY

BOLLIN

Stockport

S H I R E

RIVER
MERSEY

WEAVER

Northwich

WEAVER

Macclesfield

C   H   E   S   H   I   R   E

Chester

LOCATION
MAP

Middlewich

DANE

TO WARWICKSHIRE

Nantwich

TO SOUTH WALES

S T A F F O R D S

Burslem

Hanley
AUG. 15, 1842

Newcastle-
UNDER-LYME

Stoke-
ON-TRENT

10 MILES

10 KILOMETERS

T H E   P O T T E R I E S

Longton

TRM

The rioters proceeded to turn out workpeople in the towns of Ashton and Oldham, and the various mills in the vicinity; and the next morning proceeded with the same intention to Manchester. They arrived at Holt Town, in number about 5,000, at ten o'clock, but were met in Pollard-street by a troop of cavalry, under the command of Colonel Wemyss, a company of rifles, and a large body of police. This force arrested their progress for some time: but, after having agreed to disperse, they eluded that course by breaking up into several detachments, which continued their arbitrary levies upon the mills, laid contributions on the provision shops, and at length met in large numbers on a vacant spot of ground near Granby-row, where they were addressed by several popular orators, and declared their resolution not to return to work until wages were restored to the rate which they bore in the early part of 1840. In the afternoon a contest took place at Messrs. Birley's mill, the windows of which were entirely destroyed, and a girl was killed by a missile thrown from the roof. Similar riots took place in various parts of Manchester on the 6th, and a police-station at Newton was wholly demolished. Two policemen, who were severely wounded, died the next day in the Infirmary.[9]

In Manchester, the "turn-outs" closed down some 130 cotton mills and perhaps as many dyeworks, foundries, and machine shops, involving in all some 50,000 hands; there was no pillaging except of bread, and remarkably little disorder.[10] But at Stockport, on the seventh, there were riots in the course of which the workhouse was attacked and 672 seven-pound loaves and £7 in copper were taken away. At Preston, the next day, the military opened fire and shot four strikers dead. At Salford, troops defending the Adelphi Works fired and wounded five. By now (it was a bare week since the movement had begun), the *Annual Register* reported, "the rioting had . . . extended to Rochdale, Bury, Macclesfield, Bolton, Huddersfield, and all the surrounding districts; several attempts were made to injure the railroads, but fortunately without success." Two days later, the strikes had spread to Halifax, Bradford, and Leeds in Yorkshire and into the mining districts of Staffordshire and Warwickshire.

By now, however, under the influence of local Chartists, the movement had assumed a political form. Already on August 7, a great meeting of Lancashire and Cheshire "turn-outs" on Mottram Moor, near Stalybridge, had resolved that "all labor shall cease until the People's Charter becomes the law of the land." During the next week, the motion was taken up by strikers' meetings in numerous factory towns; and a conference of the combined trades, meeting in Manchester to direct the strike, decided to give it support. On August 15, the resolution was passed at a meeting of miners at Hanley in the Potteries, addressed by the Leicester Chartist Thomas Cooper. Two days later, the National Charter Association also met in Manchester, and though the leaders were divided they could not evade the issue: should the "turn-outs" be discouraged, or should the strike be extended under the banner of of the Charter? Julian Harney, though a firm advocate of "physical force," feared a trap and recommended no cooperation; and O'Connor himself, whose opinion carried more weight than any other's, blamed the strikes on the Machiavellian intrigues of the Anti-Corn Law League. "They have gotten the people out! How will they get them in again?" However, others took a contrary view: among them Thomas Cooper, lately returned from Hanley, and Dr. McDouall, who had close connections with the trade unions. O'Connor for a brief while changed his mind ("you have no alternative but to bow or to resist the tyrant's will"); and McDouall was empowered to issue a manifesto pledging the conference's support for a general strike. So an important step had been taken: the Chartist leaders, under the pressure of events and their own followers "from below," had once more given their blessing to a political strike. Yet their decision came too late to be effective; Harney opposed the strike at Sheffield; and O'Connor changed his mind again and condemned McDouall for his "wild strain of recklessness" in the *Northern Star*. The Plug-Plot Riots ended in a flood of mutual recriminations; the strikers returned to work (though some not till the spring of 1843); and political Chartism and the trade unions, briefly brought together, drifted once more apart.

Even if the alliance had been short-lived, the experience would not be entirely wasted for the future. In more senses than one, the events of 1842 were an important landmark in British labor history. But they had also shown that, alongside modern-type labor disputes and working-class political movements, other forms of mass action appropriate to an earlier age still persisted, and might even on occasion prevail. The case is perhaps best illustrated by the example of the Pottery towns. The Staffordshire miners and iron workers had already been on strike in July over a cut in their wages; and in August they and the potters readily joined the "turn-outs" that marched into the Potteries from the neighboring manufacturing districts. As we have seen, the call to extend the strike and to link it with the People's Charter reached Hanley on the very day that Thomas Cooper was addressing a great miners' meeting. A local Chartist blacksmith, Joseph Capper, put the resolution, which was carried with acclamation; the pumps were stopped in the mines, the potters were all called out, and every factory in the district was closed down. But Cooper, who, though he had inflamed his listeners with violent words, had no intention of provoking riots, had gone off to attend the Chartist conference in Manchester; Capper and the local Chartist committee lost control of events; and a wild and spontaneous outburst of rioting followed at Hanley, Fenton, Longton, Burslem, Stoke-on-Trent, and other Pottery towns. Police stations were raided for arms and prisoners released, police records and poor rate books seized and destroyed, and the houses of local magistrates, coal-owners, parsons, and rate collectors "pulled down" or set on fire[11] The account of the trial of twenty-nine prisoners ("mostly young men, or even boys"), charged with demolishing the Rev. Benjamin Vale's house at Longton, near Stoke-on-Trent, reads like a scene from the Gordon Riots or the attack on Priestley's house in Birmingham in 1791.

The first witness [wrote the *Annual Register*] was Mary Anne Vale, who described the attack on the house. On the 15th August, she saw a mob approaching the house, and immediately proceeded to close the shutters. The mob, however, reached the house before she was able to do so. She was greatly alarmed, her husband not being at home. They demanded money and drink; which at first she refused; but she after-wards gave them her purse, containing about 5s. or 6s., and desired the servant to give them some drink. They then proceeded to the study, and commenced destroying and burning the books and furniture. Some of them went upstairs and set fire to several rooms; others followed the servant to the cellar with a sheet, which they set on fire; and they then commenced drinking whiskey. Witness fled as soon as she saw the whole house in flames, and took refuge in an adjoining cottage; when Jabez Phillips, one of the prisoners, came up and said, "They were going to London to burn, and bring all things to their proper level."

Dr. Vale returned while the house was burning; but a friend prevented his entering it. The mob made a bonfire of the furniture in front of the house, and were with difficulty stopped in their rough sport. . . .

When I saw the house on fire [said George Bailey, a bricklayer], I went to fetch the engine, and helped to work it and put out the fire . . . Williams came to stop us from working the engine. He first set his foot on the hose, and then be borrowed a knife from Cartledge to cut the hose; but he was taken into custody before he could do it by Mr. Richard Cyples. . . . I saw Wright put a bed upon the fire in front of the house. I had known him before. I also saw Joseph Whiston, who was known by the name of Joco. I saw him take a piano and put it on the fire. He said the Lord was at his side, and the flames would not hurt him. . . .

At this time there were about four or five hundred persons present. One of the prisoners was detected in pilfering small articles, caps, scissors, and the like, and putting them in his pocket. The people who brought the engine were putting out the fire, when the military came to the spot, and several of the rioters were taken into custody.[12]

Defense counsel pleaded that several of the prisoners had been in a state of intoxication: they had found a barrel of whiskey in the cellar and (he argued) the jury could well imagine "that such a stimulus applied to persons who were on the verge of starvation must have driven them into a state of temporary madness, rendering them in a great measure unaccountable for their acts." The jury, however, found all but one of the prisoners guilty; and the same verdict was returned against a great many more of the further 274 persons brought to trial before the Staffordshire Special Commission for similar attacks on the houses of the Rev. Charles Ellis Atkins of Hanley; Lord Granville, a coal owner, and his agent, Forrest, of Shelton; Mr. Barwell of Burslem; and William Parker, a county magistrate and squire of Shelton. 146 of them were sentenced to prison with hard labour and 75 to be transported for terms varying from seven years to life. Of the latter, 30 appear in the convict records of Tasmania. They include 20 colliers, 14 potters, 8 labourers, 2 bakers, 2 carpenters, a shoemaker, a carter, a groom, an engine driver, and an engine turner.[13]

This was by far the largest batch of prisoners arrested, imprisoned, and transported for participation in any single event in the course of the Chartist disorders. Yet these disturbances were by no means typical of Chartist popular movements and outbreaks as a whole. They were, like the occasional raids on food shops and threats to railways, mills, and machinery, archaic survivals from the past rather than characteristic of the workers' movements of the 1840's. In 1842, police, magistrates, and troops in Manchester and other manufacturing towns would have been quite incapable of preventing far more violent disorders if the strikers or their leaders had been determined to repeat on a larger scale the methods of the "No Popery" rioters in London or the "Church and King" rioters in Birmingham of fifty years before.[14] But the nature of industrial disputes and popular demonstrations was changing, and though there were elements in Chartism that looked back to both the violence and the "golden age" of an idyllic past, there were others for whom the present held other prospects and offered other methods of redress. Among both leaders and followers there were many who dreamed of returning, through the Charter, from the grim social realities of the present to the old Jacobin ideal of a society of small masters and skilled craftsmen; and O'Connor, for whom machinery and the industrial age were an anathema, thought he could solve the workers' problems by skimming off the surplus urban population and putting it back on the land. Yet, for all these Utopian yearnings and speculations, Chartism, as the product of an evolving industrial society, was bound, in order to survive so long, to seek out new means to impress itself on the nation's conscience. It found them in the political agitation for the Charter, in the National Charter Association, an early forerunner of a "labor" party, and in the workers' industrial movement, particularly that of 1842. These, too, had deep traditional roots: the Charter itself, as we have seen, derived from earlier radical models, and the industrial movement might still, as in the Potteries, develop into old-style attacks on property. But in neither case was there really a reversion to the past. The Six Points meant something very different when addressed to the "black hands" of the industrial areas from what they had meant when addressed to the clergy, gentry, and "middling" householders of Westminster; and the potters and colliers of Hanley, for all their antiquated forms of action, had, through the Charter, acquired a political purpose and vision of the future that were denied to the rioters of

1780 and 1791. In short, while Chartism mirrored the death throes of a dying society, it was even more the expression of the birth pangs of a new.

REFERENCES

1. Quoted by Asa Briggs, in *Chartist Studies* (London, 1959), p. 10.
2. *Ibid.*, pp. 1-28.
3. For the best purely factual and descriptive account of Chartism, particularly in its earlier stages, see M. Hovell, *The Chartist Movement* (London, 1918).
4. Quoted from F. C. Mather, *Public Order in the Age of the Chartists* (Manchester, 1959), p. 1.
5. *Ibid.*, pp. 8-28. Mr. Mather adds a fourth cycle: that of the Rebecca riots, November 1842-October 1843 (see my Chapter 10).
6. G. D. H. Cole and R. Postgate, *The Common People 1746-1938* (London, 1945), pp. 296-9; G. Kitson Clark, "Hunger and Politics in 1842," *Journal of Modern History*, XXV (1953), 355-74.
7. For wheat prices in 1842, see *Gentleman's Magazine*, new series, XVII, 119, 231, 343, 455, 567, 674; XVIII, 111, 223, 335, 447, 559, 679.
8. For a detailed account, see A. G. Rose, *The Plug Riots*, Lancs and Cheshire Antiquarian Society, 1957.
9. *Annual Register*, LXXXIV (1842), 133-4.
10. See "Chartism and the Trade Unions" in *Our History*, pamphlet no. 31, autumn 1963, pp. 6-7.
11. For a vivid account, based partly on local documentary materials, see Frederick Harper's novel, *Joseph Capper* (London, 1962), pp. 138-56.
12. *Annual Register*, LXXXIV (1842), 157-9.
13. *Ibid.*, p. 163; Tasmanian State Archives, CON 33/38, 54, 61.
14. Mather, *op. cit.*, pp. 14-16.

PART TWO

The Pre-industrial Crowd

THIRTEEN

Faces in the Crowd

We have seen something in earlier chapters of the changing composition of what I have called the pre-industrial crowd. We noted, for example, the role played by peasants and rural craftsmen in French country riots and industrial workers in the English; the particular disposition of weavers and miners to break machinery in English industrial disputes; the youth of some rioters and not of others; the part played by women in certain of the great *journées* of the French Revolution; and the respective role of farmers and farm laborers in the English rural riots of the 1830's and 40's and that of the workers from the railway repair shops in Paris in June 1848. All these examples suggest that the nature of disturbances and of the crowd's activities are intimately connected with the composition (social, occupational, and other) of those taking part in them. Yet this is an aspect of the question that has been almost entirely neglected by historians and sociologists alike. Historians have, as we saw, been inclined to take refuge behind such omnibus and prejudicial or "value-oriented" labels as "mob" or "the people"; and, adopting as their models Clarendon's "dirty people without name," Taine's *la canaille,* or Michelet's *le peuple,* they have appeared to assume that, whether the crowd's activities were praiseworthy or reprehensible, the crowd must remain an abstract phenomenon without face or identity. And social scientists, for all their serious concern with the crowd's behavior and its underlying motives, have in this respect not done much better.°

° See, for example, Neil Smelser, who, while recognizing the importance of the changing composition of crowds in the course of disturbances, limits its discussion to a few lines (*Theory of Collective Behavior* (London, 1962), pp. 253, 260-61).

As we noted in an introductory chapter, the problem is a difficult one to tackle. Not only does the historian have to rely for his answers on "dead" parchment, but the records most often lack both adequacy and precision. If we are concerned with social as well as occupational distinctions, how do we tell whether a "carpenter," for instance, is a master or a journeyman? As Professor Soboul reminds us, Maurice Duplay, at whose house Robespierre lodged in the Rue St. Honoré in Paris, is simply described as a *menuisier* (cabinet maker); yet he employed thirty workpeople, had an annual income of 10–12,000 livres, and (so his own daughter tells us) would never dream of allowing any of his journeymen or *garçons* to sit down to eat at his table.[1] The point is not, of course, that the compilers of contemporary records were just careless in such matters, but that our present "language of class" (to use Professor Briggs's term) has evolved only slowly and that observers of the social scene in the eighteenth and early nineteenth centuries, even those as methodical and diligent as the Parisian *commissaires de police* and their scribes, thought in terms of different social categories from those in common use today. As long as society was still hierarchical and "aristocratic" and mobility between classes was comparatively unusual—or, if not unusual, officially frowned on—it was normal to think of society in terms of differing "orders," "ranks," "degrees," or "stations" rather than of differing "classes"; and this continued to be the case, due to differing historical circumstances, longer in France than in England.

In France it was generally assumed before the Revolution that the significant divisions were those separating *privilégiés* (nobles and higher clergy) from *roturiers* (commoners), the latter being lumped together for official purposes, whether they were peasants, bankers, masters, or journeymen, under the common label of Third Estate. Unofficially, it is true, distinctions were in fact already being made between proprietors or *honnêtes gens* (whether noble or other) and manual producers, and peasants were generally seen as belonging to a category of their own; but the term *ouvrier* continued to be applied as readily to masters as to their workpeople, and it was not until the present century that an *ouvrier* became by definition one who not only worked with his hands but worked for wages for an employer.* In England, where industrial society emerged earlier and developed more rapidly, the transition to the modern "language of class" was less prolonged, but it went through similar stages of evolution. In the 1820's and 1830's, a "manufacturer" could as well be a wage earner as an employer; the word "class" was not used as a term of purely social distinction until 1805; and even when terms like "working class" and "middle class" came into use after 1812, they continued to be obscured by such terms as "industrious classes" (note the French equivalent of *classes laborieuses*) until the middle of the century; and it was another thirty years before old phrases like "orders," "ranks," and "degrees" were finally abandoned.[2]

Such considerations are a reminder that even where the documents are reasonably adequate in recording names, identifying faces, and distinguishing between one type of rioter or striker and another, we still have to make the effort to interpret them correctly. On the one hand, we must avoid the temptation to read the past too closely in terms of the present and to apply to the pre-industrial crowd labels only appropriate to later times: it was precisely for this reason that a French writer, Daniel Guérin, was taken to task by his critics when he presented the Parisian sans-culottes of 1793–5 as though they were a modern industrial proletariat in embryo. But, equally, we have to avoid falling into the opposite error, which is to be bound too closely and literally by the social labels used by contemporary writers and observers. The fact that a memorialist or police agent of 1789 may, in using such terms as *ouvriers* or "industrious classes," make no distinction between employers and wage earners, does not oblige us to do the same. Whatever contemporaries may have thought about it, society is continuously evolving and developing and there is bound to be a time lag separating the emergence of new social forms and forces and their recognition in the "language of class" used by dictionaries and encyclopedias. To take an obvious example: the appearance of new classes of factory workers and manufacturing entrepreneurs in England, the product of her industrial revolution,

* See *Dictionnaire de l'Académie française*, 1935; and contrast with the definition of *ouvrier* given in the previous (1878) edition.

was a social reality long before contemporary opinion was fully aware of what was taking place. Here, of course, the historian, though so often at a disadvantage, has the advantage of being able to look back at the whole course of development, and can thus gauge more precisely the exact point of transition and devise social labels appropriate to the occasion. Even so, the pitfalls are many and he must tread warily; and any conclusions that we draw from the documents on the composition of the pre-industrial crowd must be tentative and lay no claim to finality.

First, let us attempt to dispose of a common fallacy. The typical riotous or revolutionary crowd, writers like Taine and Gustave Le Bon have suggested, is composed of criminal elements, riffraff, vagrants (the French *gens sans aveu*), or social misfits. Le Bon even wants to have it both ways: on the one hand, he argues that the crowd reduces its sane and rational elements to a common level of animality; on the other, that it tends to attract criminal types, degenerates, and persons with destructive instincts.[3] Social historians of the eighteenth century in England have tended to adopt this view: though avoiding the more prejudicial of these labels, they have been inclined to see the urban "mob" in terms of the "slum population" of large cities or the poorest of the poor. Dr. Dorothy George, for example, ascribes a major part in the Gordon Riots of 1780 to "the inhabitants of the dangerous districts in London who were always ready for pillage." More recently, Dorothy Marshall has made the bolder claim that the "mob" was in large measure composed of social dregs, pimps, prostitutes, thieves, and receivers.[4] And there is certainly ample evidence to suggest that this was the prevailing view of contemporary observers, whether of the aristocracy or of the middle class.

But, backed as it is by such a solid body of opinion, is the view for all that valid? Do the common run of rioters, strikers, and insurgents of these times tend, in fact, to be drawn from social riffraff, from Dr. George's "dangerous districts," or what Louis Chevalier has termed *les classes dangereuses*?[5] In the present state of our knowledge, it would be ludicrous to claim to give any final answer to this question: neither the nature of the documents available nor the extent of the inquiries made so far would warrant it. Yet there are solid reasons for arguing that the traditional view

is on the whole a false one. At first sight, no doubt, there is a great
deal to recommend it. It can hardly be denied that the conditions
of social commotion under which riots occurred at this time, as
at any other time, provided admirable opportunities for petty
thieves and looters to join in the fray and, under cover of riot or
revolution, reap a golden harvest. We have already quoted
numerous cases in our earlier chapters to illustrate this point.
In the Gordon Riots, for example, the jails were broken into by
the "No Popery" demonstrators and several hundred prisoners—
including 134 from Newgate and 119 from the Clerkenwell Bride-
well—were let loose on the streets of London; and Horace Walpole
may not have exaggerated when he wrote at the height of the
disturbances that "as yet there are more persons killed by drinking
than by ball or bayonet." Again, one of the most spectacular of
the incidents of the Paris revolution of July 1789 was the methodical looting by local poor and unemployed of the St. Lazare
monastery on the northern outskirts of the city; and in the long
history of revolutions this was certainly no exception. Yet such
incidents, although providing useful illustrative material for those
sharing Taine's and Le Bon's views on the nature of the "mob,"
are quite insufficient to prove their point. In fact, the evidence of
the police and judicial records—admittedly inadequate, but more
reliable than the casual and often prejudiced accounts of chance
observers—tends to refute it.

Here are a few examples. Of the 160 persons brought to trial
after the Gordon Riots, only a handful were found to have had
previous convictions; and it is remarkable how many of these
prisoners received testimonials of good character from their
neighbors or employers, a fact all the more striking as it contrasts
sharply with the bad records of many of those who informed
against them. These prisoners, besides, were almost without exception men and young lads of settled abode and occupation; only
fifteen of them were specifically charged with theft, and in eight
of these cases the charge remained unproven.[6] The records relating
to the French grain riots of 1775, which we described at length
in an earlier chapter, are far more detailed and allow us to arrive
at more confident conclusions. Several hundreds of persons were,
as we have seen, arrested at the end of this affair and were

thoroughly searched and cross examined by the police, who had therefore ample opportunities to discover how many of their prisoners had been bribed or had been branded or imprisoned for previous felonies or misdemeanors. From these investigations it appeared that nearly all were local people; few were vagrants, though many (particularly those arrested in Paris) lived in lodgings; and only a handful had served previous prison sentences —and only in one instance for an offense that could be described as anything but trivial.[7]

Similar facts emerge, though the evidence is not always so complete, from the official records relating to those arrested, killed, or wounded—or even just participating—in the various *journées* of the French Revolution of 1789–95. In the early months of 1789, Paris was flooded with unemployed country workers and urban poor, a fact that caused both the old and the new city authorities considerable concern. Yet, apart from the incident at the St. Lazare monastery that we have noted, vagrants, *gens sans aveu*, and criminal elements played only a minor, marginal role in the disturbances of that year. Among 68 persons arrested, wounded, and killed in the Réveillon riots in the Faubourg St. Antoine at the end of April, only three were without fixed abode and only three had served previous terms of imprisonment; and of these only one was found to be branded with the "V" of the convicted *voleur* or thief. No arrests were made after the fall of the Bastille (the sure sign of a successful operation), but we know the names of each one of the 662 so-called *vainqueurs de la Bastille*, and of these all were of fixed abode and settled occupation, the great majority of them being drawn from the Faubourg St. Antoine and adjoining districts. In later upheavals the pattern remained much the same. The next great popular demonstration was that of July 17, 1791, when thousands gathered in the Champ de Mars, at the invitation of the Cordeliers Club, to sign a petition calling for the abdication of Louis XVI. In the course of the whole agitation surrounding this affair, some 250 persons were arrested by the police and National Guard on a multiplicity of charges: of these, two were beggars, three others were found to be without settled occupation (*sans état*), four had had previous convictions (all of a trivial nature); and, once more, the overwhelming majority were men and women of fixed abodes and settled jobs. The same was undoubtedly true of the armed citizens who reduced the Tuileries and overthrew the monarchy in August 1792: quite apart from what the records tell us about their past history and occupations, it could not have been otherwise, as all but householders were excluded from the military units that carried through the operation. The evidence is less conclusive in the case of the disturbances of 1793–5; but, such as it is, it tends to confirm the impression that the crowd in the French Revolution—and not only that engaged in the great political *journées*—was largely composed of sober householders and citizens, admittedly of humble station and often temporarily unemployed, but among whom vagrants, thieves, prostitutes, and social riffraff played an altogether insignificant part.[8]

In the case of English country riots, particularly those of the eighteenth century, the evidence is far less detailed and impressive: we generally have to depend on the piecemeal and casual observations of eyewitnesses, magistrates, or newspaper correspondents. Yet, here again, we have the impression that riot and crime, though occasionally brought together, were casual rather than close companions. After the riots that swept through the southern, southeastern, and western counties in 1766, the *Gentleman's Magazine* reported from Berkshire:

William Simpson and *John Skelton*, two criminals convicted at the Assizes, held by special commission at *Reading*, for robbery on the highway, were executed there. *They were not among the number of rioters.*[9]

Admittedly, this tells us nothing of the police records of those taking part in the disturbances, though it is perhaps significant that the correspondent should so deliberately underline the distinction between the one type of popular activity and the other. Again, we have seen that the Rebecca riots in West Wales and the Luddite disturbances in the north of England were, at a certain stage, attended by outbreaks of gangsterism, robbery, and undiscriminating attacks on persons and properties; but these appear to have lain on the fringe rather than at the center of the movements and to have been the work of persons taking advantage of the unsettled conditions that the riots had brought about.°

However, the evidence relating to some of these later disturbances is more complete, for in the Australian convict records of the 1830's and 1840's we rediscover the precision of the French police reports of half a century before. So we find that among the thirty potters, miners, and others transported to Tasmania for wrecking houses and property in the pottery towns of Staffordshire in 1842, eight had had previous convictions: some for assault, others for breaking fences or vagrancy or leaving their employer's service, and two for the more serious offenses of rape and embezzlement.† Again, among the far higher number (464 in all) transported to the Australian colonies for taking part in the "Swing" riots of 1830, 94 of 325 sent to Tasmania and 11 of 139 sent to New South Wales had been previously arrested or convicted: among the former group, by far the most common offense was poaching (in 32 of the 94 cases), and only 8–10 had served sentences of six months or more, mainly for assault or larceny.[10] Thus roughly one in four of the convicted rioters of 1842 and two in nine of those of 1830 had been arrested before or had served earlier prison sentences.‡ While this is a considerably higher proportion than among those arrested in the grain riots of 1775 or in the riots of the French Revolution in Paris, we can in this case get a more balanced picture by comparing the criminal records of these men with those of the general run of male convicts sent

---

° See pp. 88 and 161 above; and note Dr. Darvell's comment on the Luddites: "The Luddites proper rigidly confined themselves to their specific offences, breaking machinery and (in the north) collecting arms. . . . They were not to be held responsible for ordinary robberies which were clearly the work of different groups of men, gangs of common thieves using the Luddite name, knowing that it saved them from all danger of resistance or pursuit." (F. O. Darvall, *Popular Disturbances and Public Order in Regency England* (London, 1934), p. 184.)

† Tasmanian State Archives, 2/44, 2/60, 2/67, 2/79, 2/83, 2/88. One of the thirty—the rapist—was transported for "breaking and entering a shop, and stealing therein."

‡ It should be noted, however, that such offenses as poaching, arson, stealing firewood, assaulting a gamekeeper, or leaving the service of an unpopular employer (which account for most of these convictions) were not considered reprehensible by even the respectable poor (see also pp. 224-5 below).

to the two Australian colonies for a wide variety of offenses during the whole period of transportation: in their case the "former-offense" rate has been calculated by Dr. Lloyd Robson as amounting to some 61 percent of all those transported.[11] Moreover, in the case of the rioters sent to Tasmania, we can go even further by comparing the number of misdemeanors they subsequently committed in the colony with those committed by convicts as a whole. The results show that the rioters of 1842 incurred reprimands or penalties for a total of 91 offenses, or an average of about 3 offenses per man, and the "Swing" rioters of 1830 for a combined average of 1.7 per man; whereas Dr. Robson's overall estimate for male convicts of all types transported to Tasmania between 1803 and 1852 is as high as 6 offenses per head up to 1840 and 4 thereafter. Of course, in both of these groups of transported rioters there was a minority that committed far more than their share of misdemeanors in the colony, rising in some cases to twelve or fifteen per man and involving serious cases of rape, assault, and robbery; but the general reputation of the men of 1830, in particular, was extremely high among those in authority, and Governor Arthur on more than one occasion singled them out for special praise as men of exemplary character and as convicts of "the better sort."[12] By and large, then, we may conclude with a fair degree of certainty that in this case, too, crime and riot, far from being inseparable companions, were only occasional and somewhat uneasy bedfellows.

Admittedly, such evidence does not go far enough to dispose of the argument that the pre-industrial crowd was most frequently recruited from the "slum population" of great cities or from their "dangerous" districts or social classes. A final answer can be given only after far more extensive researches have been carried out. The gap is a particularly serious one, as it includes the detailed study of London and Paris riots in the early nineteenth century. M. Rémi Gossez' work on Paris in 1848 has yet to appear; and M. Louis Chevalier's book on the "industrious" and "dangerous" classes of Paris of the 1820's to 1840's, while an excellent social and demographic study of the population as a whole, throws little light on the components of the riotous and rebellious crowd; [13] while nineteenth-century London still awaits its "sociological" historian. In consequence, we have to make do with such studies as have already been made of the French Revolution and of the London "mob" of the eighteenth century. These, at least, suggest strongly that there is little concordance between the main city strongholds of crime and over-crowding and those in which popular outbreaks, strikes, and revolutionary *journées* most frequently occurred. It would perhaps be comforting to the moralist or to the champion of a traditional social order that it should be otherwise, but for this the evidence gives little support. In Paris, during the French Revolution, the main centers of revolutionary agitation and response were undoubtedly the main centers of petty trades and crafts and shops, like the Faubourgs St. Antoine and St. Marcel and the Section des Gravilliers, though it is true that the crowded districts around the central markets and the Hôtel de Ville ran them pretty close. In London, the lack of concordance is even more sharply marked. The denizens of St. Giles-in-the-Fields or of the shadier quarters of Holborn (such as Field Lane, Chick Lane, or Black Boy Alley)—centers of gin-swilling, petty larceny, casual labor and of the poorest immigrant Irish—may, as Francis Place deplored, have been among those who flocked most eagerly to Tyburn Fair to witness public executions; but it was not they but their fellow citizens of the more sober districts of settled occupation, like the City of London, the Strand, Southwark, Shoreditch, and Spitalfields, who most conspicuously took part in riots.[14]

If, then, slum dwellers and criminal elements were not the main shock troops of the pre-industrial crowd or the mainstay of riot and revolution, who were? The short answer will hardly come as a surprise. Basically, they were the "lower orders" or *menu peuple* of the towns and countryside, or those who, in Paris and other cities during the French Revolution, were called the sans-culottes. Exceptionally, they might be recruited from other social groups: there are plenty of examples in the disturbances of 1787-95 in Paris of occasional students, teachers, professional men, civil servants, small *rentiers*, and lawyers' clerks taking part: on one occasion, that of the royalist uprising of October 1795 (the 13th Vendémiaire), such elements appear even to have played the dominant role. In London, too, it was noted during the Wilkite disturbances of 1763-71 that citizens of "the better sort" on occasion mingled with the vulgar "mob." But, normally, merchants, capitalists, or the more prosperous householders did not demonstrate, riot, or shoulder muskets to besiege a Bastille or capture a royal palace by force of arms. In strikes and food riots the point is so obvious as to be hardly worthy of mention; but even where the sympathies of a substantial part of the propertied classes were evidently enlisted on the side of those taking part, such activities were generally left to the common herd. So it was in Paris in the revolutionary events of 1789 and 1792, and again in July 1830 and February 1848; and in England (though the parallels are not exact) during the Wilkes "affair," in the opening stages of the Gordon Riots, and in the Reform Bill agitation of 1831. (But in England the "lower orders" most often found themselves without effective middle-class support—with political consequences that will be considered in a later chapter.)

In France, then, those taking part in pre-industrial riots and disturbances were, in cities, predominantly small workshop masters, shopkeepers, apprentices, independent craftsmen, journeymen, laborers, and city poor; and in the countryside, wine-growers, small peasant proprietors, landless laborers, and rural craftsmen. In England, they were small shopkeepers, peddlers, artisans, journeymen, servants, and laborers in the one case and weavers, miners, woolcombers, small tenant farmers and freeholders, farm laborers, and village craftsmen in the other. Factory workers only begin to appear in large numbers in English disturbances (apart from strikes) in the 1830's. In France, they were nonexistent in the riots of the Revolution of 1789-95 and virtually so in those of February and June 1848; and in 1789, at least, even workers in manufactories (textiles, glass, tobacco, tapestries, porcelain) played a far less conspicuous role than craftsmen or building and riverside workers.

To say so much is, of course, to say little more than that the composition of rioters in towns and villages tended to reflect the social patterns of a pre-industrial age. Yet this is by no means all that can be said, as there were considerable variations in the composition of these rioters of the "inferior set" as between one popular outbreak and another; and such variations may be highly significant in that they may throw further light on the nature of the disturbances themselves. In industrial disputes, the point may appear to be so obvious as to be the shallowest truism; yet even here we should know more about the exact nature of a grievance if the documents were to tell us whether those who voiced it were among the lower-paid or more highly paid members of their craft: certainly the London coal heavers, weavers, glass grinders, and hatters who went on strike in 1768-9 already received higher wages than most workers in that city.

In the French Revolution, we find only one occasion in which wage earners, as opposed to other groups among the sans-culottes, appear to have predominated in what was not primarily an industrial dispute; but that was in the Réveillon riots of April 1789, where the issue of wages, though secondary to that of food prices, played a certain part. Similarly, we find that women played a more conspicuous role on those occasions—as in the march to Versailles in October 1789, the food riots of 1792-3, and in the final upsurge of the sans-culottes in May 1795—when food prices and other bread-and-butter questions lay immediately to the fore. On other occasions, it was the craftsmen of the small workshops—masters, independent artisans, and journeymen—that played the principal part. This was particularly so in the more highly organized affairs such as the demonstration on the Champ de Mars and the armed attacks on the Bastille and the Tuileries: in such cases, the small shopkeepers and workshop masters, who were the main carriers of revolutionary ideas and slogans among the *menu peuple*, often brought their journeymen, *garçons*, and apprentices along with them as companions in a common enterprise.[15]

In the English rural riots of the early nineteenth century, we have already seen that the composition of villagers taking part might change sharply from one incident to another: in 1830, it was the farm laborers of the southern counties that wrecked machinery and burned the landlords' and farmers' ricks; whereas in the riots of the 1840's in Wales it was the tenant farmers that both planned Rebecca's nocturnal operations and carried them through. Where riots were widespread we may note a similar diversity among those taking part in different parts of the country. Such a diversity is obvious enough in movements like the French flour war of 1775, where the common interest of small consumers of town and countryside involved not only the wine-growers, small peasant proprietors, and rural craftsmen of the village and market town but the porters and laborers of the city. It is less obvious, though certainly no less significant, in a purely rural movement like that of the

English laborers of 1830. Here the majority of those taking part were undoubtedly farm laborers in the strictest sense of the term: ploughmen, reapers, mowers, milkmen, grooms, shepherds, and the like; but a substantial minority were rural craftsmen: carpenters, joiners, bricklayers, masons, cobblers, tinsmiths, tailors, weavers, and paper makers. Among those transported to Australia, there were significant variations between one county and another; but, taking them as a whole, about one in three of those sent to New South Wales and between one in four and one in five of those sent to Tasmania were of this kind.

Sometimes diversity might take another form, and the entry of new social elements into a riot already under way might change its whole direction. In the Gordon Riots, for example, the "better sort of tradesmen" who followed Lord George Gordon to Westminster to present the Protestant Association's petition were soon elbowed out of the way by London's "lower orders"—small traders, journeymen, apprentices, and servants—who passed from words to deeds and began to burn down Catholic houses, schools, and chapels; and these, in turn, were reinforced a few days later by prisoners released from Newgate and other "undesirables," which may account for the less discriminating orgies that marked the closing stages of the rioting. We noted, too, the turn taken by the Rebecca riots, when the small tenant farmers, who up to the summer of 1843 had held the movement firmly under their control, began to lose its direction to the unemployed workers of Glamorgan and "professionals" like Dai'r Cantwr and Shoni Sgubor Fawr: it was at this time that it both entered its "lunatic" phase and began to voice the claims of the laborers against the farmers.[*] In both cases, we noted that the appearance of these new elements caused a change of heart among the more "respectable" of the movement's original supporters: in the first, among the City householders, who rallied to the side of government once their own properties, and not only those of Roman Catholics, appeared to be endangered; and, in the second, among the farmers, who had become alarmed by the growing militancy of the laborers.

On a larger scale, we see a similar process developing in Paris in 1848. It was the entry of the faubourgs on February 23, 1848

[*] See pp. 160-61 above.

that turned a political demonstration against the Ministry into an insurrection that forced the King to abdicate; and a great deal of what happened between February and June can be explained in terms of the desire of the more "respectable" revolutionaries to rid themselves of their embarrassing allies of the "inferior set." Or a similar process might take place in reverse, and insurgents of a higher social class take over a movement started by wage earners or urban poor. Something of the kind happened in Paris in October 1789 and again in September 1793. In the first case, a food riot launched by the women of the markets was converted into a political demonstration with far-reaching aims by the entry on the scene of Stanislas Maillard's *volontaires de la Bastille* and the battalions of the National Guard. In the second, a demonstration by the "lower orders" of sans-culottes for a general *maximum*, or ceiling on the price of food, was temporarily diverted by Hébert and the Commune's leaders into a massive march of the Paris Sections to impose their own political demands on the National Convention. In April 1848, a great workers' rally called together by the leaders of the clubs was eclipsed and overshadowed by a counter-demonstration of the petty-bourgeois National Guard, mustered to display their loyalty to Lamartine and the provisional government. And doubtless every revolution is rich in similar illustrations.

This by no means exhausts the variety of components to be looked for in the pre-industrial crowd. Other variables, such as age, literacy, religion, or geographical and occupational distribution, may be equally significant. Here a few examples must suffice to illustrate the point. In the "No Popery" disturbances in London, it is reasonably certain that a high proportion of those who destroyed Roman Catholic and other properties were youths or boys: contemporary observers like Horace Walpole, later chroniclers like Charles Dickens, and the judicial proceedings relating to the affair all agree on this point. Walpole stresses the part played by "apprentices," and the number of apprentices, journeymen, and young workers of every kind among the 160 persons brought to trial bears him out. Though the Old Bailey records give no complete picture of the prisoners' ages, it is striking how often a witness refers to the accused as "a young fellow," "a boy," or "a child," or gives his age as 15, 16, or 18, or even (in one instance) as "not

yet 14"; and of the twenty-five persons hanged one (and certainly
not as many as suggested by Walpole) was a boy of 15. But this
youthfulness was by no means a feature common to all such dis-
turbances.The average age of 42 Luddites transported to Australia
between 1812 and 1817 was 30.7; that of 75 Chartists transported
in 1842 was 26.5 and of the 16 sent out in 1848 it was 31. That of
the far greater number transported machine-breakers and arsonists
of 1830 was not so high, but higher than Dr. Robson's mean
for the convicts as a whole: with an average of 29 in the case
of several hundred sent to Tasmania and of 27 for those sent
to New South Wales, and of these over half were married
men with families.*[16] The point is of some importance, as it
may perhaps be assumed that settled family men might not so
readily be drawn into such desperate ventures without the spur
of some overwhelming grievance or deep conviction. The ages of
persons wounded or arrested, or simply taking part, in the disturbances of the French Revolution may also be significant in this
respect. The average age of the 662 *vainqueurs de la Bastille* was
34, of those killed and wounded in the assault on the Tuileries in
1792, 38; and of those arrested after the insurrection of May 1795,
36. Such men were appreciably older than those arrested for
taking part in the French grain riots of 1775 (average age 30), in
the pro-*parlement* disturbances (23) and Réveillon riots (29) on
the eve of the Revolution, and in the Champ de Mars affair of 1791
(31). The proportion of persons who may be termed literate from
their ability to sign the police magistrate's report on similar occasions also varied considerably from one disturbance to another:
from 33 percent in the grain riots of 1775 to 62 percent in the
Réveillon riots, to 80 to 85 percent respectively in the case of the
journées of July 1791 and May 1795.† Such differences no doubt
suggest that participants in one type of disturbance were more

* Compare with Dr. Robson's estimated mean of 25.9 years for all English
male convicts transported to the two Australian colonies between 1787 and
1852, of whom a little over one quarter only were married (*op. cit.*, pp. 25-6).
† *The Crowd in the French Revolution*, p. 249 (Appendix V). In the case
of the "Swing" rioters of 1830, the percentage of those able to read or to read
and write ranged between 66 and 75, according to the ship on which they
traveled; but there is no certainty that the methods of testing literacy were
the same in each case. (See reference 12).

sophisticated than they were in others. But, unfortunately, in such cases the evidence is piecemeal and inadequate and does not allow of more than the most tentative conclusions.

Equally significant perhaps is the tendency of certain occupations to be more radical, riotous, or revolutionary than others. We have already noted the proneness of Cornish tin miners, West Country weavers and wool combers, Spitalfields silk weavers, and English colliers in general to be drawn into both food riots and violent disputes with their employers; and writers have stressed the reputation for radicalism, either at this time or at others, of French fishermen, Swedish lumbermen, Australian sheepshearers, and Viennese cobblers.[17] In the course of my own particular researches, I have noted that the Paris craftsmen most conspicuous for their participation in the revolutionary events of 1789-95 were locksmiths, joiners, cabinet makers, shoemakers, tailors, and stone masons; and, among those of less skilled occupations, wine merchants, water carriers, porters, cooks, and domestic servants. It is remarkable how many of these trades reappear half a century later among the thousands arrested and convicted for taking part in the June "days" of 1848.[18] There is, of course, no particular mystery about this: French fishermen (to take an example) may, over their long history, have suffered from more than their fair share of insecurity of employment; and it is not surprising that under the historical conditions with which we are here concerned craftsmen should be more vocally militant than factory workers or domestic workers and that, among them, the most vocal of all should be those belonging to such populous crafts as joinery, tailoring, and shoemaking. Equally, as historical conditions change, it is likely that similar inquiries into the composition of the crowd in the more fully developed industrial society of the 1860's or 1880's would yield quite different results.

This last point raises a further question: how far is the crowd representative of the social groups from which its component parts are drawn? It is, of course, clear enough that because a certain number of locksmiths or engravers took part in the siege of the Bastille (and, in this case, we know the exact number that were officially recognized as having done so) it does not follow that they carried with them the support and good will of Paris locksmiths and engravers as a whole. Michelet assumed that they did and, although he probably exaggerated, his optimism is likely to have been more justified on this occasion than on others. More often, historians have been inclined to treat the rebellious or revolutionary crowd as a militant minority to be sharply marked off from the far larger number of citizens of similar class and occupation who, even they were not overtly hostile, played no active part in the event. Thus it is common to draw a line of distinction between militants, or "activists," and the passive majority. Is such an assumption justified? It is a knotty problem and one even less susceptible of solution by parading statistical evidence than several others that we have treated in this chapter. For a statistical calculation to have even the remotest chance of carrying conviction it would have to be based on a sort of Gallup poll conducted among the population at large: a course that is, unfortunately, not open to the historian.

Even without such resources, it may perhaps be argued that this distinction between militants and "passives" should not be carried too far. It is no doubt valid in the case of the small groups of "activists" or *meneurs* who, even in the most seemingly spontaneous of all such movements, played a distinctive role: we shall return to them in a later chapter. Again, the crowd might be composed in the main of a body of dedicated militants, who had deliberately elected to concert together and whose devotion, determination, and political acumen or sophistication marked them off more or less sharply from their more passive fellow citizens. This may have been the case in such quasi-military operations of the French Revolution as the assault on the Tuileries in August 1792 or the march on the Convention of the sans-culotte battalions in May 1795. This, however, could only happen after the Revolution had had time to produce a political élite from among the sans-culottes themselves, trained in the clubs, Sectional assemblies, and National Guard and by the experience gained from a succession of popular *journées;* it could not happen in the earlier years, nor could it happen until much later in England, where riot never reached the stage of revolution. In other cases, in strikes and food riots in particular, it is doubtful if any clear-cut and valid distinction of this kind can be made between the bulk of those who join the crowd and those who line the sidewalks as mere spectators or even stay at home. The case is further complicated by the fact that on such occasions innocent bystanders or casual participants may be shot down by bullets or, if they give way to a momentary display of enthusiasm, may be arrested as "leaders": the French police records are rich in such examples.*

A related problem is how far the minority of active participants enjoys the sympathy of the passive majority. It is impossible, once more, to discuss this in any but the most general terms. There are occasions when the crowd (using the term in its broadest sense) is only able to impose its authority or enlist silent acquiescence among the majority by the terror of destructive violence or the display of superior force. It was undoubtedly only by such means that the bands of *armées révolutionnaires* recruited in Paris and other cities were able to impose their will on the French rural population in the autumn of 1793; and a similar fear of the consequences probably contributed to the inactivity of London constables and magistrates during the "No Popery" riots of 1780. Nevertheless, this was not so in the case of the Réveillon riots in Paris in April 1789; and yet, long after the disturbances were over, the local population showed where its sympathies lay by refusing to hand over known participants to justice. We have noted similar examples from the Luddite outbreaks in the midlands and north of England and the Rebecca riots in West Wales. In such cases, there is an evident bond of sympathy and common interest linking the active few with the inactive many. More light may perhaps be shed on this matter when, in subsequent chapters, we come to consider the motives underlying popular disturbances and the causes of their success or failure.

REFERENCES

1. A. Soboul, *Les sans-culottes parisiens en l'an II* (Paris, 1958), p. 440.
2. A. Briggs, "The Language of 'Class' in Early Nineteenth-Century England," in A. Briggs and J. Saville (eds.), *Essays in Labour History in Memory of G. D. H. Cole* (London, 1960), pp. 43-73.
3. G. Le Bon, *The Crowd: A Study of the Popular Mind* (London, 1909), pp. 36 ff.; *La Révolution française et la psychologie des révolutions* (Paris, 1912), pp. 53-61, 89-93.

* See pp. 250-52 below.

4. M. D. George, *London Life in the Eighteenth Century* (London, 1951), pp. 118-19; Dorothy Marshall, *Eighteenth-Century England* (London, 1962), pp. 36-7.

5. L. Chevalier, *Classes laborieuses et classes dangereuses* (Paris, 1958).

6. G. Rudé, "The Gordon Riots: A Study of the Rioters and their Victims," *Transactions of the Royal Historical Society*, 5th series, VI (1956), 104-105.

7. G. Rudé, "La taxation populaire de mai 1775 à Paris et dans la région parisienne," *Ann. hist. de la Rév. franç.*, no. 143, April-June 1956, pp. 139-79; and "La taxation populaire de mai 1775 en Picardie, en Normandie, et dans le Beauvaisis," *ibid.*, no. 165, July-Sept. 1961, pp. 305-326.

8. See my *The Crowd in the French Revolution* (Oxford, 1959), pp. 186-90, 249.

9. *Gentleman's Magazine*, XXXVII, 48 (February 26, 1767) (italics in original).

10. Tasmanian State Archives, 2/132-2/178, 53/4328; *The Names and Descriptions of All Male and Female Convicts Arrived in the Colony of New South Wales during the Years 1830 to 1842* (11 vols. Sydney, 1843), II, 43-52.

11. L. L. Robson, *The Origin and Character of the Convicts Transported to New South Wales and Van Diemen's Land 1787-1852* (unpublished Ph.D. thesis, Australian National University, Canberra, 1963), pp. 28-9.

12. See my article, " 'Captain Swing' and Van Diemen's Land," shortly to appear in *Tasmanian Historical Research Association: Papers and Proceedings*.

13. L. Chevalier, *op. cit.*, pp. 551-3.

14. G. Rudé, *The Crowd in the French Revolution*, pp. 185-6; *Wilkes and Liberty* (Oxford, 1962), pp. 13-16; "The London 'Mob' of the Eighteenth Century," *The Historical Journal*, II, i(1959), 1-18.

15. *The Crowd in the French Revolution*, pp. 179-85.

16. G. Rudé, *Protest and Punishment* (Oxford, 1978), pp. 250-51.

17. E. J. Hobsbawm. *Primitive Rebels* (Manchester, 1959), p. 122 (quoting Dr. Ernst Wangermann); W. G. Runciman, *Social Science and Political Theory* (Cambridge, 1963), pp. 95-6 (quoting André Siegfried).

18. *The Crowd in the French Revolution*, pp. 185, 234-5, 246-8 (Appendix IV).

FOURTEEN

Motives and Beliefs

As long as the crowd in history was considered unworthy of serious attention, it was natural that the study of its motives should have been somewhat superficial. Explanations of why the crowd rioted or rebelled have naturally tended to vary with the social attitudes or *values* of the writer. To those to whom the crowd's actions were wholly reprehensible, the crowd would appear to be prompted by the basest motives, by the lure of loot, gold, rape, or the prospect of satisfying other lurking criminal instincts. To those to whom the crowd seemed, on balance, to be an object worthy of sympathy or compassion rather than of reprobation (though this would vary with the occasion), noble ideals, particularly those of sound middle-class and liberal inspiration, would play an important part. To others again, those whom Marx in his day termed the proponents of a "vulgar" materialism, short-term economic factors seemed the most valid explanation of all types of popular unrest, and every disturbance became almost by definition a hunger riot, or *émeute de la faim.*

None of these explanations are wholly without merit, yet all are either superficial or misleading. Why this is so will, I hope, appear in the course of the present chapter. But a preliminary word needs to be said about the first of these interpretations, which, being the most pervasive of the three, calls for a separate comment. Its underlying assumption appears to be that the masses have no worthwhile aspirations of their own and, being naturally venal, can be prodded into activity only by the promise of a reward by outside agents or "conspirators." "In most popular movements," writes Mortimer-Ternaux, a historian of the French Revolutionary Terror, "money plays a greater role than feeling or conviction (*la passion*)"; and Taine and his school offer similar explanations of why the Bastille fell or the French monarchy was overthrown.[1] But such a view, with its evident social bias, was by no means the invention of these writers: on the contrary, it receives ample confirmation from the opinions of contemporary observers. For as long as no serious attempt was made to probe the deeper aspirations of the poor, their periodic outbursts in riot or rebellion were liable to be attributed to the machinations of a political opponent or a "hidden hand."

Such an attitude was shared by all in authority, whether aristocratic or middle class, conservative, liberal, or revolutionary, though the sort of outbreak that might, exceptionally, be condoned would naturally vary from one class or party to the other. Where Sir Robert Walpole, the King's Chief Minister, attributed the riots of 1736 in England to a Jacobite conspiracy and some of his agents spoke darkly of "high church" or "popish priests," Lord Granville, an opposition peer, was willing to ascribe such "tumults" to "oppression." Again, where George III's ministers and their agents hinted that the Gordon Riots might have been instigated by French or American gold, some opposition leaders were inclined to blame the government itself for deliberately fostering riot as a pretext for calling in the army and imposing martial law. Indeed it was common in eighteenth-century England for one party to accuse the other of "raising a Mob." In France, Voltaire, being a critic of aristocracy and a friend of Turgot, convinced himself that the grain-rioters of 1775 were in the pay of Turgot's enemies at Court. During the French Revolution, both revolutionary leaders and their royalist or aristocratic opponents were remarkably liberal with such charges when it suited them: Montjoie, a royalist journalist, claimed to have first-hand proof (which proved to have little foundation) that the Réveillon rioters of 1789 had been bribed with *louis d'or;* and Girondins and Jacobins alike were disposed to believe that food rioters like those that invaded Paris grocery shops in February 1793 had been paid by agents of Pitt or the "aristocrats."[2] Thirty or forty years later, such simple explanations had lost much of their force: we have but to read English parliamentary debates on the Luddites and Chartists to appreciate the difference; but, throughout the eighteenth century, the police—the French perhaps more stubbornly than the

English—clung to their conviction that the twin agents of riot and rebellion were bribery and "conspiracy."

To illustrate the point, we quote the remarkable cross examination by the Beauvais police of a woolen worker arrested in the market town of Mouy at the time of the corn riots of 1775:

Q. How was it known that there were riots elsewhere?
A. Everybody said so in the market at Mouy.
Q. Did any "strangers" come by who urged the people to riot?
A. He saw none.
Q. What did these "strangers" look like?
A. Repeats that he saw none.
Q. What did they talk about?
A. Repeats that he saw no "strangers."
Q. Did they claim to be bearers of the King's orders and did they produce papers purporting to prove it?
A. Repeats that he saw no "strangers."
Q. Did they give, lend, or promise money?
A. He saw no one offering money.
Q. Did any of them produce mouldy bread . . . to stir up the people?
A. He saw no mouldy bread.
Q. Does he know where and by whom this mouldy bread was baked?
A. Repeats that he saw no mouldy bread.
Q. How was it that the inhabitants of each village assembled on the same day and at the same hour?
A. This was always so on market days.
Q. Had he seen bills posted up or distributed?
A. No.
Q. Were they printed or written by hand?
A. Repeats that he saw none.
Q. Does he know where they were printed?
A. Repeats that he saw none.
Q. Does he recognize the writing on those written by hand?
A. Repeats that he saw none.
Q. Where had they been drinking, with whom, and who paid for the drinks?
A. Repeats that he saw no one.[3]

It is remarkable that such searching and persistent questioning should, in this and other cases, have yielded almost entirely negative results. Occasionally a prisoner or a witness, unlike the prisoner in the present instance, admits to having heard rumors about money having been distributed to provoke disorder; but never once does he appear to have been present at the transaction or to have been personally involved. This is not to argue that such rumors were all equally without foundation, though it strongly suggests that cases of bribery in popular movements were not so frequent as the authorities supposed they were.[4] Nor does it exclude the fact of bribery in other cases, as when gangs of strongarm men were recruited by a man of "quality" to beat up or intimidate a political opponent. Such was the case at the Middlesex election of December 1768, when the Court candidate, Sir William Beauchamp Proctor, hired a band of Irish chairmen—at the rate of 2 guineas a day, it was claimed by their leader—to drive his radical opponent's supporters off the hustings.[5] This was the well-known device of "raising a Mob"; but it has nothing to do with the sort of popular movement we are here discussing.

In any case, such explanations, even where they contain a more solid substance of truth, are grossly over simplified. The crowd may riot because it is hungry or fears to be so, because it has some deep social grievance, because it seeks an immediate reform or the millenium, or because it wants to destroy an enemy or acclaim a "hero"; but it is seldom for any single one of these reasons alone. Of course, it would be ludicrous to reject the simple and obvious answers merely because they are so. Economic motives, for example, may be presumed to be dominant in strikes and food riots, as political issues play a part of varying importance in both radical reform movements and movements directed against radical reform, such as the Priestley riots in Birmingham in 1791. When Cornish tin miners or West Country weavers burn down their employer's house or mill or destroy his machinery in the course of an industrial dispute, we need no particular powers of divination to conclude that, whatever the form of disturbance, it is higher wages that they are after. Similarly, when food rioters threaten bakers, invade markets, and rip open sacks of flour or grain, we may assume that the real purpose is not so much to intimidate or destroy as to bring down the price of food. Again, when Parisians assault and capture the Bastille and Londoners "pull down" Catholic houses and chapels, we must suppose that they intended to do precisely this. In looking for motives we must, therefore, not be so subtle or devious as to ignore the overt or primary intention.

The latter, however, only gives us a clue to the general nature of a disturbance; and here we are not so much concerned with this as with what prompted people, often of different social groups, occupations, and beliefs to take part in the event. Even if the immediate or overt motives leap to the eye, we still have to explore those that lie beneath the surface; and if persons of differing classes or creeds are involved, some may be impelled by one motive and some by another. Motives will, therefore, vary not only between one action and the next but between different groups participating in the same disturbance. Even so, we shall become hopelessly confused if we do not attempt to make some distinction between what we may term dominant and underlying motives or beliefs. Here, for the sake of clarity, it is proposed to divide the former into "economic" and "political" and to consider what part they played, both separately and in association, in the activities of the pre-industrial crowd.

Let us begin with those disturbances in which economic issues were clearly paramount. Such were food riots (at this time, the most frequent of all), strikes, peasant attacks on châteaux, the destruction of gates and fences, the burning of hayricks and the wrecking of industrial and agricultural machinery. These account, as we have seen, for the vast majority of disturbances in which the pre-industrial crowd in France and England was actively engaged. And in these we must assume (unless we have evidence to the contrary) that the common people of town and countryside were impelled by the urge to maintain or improve living standards, to raise or prevent reductions in wages, to resist encroachments on their holdings in land or their rights of common pasture, to protect their means of livelihood against the threat of new mechanical devices, and, above all, to ensure a constant supply of cheap and plentiful food, Yet bad, even abysmal, economic conditions were not an automatic "trigger" to disturbance. In England, strikes and trade-union activity tended to occur not at moments of deepest trade depression and unemployment, but rather on the upswing of a boom: as in 1792, 1818, 1824, and 1844-6[6] (the year 1768 appears to have been an exception). During the French Revolution, we noted, the most protracted industrial disputes were those of 1791 and 1794, which were years of comparative prosperity; and that when runaway inflation and unemployment set in, as in the winter of 1794-5, strikes came to an end and food riots took over. Food riots, unlike strikes, were the direct product of bad harvests and trade depression, rising prices and shortage of stocks; but they did not necessarily occur at the peak of a cycle of rising prices: we saw rather that they tended, as in the largest disturbances of their kind before 1789—those of 1766 in England and 1775 in France—to arise as the result of a sudden sharp upward movement leading to shortage and panic buying. Again, strikes, food riots, and peasant movements, even when the prevailing issues were purely economic, might take place against a political background that gave them a greater intensity or a new direction. In London in 1768, already existing industrial disputes were touched by the Wilkite political movement: we find striking weavers and coal heavers acclaiming John Wilkes; and, in France in 1789, it seems unlikely that the peasants would have chosen that particular moment to settle accounts with their landlords if the general political conditions had not been what they were.

Conversely, economic motives often impinged on movements that were, in their essence, political. City riots, upon which political issues usually obtruded, frequently took place against a background of rising prices or food shortage: we saw examples from Paris in 1720, 1752, and 1788, and from London in 1736, 1768, and 1794; though, here, the Gordon Riots and the later Wilkite disturbances appear to have been exceptions.* Similiarly, the French revolutions of 1830 and 1848 broke out during periods of food shortage and trade depression; and we have noted the particular part played by the unemployed in Paris in June 1848. The same intrusion of economic issues is evident in English disturbances of the early nineteenth century; Professor Rostow has vividly illustrated the point in his "social tension chart" for the years 1790 to 1850.[7]

On such occasions, the shortage and high price of bread and food appear to have acted as a stimulus to popular participation in movements that were obstensibly concerned with other objects and issues. During the first French Revolution concern for the price of bread runs like a constant thread through every phase of the struggle of parties and through nearly every

* See Chapter 3.

one of the great popular *journées,* and accounts, perhaps more than any other factor, for the unity and militancy of the Parisian sans-culottes. The revolutionary crisis of 1789 broke out against a backcloth of steeply rising bread prices: we saw how the peasant movement began with raids on markets, millers, and granaries before turning into a war against the landlords; and the Réveillon rioters, who destroyed the houses of two unpopular manufacturers, also raided food shops and demanded a reduction in the price of bread. In October, the women of the markets who marched to Versailles to fetch the royal family to Paris chanted as they marched (or, at least, so tradition has it), "let us fetch the baker, the baker's wife and the little baker's boy"; and Barnave, in describing the day's proceedings to his *Dauphinois* constituents, wrote that while "the bourgeoisie" were mainly preoccupied with the political issues, "the people" were equally concerned with the shortage of food. The outbreak of war brought further problems: not only bread, but meat, wine, coffee, and sugar began to disappear from the shops, and in Paris food riots preceded or accompanied each one of the political *journées* of 1792 and 1793. In September 1793, as we saw, it was as the direct result of the popular agitation in the markets, streets, and Sections that the National Convention adopted the law of the General Maximum that placed a ceiling on the prices of most necessities. And, after the Jacobins had fallen and the *maximum* had been abandoned, the insurgents of May 1795 wore on their caps and on their blouses the twin slogans, "The Constitution of 1793" and "Bread."[8]

We are certainly not arguing that short-term economic factors eclipsed all others and that all popular movements of this period, even such politically oriented movements as those of the French Revolution, were really food riots in disguise. We saw in an earlier chapter that even before 1789 the political ideas of the *parlements* in Paris and of the Common Council of the City of London played a part in popular disturbance. Mr. Edward Thompson claims that the London crowd of the 1760's and 1770's "had scarcely begun to develop its own organization or leaders" and, that, having little theory distinct from that of its middle-class "managers," was as yet an unreliable instrument of radical policies.[9] This is true enough, and the proof lies in the fact that the same crowd that had shouted for "Wilkes and Liberty" in 1768 was, a dozen years later, directing its energies into channels that were hardly propitious for the radical cause—destroying Catholic houses and chapels. Nevertheless, the political lessons learned were not entirely forgotten, and they revived and were enriched under the impact of the French Revolution. For, both in England and France, the Revolution of 1789, by posing sharply in their multiform aspects the new concepts of the "rights of man" and the "sovereignty of the people," added a new dimension to popular disturbance and gave a new content to the struggle of parties and classes.

Some historians have doubted the depth of the penetration of these political ideas among the common people. Professor Cobban, for example, has questioned the importance of the circulation of a few political slogans, for (he writes) "one knows how easily a crowd can be taught to chant these and how little serious political content they can have."[10] This would be true enough if it were only a matter of mouthing borrowed slogans, though even these were of some importance in mustering popular support for a radical cause: it is surely significant, for example, that even before the Estates General assembled at Versailles on May 5, 1789, Parisian crowds had taken up the rallying cry of *Vive le Tiers Etat!* and (like Arthur Young's peasants of a few months later)[11] given it a special meaning of their own. And such ideas and slogans were certainly not kept on ice, as it were, for the great political occasions: on the contrary, there is ample evidence that they permeated ever more deeply and widely as the Revolution progressed. Already in August 1789, we find a journeyman gunsmith arrested at Versailles for speaking slightingly of General Lafayette supporting his claim to a fair hearing with an appeal to the "rights of man"; and Malouet, a hostile observer, relates how at this time chairmen at the gates of the National Assembly were eagerly discussing the rights and wrongs of the case for a royal right of "veto." A year later, the democrats of the Cordeliers Club were forming popular clubs and societies through which they began to give systematic instruction to small craftsmen and wage earners in the more advanced revolutionary doctrines; and, in police records, we read of journeymen and domestic servants subscribing to the radical press and even taking out subscriptions to the more exclusive Jacobin Club.[12] Under this impetus, the sans-culottes not only formed political organizations of their own but later, when

they dominated the Paris Sections and Commune, began to advance policies and solutions that proved highly embarrassing to
their Jacobin allies. And not only that; for, having assimilated their
ideas, they gave them a new content that corresponded more with
their own interests than with those of their middle-class teachers.[13]

The sans-culotte movement ended, as we have seen, in the final
outbreak and disaster of May 1795, and when it reappeared in the
1830's it had acquired a new social content and new battle cries
and slogans. As we noted in Chapter 11 it was the advent of the
industrial revolution and the growth of a working-class movement
in the intervening years that were largely responsible for the
transformation. Babeuf had already, during the first of the political
revolutions, given a new socialist twist to the ideas of 1789, but
he had come too late to find an effective audience among the
sans-culottes. It was only after 1830 that his ideas and ideas
similar to his evoked a deep response among the clubs and workers'
organizations that sprang up in Paris and played so large a part in
the events of 1848. What was new now was not only the content
of the ideas themselves but the class of men who voiced them.
Among those arrested after the June "days" of that year was
Antoine Bisgambilia, an obscure and illiterate mechanic (*mécani-
cien*), who, in a note dictated to the police from La Roquette
prison, expressed his political convictions as follows:

> Everybody knows that I don't compromise with my conscience and
> that, as long as I have breath left in my body, I shall use it for the
> triumph of the Democratic and Social Republic.[14]

Admittedly, this declaration appears in an isolated document and
we should hardly expect to find many others of the kind; but the
nature of the June revolt and the large number of those arrested
and convicted suggest that such views were shared by many
others. What is certain is that, by now, wage earners—railwaymen,
building workers, and journeymen of the traditional crafts—were
playing a far larger part in political movements than they had in
the first revolution, and were even (like the shopkeepers and
craftsmen of 1793) voicing political demands of their own.

A similar evolution had taken place in England; and in some
respects it had proceeded more rapidly than in France. As England
went through no revolution of her own, the new revolutionary

ideas of the rights of man and popular sovereignty were largely borrowed from across the Channel. Through the works of Thomas Paine and others, these began, from early in 1792, to circulate among democrats, dissenters, and the master craftsmen, and journeymen of the big cities and industrial towns. This was also the year that Thomas Hardy's London Corresponding Society began to meet at The Bell in Exeter Street, with its membership of small urban tradesmen and artisans: similar in its social composition to those who met in the clubs and committees of revolutionary Paris. Yet, in some of the English societies like that of Sheffield, there appears to have been a larger percentage of "the inferior sort of Manufacturers and Workmen" than in similar bodies in France.[15] To that extent, it may perhaps be claimed that in England the new revolutionary ideas met with a proportionately greater response among wage earners than in France herself. The English societies were, however, short lived, succumbed to early repression, and had little opportunity of making recruits among the newly emerging factory population.

Jacobin ideas survived, however, gradually found a wider audience and, "driven into weaving villages, the shops of the Nottingham framework knitters and the Yorkshire croppers, the Lancashire cotton-mills, were propagated in every phase of rising prices and of hardship." [16] They emerged on the surface again in the freer political atmosphere of the Westminster election of 1807, when the radicals Burdett and Cochrane were borne to victory by the popular vote; and they inspired the Lancashire weavers who were cut down by the Manchester yeomanry at the great parliamentary reform meeting in St. Peter's Fields in August 1819. After this, the Jacobin-radical tradition, enriched by memories of "Peterloo," took on a new form with the advent of the socialist ideas propounded by Robert Owen and others. It was such a mixture of ideas that moulded the political thought of men like George Loveless, the trade unionist and Tolpuddle Martyr of 1834, who, some years before Marx, wrote that "nothing will be done to relieve the distress of the working classes, unless they take it into their own hands." [17] And, on a far wider canvas, they were carried forward into the nationwide agitation for the People's Charter, which, as we have seen, both drew its inspiration from the past and looked forward to the future.

It will perhaps not escape the reader that so far we have largely dealt with the "forward-looking" aspects of the crowd's motives for riot and rebellion. If, we may appear to have been arguing, men and women were drawn into such activities, it was either because they were hungry, because they wanted to end a real or imaginary oppression, or to assure themselves of a richer and happier future; or for a mixture of similar reasons. Yet this is only a part of the story. If we limit our attention to factors such as these, how do we account for popular manifestations like the Gordon Riots, millenarial movements, Luddism, or "Church and King," or even for the paradox of the Parisian revolutionary sans-culottes who, as a vanguard of radical democracy, looked forward to the future and, for the solution of their economic ills, looked back to the idyllic conditions of an imaginary past?[18] To make such phenomena intelligible, we have also to consider some of the underlying motives and traditional myths and beliefs—what crowd psychologists and social scientists have termed "fundamental" or "generalized" beliefs°—that played a not inconsiderable part in such disturbances.

To begin with, there is the traditional "leveling" instinct, common to all such occasions, which prompts the poor to seek a degree of elementary social justice at the expense of the rich, *les grands,* and those in authority regardless of whether they are government officials, feudal lords, capitalists, or middle-class revolutionary leaders. It is the common ground on which, beyond the slogans of contending parties, the militant sans-culotte meets the "Church and King" rioter or the peasant in search of his millenium. Even in periods of comparative social peace, we find it in the traditional methods of "self-help" of the rural population, common to both France and England. As hardship presses or as opportunity offers, small farmers and freeholders, peasants and cottagers help themselves to firewood and game at the landlord's or wealthy farmer's expense and, where resistance is offered, assault gamekeepers or

---

° Thus Le Bon distinguishes between "accidental and passing ideas created by the influences of the moment" and the "fundamental ideas to which the environment, the laws of heredity, and public opinion give a very great stability" (*The Crowd* (London, 1909), p. 68). For "generalized beliefs," see N. Smelser, *Theory of Collective Behavior* (London, 1962), pp. 79-130, 202-203.

burn the farmer's ricks. Such crimes are punished severely at law —in England, progressively so after 1815—but they are not condemned, like murder and common theft, by the rural population. There was a similar elementary form of social protest in the gay abandon with which London crowds, when rioting for Wilkes, smashed the windows of lords and ladies of fashion and painted Wilkes's symbol, the "45", on the soles of the Austrian ambassador's boots. We find it in the London riots against the Corn Law of 1815, when the *Morning Post* reported that

> The mob is particularly enraged against the great parishes of St. Mary-le-Bow, St. George Hanover Square, and St. James, which comprehend the town houses of nearly all the great families of the United Kingdom.[19]

But, up to this time, the "leveling" instinct of the crowd might as readily be harnessed to an anti-radical as to a radical cause. In the Gordon Riots, the crowd's choice of targets showed that they were more concerned to destroy the properties of wealthy Catholics than of Catholics in general; and we find a rioter in Bermondsey telling his victim, who had claimed to be a Protestant: "Protestant or not, no gentleman need be possessed of more than £1,000 a year; that is sufficient for a gentleman to live upon." [20] We have noted a similar motive underlying "Church and King" disturbances: if Jacobins were attacked in the streets of Naples in 1799, it was as much because they rode in carriages as because they were allies of the "atheistical" French; and in Birmingham, Priestley and his associates were picked on not only because they were dissenters or radical reformers, but also because they were manufacturers, magistrates, and men of wealth and status.* Similarly, the peasants of the Vendée reacted against revolutionary Paris because, for quite particular reasons, their hatred of the urban bourgeois was greater than their hatred of the local landlord; and Tocqueville, though his sense of history was not as acute as Marx's, showed more than a grain of good sense when he presented the June insurrection as a conflict between the "haves" and the "have-nots," or "a sort of Servile War."[21]

---

* See pp. 138-9, 145-6 above.

Such an element was, of course, by no means peculiar to the pre-industrial crowd. Of more particular relevance was its antipathy to capitalist innovation. As commercialism and the quest of "improvement" entered the village, common lands were divided and fenced off, turnpikes were erected, and grain was stored in barns and withheld from immediate circulation, while prices were allowed to follow the whims of supply and demand and find their "natural" level. Similarly, as industry developed, labor-saving machinery was introduced into mines and mills, and wages, like prices, found a "natural" level by direct bargaining between the masters and their laborers. Thus, gradually, the old protective legislation against enclosure, engrossing, and forestalling, and the export of grain, and the old laws empowering magistrates to fix prices and wages, were rescinded; and the old notions of the "just" price and "just" wage, imposed by authority or sanctioned by custom, gave way to the new prevailing notions of "natural" wages and prices in a freely competitive market. The transformation was spread over some 150 years and followed a broadly similar course in France and England. In England it started earlier, but in France it received a sharp forward thrust in the 1760's and 1770's and in the legislation of the Revolution. In both countries, the process was largely completed by 1800; yet in both there remained a residue from ancient practices: in France, in the survival of many of the collective traditions of the village; in England, in the Speenhamland System, whereby agricultural wages continued to be subsidized from the parish poor rate until the 1830's.[22]

We have already seen how the small consumers and producers of town and countryside reacted to these innovations. Clinging stubbornly to the old paternalist and protectionist legislation as it was gradually abandoned by their rulers, they appealed to Parliament, to magistrates, and to the King himself to restore or enforce the old regulations: to forbid enclosure, to pull down toll gates, to empower justices to fix prices and wages and to regulate the supply and distribution of bread and flour. During the French Revolution, they went even further and insisted that a general *maximum* be placed on the prices of every article of consumption, thus looking forward to a more highly centralized economy than any of the old laws and statutes had envisaged. Similarly, they denounced farmers and dealers as engrossers or *accapareurs;* and in France, from Louis XV's time, there grew the persistent popular belief that a *pacte de famine* had been deliberately devised to starve the people. In England, we find a similar trend expressed in a handbill distributed at Retford in 1795:

> Those Cruall Villions the Millers Bakers etc. Flower Sellers rases Flowe under a Comebination to what price they please on purpose to make an Artificall famine in a Land of plenty.[23]

On occasion, they found allies among an older, or more conservative, generation or those in opposition to government: among magistrates and farmers, or, as in France, in the *parlements* of the Old Régime. Sometimes these allies revived or applied the old methods (we have seen examples from the riots of 1766 and 1775). If not, the people took the law into their own hands: we noted the outcome in the enclosure riots and food riots of the eighteenth century, the machine breaking of the Luddites and the laborers of 1830, the antics of "Rebecca's daughters" in the early 1840's; and even (though here the object was neither food nor wages) in the depredation of the "No Popery" rioters in London. And such acts, it was believed, far from meriting censure or savage reprisals, were morally justified and performed as a kind of solemn public duty. For if the King, misled by his ministers, "broke his Coronation oath" by allowing relief to Roman Catholics, or magistrates failed to use their powers to apply the old statutes, who but the people could set the matter right? Ned Ludd, from his office in Sherwood Forest, actually claimed the right to break the hosiers' frames under the terms of the charter of the Framework Knitters' Company.[24] The people might also expect to be paid for carrying out such duties: we saw how the "Swing" rioters charged a fee for smashing threshing machines; the Gordon rioters collected money "for the poor Mob"; and the September "massacrers" in Paris exacted their reward in terms of food and drink.

One consequence of all this was to drive a deeper wedge between the riotous crowd that clung to these old customs and the forward-looking, reforming, radical or revolutionary middle class or liberal aristocracy. Wilkes had the good fortune not to have to face this problem, as London and Middlesex were comparatively free from food and enclosure riots; but Voltaire, as we saw, could not fail to conclude that the grain rioters of 1775, who were so patently helping to undermine Turgot's reforms, were in the pay of his political opponents. Gibbon Wakefield, in 1830, managed to evade the issue by assuming that the machine-breaking and rick-burning laborers were only hostile to his enemies, the landlords and Church of England clergy, while sparing the properties of his friends, the farmers. The French middle-class revolutionaries of 1792-4 could have no such illusions: the hostility of the small peasants and sans-culottes to the freedom of trade in grain, bread, meat, and wine helped to drive the Girondins, the most determined advocates of laissez-faire, from power and a year later contributed to the overthrow of their Jacobin successors.[25]

Closely allied to the concern for "justice" was the belief in the King as the protector or "father" of his people. England being a parliamentary monarchy, the tradition there was wearing thin and appeals for protection in such instances as we have listed above were more likely to be addressed to Parliament or to the justices than to the King in person. In countries of absolute monarchy, however, the King was both the symbol and the fount of all justice and legislation, and the belief in his paternal benevolence persisted even through periods of revolution and peasant revolt, when the King's ministers may already have been long discredited and the royal power itself was on the wane. Folk myths abound about the kindly concern for their people of Emperors, Sultans, Tsars, and French Kings from St. Louis to Henri IV and Louis XVI. "Don't fire on us," cry the rebellious Volga peasantry to the general sent to shoot them down, "you are shooting on Alexander Nikoleyevitch, you are shedding the blood of the Tsar."[26] In France, the Bordeaux peasants of 1674 rioted against the salt tax in the name of the King; the grain rioters of 1775 were convinced that they were right to refuse to pay the high prices demanded by farmers, millers, and bakers because, it was firmly believed, the King had ordered that a "just" price be paid; and the peasants of 1789 produced "orders" purporting to come from Louis XVI himself to give legal sanction to their attacks on the landlords' châteaux. Of course, such a paradoxical state of affairs could not last forever: the Revolution was bound, sooner or later, either to reinforce these old notions in terms of "Church and King" (as in the Vendée) or to uproot them altogether. The war, in particular, exposed the King, and not only his ministers, to public condemnation and eventually to the merited charge of treason. It is all the more remarkable, however, that his popularity among the common people should have survived so many crises; and even as late as June 1792 (three years after the Revolution began), the crowd that invaded the Tuileries and forced Louis to toast "the Nation" combined with its vulgar familiarity a residue of reverence. But, after the fall of the monarchy in August, it was not an individual leader, but the National Assembly or the "sacred Mountain" (the Jacobins), that replaced the King as a popular father-figure. So, in the food riots of November 1792 we find the price-fixing peasants and craftsmen of the Beauce invoking the authority not, as the peasants of 1789, of the King but of the newly elected National Convention.[27]

In England, another constantly recurring theme in popular ideology is that of the Englishman's "birthright" or "liberties." The belief that Englishmen were "freeborn" and not "slaves" and did not starve or wear "wooden shoes"—like foreigners in general and Papist foreigners in particular—was deeply ingrained and had been so since the religious and social conflicts of the sixteenth and seventeenth centuries. In the campaign conducted against Walpole's Gin Act of 1736, a circular letter addressed to London distillers declared: "If we are Englishmen let us show that we have English spirits and not tamely submit to the yoak just ready to be fastened about our necks." It is a theme that runs, in one form or another, through all contemporary London riots and is also connected with the prevailing attitude towards crime, of which we have already spoken.[28] It is related, too, to the popular xenophobia or chauvinism with which London crowds, in the eighteenth century, rallied to the cause of bellicose national leaders like the elder Pitt and his City allies and rejected the more pacific overtures of men like Walpole, Bute, and the Dukes of Newcastle and Bedford. Before and during the French wars at the end of the century, it no doubt helped to promote the cause of "Church and King," as reformers like Priestley in Birmingham and Thomas Walker in Manchester were tainted as being friends of the French. Only the Americans, when at war with England, escaped this type of xenophobia. There is no evidence of anti-Americanism among all the other popular prejudices voiced at the time of the Gordon Riots. The reason is perhaps not hard to find; did not the Americans share with the English a common "birthright" and a common concern for "liberty" and the "Protestant cause"?

It was not only a matter of defending existing English "liberties" from foreign attack: there was the other, even greater, problem of restoring them to their "pristine purity" at home. Here, once more, there was a constant appeal to precedent: to the glories of a distant or imaginary past rather than to the prospects opened up by the present. Magna Carta, the Popish Plot, the Bill of Rights, and the "Glorious Constitution" of 1689 were all reminders that these "liberties" had constantly to be fought for against tyranny from within; but one of the most remarkably persistent beliefs of all was that perfect "liberties" had existed under the Saxon Kings and that these had been filched, together with their lands, from "freeborn" Englishmen by the invading Norman knights under William the Bastard in 1066. This myth of the "Norman Yoke" persisted until Chartist times and was handed down by generations of Levellers, Whigs reared on "revolution principles," London eighteenth-century radicals and democrats nurtured on the more recent doctrines of "popular sovereignty" and the "rights of man." In 1780, that same committee of Westminster reformers whose claims anticipated by half a century the Six Points of the People's Charter demanded the "restitution" of equal representation, annual Parliaments, and universal suffrage, which (it was said) "were substantially enjoyed in the times of the immortal Alfred." [29] A handbill circulated in London in 1793, protesting against the use of "crimping" houses and other oppressive government measures, asks the questions: "Would such atrocious acts have been suffered in the days of Alfred?" . . . Did Sydney and Russel bleed for this?" [30] Members of English radical societies in the 1790's wore Saxon dress and organized themselves in divisions based on Saxon *tythings;* and John Frost, the later Chartist leader, was, in 1822, attributing present inequalities in wealth to "the plunder of William the Bastard." [31] Nor were such backward-looking theories peculiar to the British. While Englishmen yearned for Saxon "liberties" and Welshmen called on the Men of Harlech to drive out the "sons of Hengist," Frenchmen of the Revolution

sought the "pristine purity" of republican manners and institutions in the days of Ancient Rome.°

Millenarial and religious ideas also clearly played a part in
popular disturbance. The millenium might assume a secular or
a religious form, though (unlike the Wesleyan ideal) it was generally to be realized on earth rather than in heaven. Millenarial
fantasies no doubt underlie many of the actions of the poor in the
course of the French Revolution; but in none are they so clearly
evident as in the sudden upsurge of hope aroused among them by
the news that the Estates General should meet in the summer of
1789. The news fostered what French historians since Taine have
called *la grande espérance:* the hope that, at last, past promises
would be fulfilled and the burdens, particularly the hated *taille*,
lifted off the peasants' backs, and that a new golden era would
begin. The state of exaltation thus engendered equally produced
its corollary, the conviction, once these hopes appeared to be endangered, that their realization was being frustrated by a *complot
aristocratique*. This dual phenomenon, it has been argued, does a
great deal to explain the almost mystical fervor with which the
menu peuple pursued their "aristocratic" enemies during the
Revolution.[32] Or, as in England, millenarial fantasies might be
clothed in the poetic imagery of Blake's "Jerusalem" or the apoc-
alyptic extravagances of a Richard Brothers, whose *Revealed
Knowledge of the Prophesies and Times* was published in London
in early 1794. This was a time when Jacobin ideas were still making
headway among the "lower orders"; and it has been suggested
that men like Brothers, who interlaced their talk of "the whore of
Babylon" and the "Antichrist" with denunciations of the high and
mighty, may have nourished similar political aspirations to those
nourished by Tom Paine's *The Rights of Man*.[33] But millenarial
ideas, while they might, under certain circumstances, stimulate
rather than weaken an already existing political movement, might
equally act as an antidote to popular militancy or as a consola-
tion for a political defeat. This may have been the case in France
after Waterloo and, in England in 1838, in the strange affair of
"the battle in Bossenden Wood."[34]

° French aristocrats before the Revolution had similarly invoked the "liberties" of the "free" Frankish nobles; but this probably played little part in
popular mythology.

In the latter case, a number of Kentish laborers believed implicitly that their leader, the spurious Sir William Courtenay, was the Messiah. But this is only one guise in which the religious motive may appear in riots. At other times, though overtly proclaimed, it might not be so profound as it was made to appear; or conversely it might lie submerged beneath the surface of events. Of the first kind "No Popery" riots, "High Church" attacks on Methodist or Presbyterian meeting halls and chapels, and urban "Church and King" explosions are obvious examples. Quite apart from their social undercurrents, such movements were never quite what they seemed. We have seen that the ill-assorted slogans "destruction to Presbyterians" and "No Popery" appeared side by side in the Birmingham riots; and one of those sentenced to death for his part in the Gordon Riots said, when questioned: "Damn my eyes, I have no religion; but I have to keep it up for the good of the cause." [35] It is not so much that in such movements the religious element is nonexistent or a mere cloak for other issues (though this was firmly believed by some contemporaries) as that in them religious, social, and political motives are bewilderingly interwoven. Perhaps, in view of their proclaimed purpose to maintain an established Church as part of an established order, we should treat them less as religious movements than as anti-radical political demonstrations.

The case is somewhat different where a dissenting religious tradition serves as an undercurrent rather than as a proclaimed object of disturbance. In London and England's West Country, in particular, religious dissent and popular radicalism had had a long association; and Methodism, even when it professed to stave off riot and lay up its treasures solely in heaven, brought with it a new fervor and moral purpose that, sooner or later, were bound to leave their mark on popular social movements. Such was certainly the case in England and Wales in the disturbances of 1830 and the 1840's: in the "Swing" and Rebecca riots and in the Welsh Chartist movement Protestant nonconformity, both Wesleyan and other, played a part. [36]

Nor must we assume that such secular, rationalist ideas as the "rights of man" and other products of the Enlightenment would, when they gripped the common people, necessarily serve as an antidote to religion. This was no doubt the intention of many rationalist thinkers and middle-class and aristocratic reformers or revolutionaries in England and France in the eighteenth century; and there were moments during the French Revolution when they appeared to have been successful. Certainly, the monopoly and authority of the established Catholic Church were successively undermined and broken—and these were never fully recovered; and Parisian crowds demonstrated to shouts of *A bas la calotte!* ("Down with the priests!") and played a part, at the height of the "de-christianization" movement in the autumn of 1793, in closing down every church in the city. Yet the popular anti-religious (as distinct from the anti-clerical) movement was comparatively short lived; as late as June 1793, Parisians in the revolutionary Faubourg St. Antoine demonstrated for the right to preserve the traditional Corpus Christi procession; and Robespierre himself sought to win further popular support for the Revolutionary Government by launching a brand-new religious cult, the Cult of the Supreme Being. This was only the most highly publicized of numerous attempts to affect a fusion between religion and the current political ideas. In many districts, the people took the initiative themselves and the Revolution saw a remarkable upsurge of new religious cults; and solemn ceremonies, accompanied by all the *mystique* of the old religious practices, were dedicated to new local "saints" or to the great popular martyrs of the Revolution, Marat, Chalier, and Lepeletier.[37] Yet once the Revolution was over, such cults appear to have left few traditions; and neither they nor the re-established Catholic Church, nor the religious minority groups, appear to have played any significant part in the revolutions of 1830 and 1848.

The analysis might be carried even further; but to spare the bewildered reader's feelings I propose to stop it here. What we have seen is a rich variety of motives and beliefs, through which economic issues and appeals to customary rights exist side by side with new conceptions of man's place in society and the search for the millenium. Such a medley of seemingly ill-assorted beliefs and aspirations is by no means a feature peculiar to the pre-industrial crowd: it appears as evidently, though with different emphases and variations, in the disturbances of today as it does in those of ancient or medieval times. But through the confusion a certain common pattern peculiar to the age emerges. We shall, however, hardly be aware of it unless we place the riots and rebellions in their historical context and compare those of the early and middle years of the eighteenth century with those of the French Revolution and those that followed later. Even when we do so, we shall not see a steady, gradual disappearance of appeals to custom and millenarial fantasies: these persist, though at times with abated vigor, throughout the period that we are concerned with. But there are significant turning points at which new conceptions enter and, while not eclipsing the old ideas entirely, transform them or reduce their relative importance. Such turning points are the revolution of 1789 in France and the growth of independent working-class movements in the 1830's.

Professor Reinhard Bendix has stressed the contrast between types of popular protest arising in the "pre-democratic" and those arising in the "democratic" period of West European history.[38] The point is an important one, for once the new and essentially forward-looking ideas of the "rights of man" and "popular sovereignty" had gripped the popular imagination, riots and disturbances tended to acquire a new dimension and to assume a stable social-ideological content that they had lacked before. But, equally, emerging industrial society in France and England created an industrial working class, working-class movements, and working-class political ideas. Thus further new ideas and further social forces, unknown in 1789, began to come to the fore: we have seen examples in the French revolution of 1848 and in the Chartist movement in England. These stepping stones are no less significant because many of the old and backward-looking ideas persisted and old forms continued to rub shoulders with the new. Moreover, traditional beliefs might, instead of becoming abandoned, be transformed and adapted to meet new needs: in this sense, there is no radical departure from the old yearning for "protection" in the socialist ideal of a more fully collectivist society.[39]

Thus, gradually, the pattern of popular protest, and the ideas that underlay it, would suffer a sea-change. In 1848, this process was by no means completed; but the new "industrial" crowd, with its richer stock of forward-looking concepts, was already clearly visible on the horizon.

REFERENCES

1. M. Mortimer-Ternaux, *Histoire de la Terreur* (8 vols. Paris, 1862-81), VIII, 455; H. Taine, *Les origines de la France contemporaine. La Révolution* (3 vols. Paris, 1878), I, 129.
2. *The Crowd in the French Revolution* (Oxford, 1959), pp. 191-3.
3. Archives de l'Oise, B 1584 (my translation).
4. For a fuller discussion of the evidence, see my *The Crowd in the French Revolution*, pp. 191-6.
5. See my *Wilkes and Liberty* (Oxford, 1962), p. 59.
6. E. J. Hobsbawm, "Economic Fluctuations and Some Social Movements since 1800," *Economic History Review*, 2nd series, V, i (1952), 8.
7. W. W. Rostow, *British Economy of the Nineteenth Century*, (Oxford, 1948), p. 124.
8. *The Crowd in the French Revolution*, pp. 201-207.
9. E. P. Thompson, *The Making of the English Working Class* (London, 1963), pp. 70-71.
10. A. Cobban, *The Social Interpretation of the French Revolution* (London, 1964), p. 127.
11. A. Young, *Travels in France and Italy* (Everyman Library, London, 1915), pp. 172-3.
12. *The Crowd in the French Revolution*, pp. 196-9.
13. A. Soboul, *Les sans-culottes parisiens en l'an II* (Paris, 1958), pp. 505-648.
14. Arch. de la Préfecture de Police, Aa 429, fo. 441.
15. Thompson, *op. cit.*, pp. 149-57.
16. *Ibid.*, p. 185.
17. G. Loveless, *The Victims of Whiggery: A Statement of the Persecutions Experienced by the Dorchester Labourers* (London, 1837), p. 23.
18. See G. Rudé, J. Zacker, Sophie A. Lotte, and A. Soboul, "I Sanculotti: una discussione tra storici marxisti," *Critica Storica*, I, iv (1962), 369-98.
19. Quoted by D. G. Barnes, *A History of the English Corn Laws from 1660 to 1846* (New York, 1961), p. 136.
20. *Old Bailey Proceedings* (Surrey Special Commission) (London, 1780), p. 11.
21. *The Recollections of Alexis de Tocqueville*, ed. J. P. Mayer (Meridian Books, New York, 1959), p. 150.
22. See pp. 44, 67 above; and Thompson, *op. cit.*, pp. 67-8.
23. Quoted by Thompson, *op. cit.*, p. 67.
24. F. O. Darvall, *Popular Disturbances and Public Order in Regency England* (London, 1934), p. 170.
25. A. Soboul, *op. cit.*, pp. 1025-1031.
26. Quoted by E. J. Hobsbawm, *Primitive Rebels* (Manchester, 1959), p. 121.

27. M. Vovelle, "Les taxations populaires de février-mars et novembre-décembre 1792 dans la Beauce et sur ses confins," *Mémoires et documents,* no. XIII (Paris, 1958), p. 137.

28. G. Rudé, "The London 'Mob' of the Eighteenth Century," *The Historical Journal.* II, i (1959), 13-14; Thompson, *op. cit.,* 59-61.

29. Cited by S. Maccoby, *The English Radical Tradition 1763-1914* (London, 1952), p. 36.

30. Old Bailey *Proceedings* (1794), p. 1327.

31. C. Hill, "The Norman Yoke," in *Democracy and the Labour Movement,* ed. J. Saville (London, 1954), pp. 11-66; Thompson, *op. cit.,* pp. 84-8, 150; D. Williams, *John Frost: A Study in Chartism* (Cardiff, 1939), p. 50.

32. G. Lefebvre, *Quatre-Vingt-Neuf* (Paris, 1939), pp. 112-14.

33. Thompson, *op. cit.,* pp. 116-19.

34. P. G. Rogers, *Battle in Bossenden Wood* (London, 1961). See p. 149 above.

35. Old Bailey *Proceedings* (1780), pp. 446-52.

36. See pp. 155, 156 above; and Thompson, *op. cit.,* pp. 350-400.

37. A. Soboul, "Sentiment religieux et cultes populaires pendant la Révolution: saintes patriotes et martyrs de la liberté," *Archives de sociologie des religions,* July-Dec. 1956, pp. 73-86.

38. R. Bendix, "The Lower Classes and the 'Democratic Revolution'," *Industrial Relations,* I, i (Oct. 1961), 91-116.

39. For an attempt to go beyond the piecemeal study of motivation in individual movements and to present the full range of ideas and beliefs underlying social and political action of the day, see my *Ideology and Popular Protest* (London, 1980).

FIFTEEN

The Pattern of Disturbance
and the Behavior of Crowds

So far, we have considered the crowd's components rather than the crowd itself. We have discussed the social classes, groups, and individuals from which the pre-industrial crowd was drawn, the occupations to which they belonged, and the ideas and motives that underlay their actions; but little has been said as yet of the crowd as a collective entity, of the reactions and behavior of its components as a group, or of what Le Bon, and Georges Lefebvre after him, have termed the "mental unity" or "collective mentality" of crowds.[1] Admittedly some writers, including Le Bon himself, stress these factors at the expense of all others and so tend to reduce the crowd to a pure abstraction or inchoate mass, torn as it were from its social and historical moorings. Yet to neglect them altogether is to be hardly more realistic, as it is only in its most highly organized or regimented form, as on strictly ceremonial occasions, that the crowd may be said to be no more than the sum total of its parts.[2]

This being so, we still have to ask certain questions regarding the crowd's actions and behavior. What was the behavioral pattern of the pre-industrial crowd and why did it tend to behave in certain ways rather than in others? How did individuals or groups grow into crowds, and how did one type of disturbance become transformed into another? How did the crowd's "collective mentality"—its moods of violence, audacity, or heroism—develop? To what extent were its actions organized or spontaneous? What were the crowd's relations with its leaders, and how were the slogans or marching orders transmitted? And what justice is there in the view that these crowds, like any others, were fickle, irrational, and prone to destructive violence? These are some of the problems that will be discussed, or merely briefly touched on, in the present chapter.

In earlier chapters we have already noted the general pattern of the crowd's behavior. While the crowd behaved differently in different situations, the common elements were direct action and the imposition of some form of elementary "natural" justice. Strikers tended to destroy machinery or "pull down" their employers' houses; food rioters to invade markets and bakers' shops and enforce a popular price control or *taxation populaire*; rural rioters to destroy fences and turnpikes or threshing machines and workhouses, or to set fire to the farmer's or landlord's stacks; and city rioters to "pull down" dissenters' meeting houses and chapels, to destroy their victims' houses and property, and to burn their political enemies in effigy. On the great revolutionary occasions, as on those of 1789–95, 1830, and 1848 in France, such forms of action were supplemented by others on a more heroic scale, such as armed assaults on the Bastille, Tuileries, or Hôtel de Ville, or the manning of barricades; but the general pattern remained substantially the same. There were, however, important deviations from this norm, and forms of action associated with later times were already emerging in the riots and disturbances of the pre-industrial age. In Manchester, for example, in 1810, there was a strike of cotton spinners that already closely resembled strikes of more recent times;* and in France the modern type of industrial dispute appears to have been more frequent than in England. The petition had already appeared as a focus for popular action: we have seen examples from London workers' disputes of the 1760's; and in Paris, in July 1791, such a petition conceived on perfectly "modern" lines was the occasion of the great meeting and massacre on the Champ de Mars.

Besides these, there were other more traditional forms of action that were also intended to persuade by peaceful demonstration rather than by violence. Such were the great popular parades and colorful ceremonies that were almost as typical of the times as the resort to "natural" justice. During the Wilkite agitation in

* See p. 67 above.

London, Wilkes's followers of both the "middling" and "lower" sort frequently paraded with flags flying and drums beating, shouting slogans and displaying their hero's colors; and on one occasion among many "a great body of [Middlesex] freeholders, preceded by a band of music, with colours flying, marched along Pall Mall, and stopped fronting the Palace, where they gave 3 loud huzzas, and the music began to play"; a week later, Wilkes's election victory over his opponent Colonel Luttrell was greeted in the small town of Somerton in Somerset by the ringing of bells, illuminations, and a solemn procession, headed by "2 ushers of the Grammar School representing Liberty" and "45 gentlemen scholars with blue favours." [3] Similar manifestations, attended by pageantry and discipline, were a common feature of Paris both before and after the outbreak of the Revolution in 1789, and it was a similar display of fluttering flags and pennants that thirty years later was so savagely broken up by yeomanry on St. Peter's Fields in Manchester. For, despite their peaceful pretensions, these colorful and massive displays alarmed the authorities and propertied classes almost as much as the acts of violence themselves. Hardy, the Parisian bookseller, who recorded the almost daily processions of tradesmen and working men and women that wound up the Rue St. Jacques to the newly built Church of Ste. Geneviève in August and September 1789, noted after one such procession that "many people found that there was something terrifying about its organization, its composition and its numbers"; and it may well be that the yeomanry of "Peterloo" was provoked to strike as much by the discipline of the Manchester weavers as by the militant slogans inscribed upon their banners.[4]

These fears were not entirely without substance, as ceremonial demonstrations might, either by an act of provocation or an unexpected turn of events, be transformed into more violent forms of action. This was all the more liable to happen at a time when the "lower orders" or sans-culottes were virtually denied all means of peaceful agitation to secure a redress of grievance. Not only had they no political rights, but "combinations" and assemblies—what the French called *attroupements*—were forbidden by law, and often rigorously suppressed. In consequence, the "hostile outburst" was no more liable to incur penalties than the more peaceful type of demonstration; besides, experience taught that a sudden attack was more likely to secure results than prolonged agitation by peaceful means: by negotiation, petition, or ceremonial displays that could in any case have little relevance outside large cities like Paris or London, Lyons or Manchester. Moreover, it was a time when direct conflicts between the governing or possessing classes and the "lower orders" was more liable to occur in country districts: it was here that fences and enclosures were erected, mills and mines were being equipped with new machinery, and sudden rises in the price of wheat were most in evidence. Hence the circumstances of the time not only were a constant provocation to popular disorder, but also tended to dictate the nature of the outburst. For what could be a more appropriate form of popular protest in rural areas, mining villages, or small market towns, or even in the outer suburbs of newly emerging factory towns, than to resort to the direct-action methods of "natural" justice practiced by Ned Ludd in Derbyshire and Cheshire, by Rebecca in West Wales, by the "Swing" rioters in the south of England, or the French and English grain rioters of 1766 and 1775?

Yet it was not only the physical factors that determined the nature of such outbreaks, for why else should they have persisted in cities like Paris and London throughout the eighteenth century, or in Bristol and Nottingham as late as 1831? A further explanation must be sought in the survival of traditional ideas and values. The circulation of radical-political ideas would, in the course of the nineteenth century, involve the small tradesmen, craftsmen, and factory workers in the struggle for political rights and for the great causes of the rights and brotherhood of man. This was already the case in the middle and later years of the French Revolution, when popular loyalty to individuals tended to give way to loyalty to causes or revolutionary institutions, and this process reached a far higher stage of development, and became more solidly grounded, in the revolutions and Chartist agitation of the 1840's. Generally speaking, however, this was still a period when popular attachment and antipathy tended to focus not so much on causes and institutions as on individual heroes and villains. As the crowd had its heroes, like Wilkes, Lord George Gordon, Marat, or the semi-mythical Rebecca, so it had its clearly identifiable villains in the shape of the individual employer, merchant, forestaller, baker, landlord, or official; and such men became the natural targets of its vengeance when wages were cut, prices were high, the harvest failed, or traditional rights were threatened. It was only by gradual stages that this personal target was replaced or eclipsed by principles or causes and, correspondingly, that the old methods of "natural" justice began to disappear.

Yet memory and oral tradition may also have played a part in prolonging the survival of such forms of action even beyond the times when they may have been most useful and appropriate. By 1831 at Bristol and by 1842 at Stoke-on-Trent, for example, the "pulling down" of houses was something of an anachronism: it had certainly not been seen in large cities like Paris and London for many years. The *mystique* of the barricades—a useful weapon of popular defense in the still largely medieval Paris of 1830 and 1848— persisted, after Paris had been rebuilt under Napoleon III, in the street fighting of 1871; and the revolution of 1848 in France was haunted, if not bedeviled, by memories of 1789 and 1793. The French peasants who in 1775 and 1789 invoked the authority of the King himself for fixing prices and burning châteaux were carrying on the tradition of their forebears at Bordeaux of a hundred years before, who had rioted to the slogan of *Vive le Roi et sans gabelle!*; and the women's march to Versailles was, in a sense, a repetition of similar demonstrations by Parisians in 1709, 1775, and 1786, though its consequences were vastly more impressive.

In England, arson, particularly the burning of the farmers' stacks of hay or corn, was a well-established weapon in agrarian disputes: "a short argument, fire," wrote Carlyle, who, like Gibbon Wakefield, could commend it for its efficacy, at least. It was widely recognized as a peculiarly British device; and as late as 1854 (when it had by no means lost its hold on the English countryside*) an Italian, a leading figure at Australia's Eureka Stockade, writes of "the wild well known English Cry 'Fire' 'Fire' " and adds that "British folk in general, the dreadful Calamity of Fire, they take it as a lark and enjoy it as a mighty fun." [5] We have seen, too, that machine breaking, the "pulling down" of houses and the

---

* Of 2,255 English male convicts sent to Australia in 1846-7, 89 were transported for arson and 32 out of 2,422 in 1852, which (except in the case of Eastern Australia) was the last year of transportation (Tas. State Arch., MSS. 2/282-2/321).

enforcement of popular price controls in food riots were all devices that had a history extending over 150 years or more. In some rural riots, as in the French of 1789, the path of disturbance actually followed well-trodden and traditional routes. Thus memory and oral tradition, as well as the material conditions or social relations of the present, served to perpetuate the forms of popular disturbance.

Yet, though riots tended to follow traditional patterns, even the most short lived of them rarely appeared entirely ready made. Even a local strike or food riot would gain in momentum from smaller beginnings and have clearly defined points of departure, climax, and conclusion. The exceptions were the more highly organized military operations, like the assault of the Tuileries Palace in August 1792, or the disciplined parades of workers summoned by the Paris clubs in 1848; but these were not typical of crowd behavior, as here participants responded almost from start to finish to the commands of recognized leaders. In its more characteristic form, the riot or rebellion developed from comparatively small beginnings in a market, a public house, a baker's, a butcher's, or a wine shop, or was "triggered" by a chance word or act of provocation, and by such and other means might assume a dimension and momentum that no one, not even the most experienced of leaders, could have planned or expected. Such were the occasions, frequent in France and England both before and after the outbreak of the French Revolution, when gatherings of small consumers in food shops and markets were transformed into massive demonstrations, attacks on property, and even full-scale insurrections or rebellions. In France, at the end of April 1775, the refusal of the porters of the small market town of Beaumont to pay the high prices demanded by the dealers "triggered" a movement that, within a fortnight of its inception, had engulfed the capital and half-a-dozen adjoining provinces. In London, in June 1780, the refusal of Parliament to consider the anti-Catholic petition of the Protestant Association transformed the crowds assembled at Westminster into bands of angry rioters that held London's streets for a week on end. In 1830, we saw how the introduction of threshing machines in a Kentish village "triggered" a widespread movement of machine breaking and incendiarism that extended to more than a dozen counties; and both the Luddite and Rebecca riots developed from similar small beginnings.°

To illustrate the point further we may, once more, take the French Revolution as a convenient model—particularly in its opening stages, before the National Guard, the popular clubs, and Sectional assemblies had created a framework within which the challenge to authority might be more systematically organized. Classic examples of the type of transformation we are describing are provided by the great Parisian insurrections of July and October 1789. In the first, a more or less peaceably disposed Sunday crowd of strollers in the Palais Royal was galvanized into revolutionary vigor by the news of Necker's dismissal from office and the call to arms issued by the orators in the service or entourage of the Duc d'Orléans. From this followed a sequence of events that could not possibly have been planned or foreseen in detail by even the most astute, farsighted, and determined of the Court's opponents: the parades along the boulevards with busts of Necker and Orléans; the assaults on the customs posts and the monastery of St. Lazare; the search for arms in gunsmiths' shops, religious houses, and arsenals; the massive demonstration outside the Hôtel de Ville, where the new municipal government was in the process of formation; the storming of the Hôtel des Invalides in search of weapons to arm the newly created citizens' militia; and finally (partly planned, though mainly the outcome of a whole series of fortuitous events) the frontal assault on the Bastille, which brought the first phase of the Revolution to a close.

In October there was a similar pattern of growth and development, though the final stages of the insurrection already bear the mark of a more conscious political direction. Certainly, to the majority of the housewives and market women demonstrating for bread in the early morning of October 5, as to the casual observer, the opening scenes of the uprising must have seemed no more than a continuation of a whole series of similar demonstrations in September. Even the mass invasion of the Hôtel de Ville was but a repetition on a larger scale of similar forms of protest in pre-

° See pp. 59, 81, 150-51, 157 above.

ceding weeks. Yet the diversion of the women to Versailles (partly
the outcome of weeks of agitation by the "patriots" and partly of
the intervention of Stanislas Maillard and his *volontaires de la
Bastille*) gave an entirely new, political, content to their demonstration. From this point, although still professing mainly economic
aims, it merged with the political insurrection launched by the
"patriots" and supported by the marching contingents of the
Parisian National Guard.[6]

Such illustrations are a reminder that even during periods of
revolutionary upheaval, when political groups were competing for
popular support, outbreaks rarely followed carefully predeter-
mined patterns: the exceptions being, of course, such highly organized military or ceremonial affairs as we have already mentioned.
Elsewhere, the fortuitous element, as we have noted, played a
remarkably persistent role and makes nonsense of the claims of
many contemporaries and later historians that such movements
were the outcome of precisely conceived "conspiracies." To that
extent, then, we must allow a considerable importance to spontaneity in the origin, development, and climax of popular disturbance.

Yet we must be careful not to press the point too far: if we have
stressed the unexpected twists and turns in the Paris insurrections
of 1789, there was nothing purely fortuitous in the events themselves. On both occasions, the provocative acts of the Court party
at Versailles clearly served as a "trigger" to unleash the disturbances that followed in the streets of the capital; but they could
not have done so if there had not been a long series of earlier incidents to lend them significance and if, above all, the political
climate for rebellion had not already been well prepared. In fact,
the prevailing political ideas and the sort of "generalized beliefs"
discussed in Chapter 14 were essential ingredients without which
there would have been no response, least of all a popular response,
to the actions taken by the Court. Again, the peasants' attacks on
the châteaux in the summer of 1789 were "triggered" by the rumors
of approaching "brigands," which, in turn, were "triggered" by the
circumstances surrounding the fall of the Bastille in Paris. But such
a sequence of events, entirely fortuitous in itself and unforeseen,
could not possibly have developed without the deep traditional

hatred of the peasants for manorial dues and obligations and the hopes of redress that had been aroused by the convocation of the Estates General at Versailles.

Almost as remarkable and seemingly incongruous is the sequence of cause and effect linking the Paris cholera epidemic of 1832 with the workers' armed insurrection of June of that year. The cholera claimed 39,000 victims, many of them from the crowded streets and tenements adjoining the central markets and Hôtel de Ville. It was widely rumored that the government or the *bourgeoisie* had deliberately infected the wells and poisoned the inmates of the hospitals and prisons; and historians have seen the June outbreak as the outcome of the panic and hatred thus engendered.[7] Here again (if we accept the proposition) we must distinguish between the "trigger" and the underlying cause; for even the terrors created by the cholera could hardly have led to the June events without the economic crisis, poverty, degradation, bitter hatreds, and defeated hopes attending the revolution of 1830.

Similarly, in even the most seemingly spontaneous of all these outbreaks a certain degree of unity was always imposed not only by the underlying ideas or "generalized beliefs," but by slogans, leaders, or some elementary or more developed form of organization. We have already noted the part played by slogans like *Wilkes and Liberty, No Popery and Wooden Shoes, Long live the Third Estate* or *For the Democratic and Social Republic* in moulding and directing opinion. While the more widely disseminated "generalized beliefs" were essential to prepare a militant climate of opinion, such slogans served to unify the crowd itself and to direct its energies toward precise targets and objectives. This was not so likely to be the case in food riots and strikes, where the issues might be clear enough, particularly to those who felt the pinch of wage cuts or rising prices; but in political demonstrations they were an effective means of rallying supporters and terrifying or discomforting opponents. Cockades and banners might serve a similar purpose: Wilkes's campaign in London appears to have owed a great deal of its success to the distribution of "favors" bedecked with the Wilkite blue (the color reappears in the "No Popery" riots of 1780); and we have seen the part played by the tricolor and *bonnet rouge* in 1789 and the red flag of the socialist clubs in 1848. By such means groups and individuals with widely varying motives and beliefs might be rallied in support of a common cause and to focus their protests on a common target.

This unity would, of course, be all the more in evidence where those taking an active part were members of a common organization. In an age before the appearance of mass trade unions, political parties, or consumers' guilds, an association of this kind would rarely be complete. The exception, once more, was where insurgents were organized in military units, like the National Guards that assaulted the Tuileries or the sans-culotte militia that ejected the Girondin deputies from the National Convention in June 1793; the case was somewhat different at the Bastille, where only a part of the insurgents were under arms. Again, there were occasions, even in the eighteenth century, where those taking part in industrial disputes were organized in trade unions: we saw in earlier chapters that this was so in the case of French paper workers, carpenters, and printers, and of London hatters, tailors, and weavers, and that, during the Revolution, the *compagnonnages,* or workers' "combinations," played some part in the carpenters' strike of 1791. In rural strikes and riots an element of organization was always provided by the village community. In Paris, by 1793, the sans-culottes had even acquired a degree of political organization through their popular societies and Sectional assemblies that was not far different from that later given to their members by political parties. Something of the kind happened to the small Middlesex freeholders at the time of Wilkes and to the London craftsmen of Hardy's Corresponding Society. In all these cases, however, the experience was comparatively short-lived, and it was not until the 1830's that stable forms of popular organization not only made a brief appearance but came to stay. Their arrival naturally affected the form and pattern of popular disturbance. The old type of food riot and such spontaneous outbreaks as that in the pottery towns in 1842 had now become the exception; and we saw the solid contribution made by the clubs and workers' organizations to the events of 1848 in Paris and by the trade unions and the National Charter Association to Chartism in England.*

---

* See Chapters 11 and 12.

Leaders, too, played a part in giving the crowd cohesion and unity and in guiding and directing its energies. Yet they probably never enjoyed the lonely eminence nor played the outstanding role ascribed to them in such events by Taine and Le Bon and other proponents of the "conspiracy" theory of revolution. Le Bon, for example, writes that "as soon as a certain number of living beings are gathered together, whether they be animals or men, they place themselves instinctively under the authority of a chief"; and he adds that the leaders of crowds are "especially recruited from the ranks of those morbidly nervous, excitable, half-deranged persons who are bordering on madness."[8] To characterize the leaders of crowds at all times and in all places in such terms is, of course, both to betray a peculiar social bias and to reduce the leaders, like the crowd itself, to a pure abstraction. In fact, the study of the crowd in history suggests not only that the role of leaders varied between one type of disturbance and another, but that they were men of differing personalities and social origins; and, above all, that a distinction must be made among leaders operating from outside the crowd, those drawn from within the crowd itself, and those acting (or appearing to act) as intermediaries between the two.

The first group of leaders are those that may more properly be called the "heroes" of the crowd—men in whose name it riots or rebels, to whose summons (or would-be summons) it responds, and whose speeches, manifestoes, or ideas serve as an ideological background or accompaniment to its activities. Such men were Chatham, Wilkes, and Lord George Gordon in eighteenth-century London; Robespierre, Danton, Marat, and Hébert in the French Revolution; Ledru-Rollin, Louis-Napoleon, and Louis Blanc in the Revolution of 1848 in Paris; and the original anonymous Rebecca, General Ludd, or even (if he ever existed) "Captain Swing" in the riots following the Napoleonic Wars in England.

Occasionally, far from exercising the "very despotic authority" that Le Bon ascribes to them, they were reluctant rather than enthusiastic leaders, or even renounced entirely the leadership that had been thrust upon them. A notorious example from earlier history is that of Martin Luther, who, far from commending the actions of German peasants rioting in his name, roundly condemned them as "murdering, thieving Hordes of Peasantry." It seems reasonable to suggest that Louis XVI played a similarly reluctant role in the rural disturbances in France in 1775 and 1789, when small consumers and peasants cited his authority in imposing food prices and settling scores with their manorial lords. These are, of course, extreme examples. More typical perhaps was the quandary of Lord George Gordon in London in 1780. His words and actions, particularly his violent attacks on Roman Catholics, undoubtedly provoked the "No Popery" riots; yet he could claim with perfect sincerity that he had never intended the consequences that flowed from them. Such ambivalent situations are liable to arise in revolutions: in 1793, both Marat and Robespierre had occasion to denounce actions undertaken in their name; and Louis Blanc, the socialist leader, conspicuously disassociated himself from the Paris insurgents of June 1848. Wilkes more than once reproved his over-exuberant followers for taking his name in vain; and even Rebecca, who kept a tighter control than most "outside" leaders over the crowd's activities, was compelled to call off her campaign when it got out of hand.

This is certainly not to suggest that the "outside" leader's or "hero's" influence in similar movements was purely casual or incidental. On the contrary: it was indispensable for giving them unity and direction. Yet, by his position "outside" the crowd, the leader was always in danger of losing his control over a protracted period, or of seeing his ideas adapted to purposes other than those he had intended. We have seen how the Parisian sans-culottes, while continuing to acclaim Jacobin leadership and Jacobin ideas, attuned them to their own with results that were most unwelcome to their original promoters. One reason for this ambivalence in leadership was that such leaders were almost invariably drawn from social classes other than those of their followers. John Wilkes was the son of a prosperous distiller; Lord George Gordon was a Scottish aristocrat and the son of a Duke; while the topmost leaders in the French Revolution were almost without exception ex-nobles, doctors, journalists, priests, or prosperous tradesmen. One result of this was that there was always a certain lack of concordance between the social and political aspirations of leaders and followers; another was that the leaders (and this was particularly the case in a protracted movement like the French Revolution) were at times compelled, in order to maintain their authority, to trim or adapt their policies to meet the wishes of the crowd. This was precisely what happened, as we have seen more than once already, when the Jacobins bowed to popular pressure in controlling the price and distribution of food. In such ways leaders, far from exercising undisputed control over their followers, might be overruled by them, and, in a sense, the role of leader and follower would be reversed!

Communication between the topmost leaders and their followers was seldom direct. Displays of mass oratory were the exception rather than the rule; though there were such occasions, as when Lord George Gordon addressed his Protestants in St. George's Fields, when meetings took place in the Champ de Mars, or when the leaders of 1848 harangued their supporters from the balcony of the Paris Hôtel de Ville. But not until 1848 in France and Chartist times in England did such displays become more than comparatively rare occurrences; and press, Parliament, and political club were more often chosen as a forum than the public square. Ropespierre's oratory was confined to the National Assembly and the Jacobin Club; Wilkes wrote his addresses and manifestoes from the King's Bench prison; Marat used the columns of his paper, *L'Ami du Peuple;* and Ned Ludd issued his directives from his headquarters in Sherwood Forest. Such appeals and messages were relayed to their followers by various means: by press and pamphlet; at public meetings; by word of mouth in workshop, pub, or wine shop; in markets and baker's shops; and, on the great political occasions, by emissaries or intermediate leaders, who acted as links between the "outside" leaders and the crowd and who may also have passed on the slogans and directives and (where the occasion demanded) drawn up the "lists" of victims and given the marching orders.

Of course, there was no mystery about such channels of communication in the highly organized operations, when military units (as in Paris in 1792 and 1793) acted under the orders of their own commanders. On some occasions, however, the mystery remains complete: who, for example, transmitted the slogans, banners, and ideas of the Protestant Association to their less "respectable" and more riotous supporters in the streets of London; and who, again, gave the order for the attack on Priestley's house in

Birmingham? On other occasions, we catch glimpses of the process of communication—at the burning of the customs posts in Paris, for example, when we learn from the testimony of numerous witnesses that local leaders—such as Du Hamel, a former blacksmith—were acting under the direct orders of the Palais Royal, the headquarters of the Duc d' Orléans. Again, in the October "days," we find Stanislas Maillard directing operations in consultation with spokesmen for the women; and Fournier l'Américain recruiting support for the marchers in his own electoral district and inciting the market women at Versailles to demand the King's return to Paris.[9] In England, in the early nineteenth century, the local Ned Ludds and "Swings" and, in Wales, the local Rebeccas and other local leaders, like the Chartists John Frost and Zephaniah Williams, who led the attack on Newport, may have played a similar part. Elsewhere, the mechanism of popular revolt may elude us completely; yet we may assume perhaps that it was through secondary leaders such as these that links were maintained between the topmost leaders and the rank-and-file participants.

But such men were also generally "outsiders." What leaders did the crowd itself throw up, either on occasions such as those we have just described or on others, as in strikes and food riots, when it was acting on its own account? In some cases there may have been quite literally none. We saw the precise answers given to the police in 1775 by a woolen worker of the market town of Mouy;° and after the July revolution of 1789 in Paris, a tallow porter asked by the police "who commanded them (the insurgents) when they went to the Palais Royal and other places," replied firmly that "they had no leader and each man was as free as any other."[10] Astonishing as it may seem, this may have been true enough of a small sector of the riots, or at least it may have appeared to be so to one of many thousands who took part. On such occasions, the police or militia were inclined to arrest and cross examine not so much leaders in any commonly accepted sense of the term as those who momentarily gave way to enthusiasm, showed more spirit, enterprise, or daring than their fellows, were heard to shout slogans, engaged in more spectacular acts of violence, or happened to be picked out and informed against by

° See p. 216 above.

their neighbors. There was, for example, the laboring woman of Yerres, who, when arrested as a ringleader in the grain riots of 1775, told the police that "she had been carried away . . . that she got excited like everybody else, and she didn't know what she was saying or doing." The same may have been true of another woman, Marie-Jeanne Trumeau, who was arrested and sentenced to death (though later reprieved) for shouting slogans and inciting to loot and burn in the Réveillon riots of April 1789. Other local leaders or would-be leaders of this kind emerge from the dusty files of the Paris police: among them the *femme* Lavarenne, an illiterate sick-nurse, who according to Stanislas Maillard acted as spokesman for the women who marched to Versailles; and Dumont (alias Cadet), a docker, who played a conspicuous role in the assault on the Paris customs posts in 1789.[11] In the French grain riots of 1775, local foraging parties were sometimes led by eminently respectable persons like farmers, schoolmasters, local officials, or even the village curé.*

In England, there were the acknowledged riot "captains," who marshaled their followers of an hour or a day to break threshing machines, pull down fences or turnpikes, or loot and destroy the houses of their selected victims. Such men were Tom the Barber, spokesman for the East London anti-Irish rioters in Goodman's Fields in 1736, and William Pateman, a journeyman wheelwright, and Thomas Taplin, a coachmaster, who led bands of rioters during the "No Popery" disturbances in London in 1780. And there were many others arrested as such among the crowds that "pulled down" Priestley's house in Birmingham, burned stacks and wrecked threshing machines in the southern counties, and attacked properties in Bristol and the pottery towns in the 1830's and 1840's.

A distinguishing feature of all such leaders is that their authority was purely local and purely temporary; and it is a remarkable fact that of the several hundreds transported to Australia for their part in the Bristol, Potteries, and "Swing" disturbances not one appears to have had any subsequent history of political or radical activity. Their militancy, like their leadership (both real and alleged, was in fact, limited to the occasion and had no future or continuity: thus, once more, the distinction between "militants" and the more

---

* See pp. 29–30 above.

casual participants in the crowd's activities virtually disappears. There were, however, exceptions—even in the eighteenth century. John Doyle and John Valline, for example, who were hanged in London in December 1769, were not mere casual rioters or men of momentary authority, but strike leaders and committeemen who had taken part in several of the weavers' "transactions." At this time such cases were confined to industrial disputes, and it is not until the French Revolution that we find this type of continuity in popular political movements. In the Champ de Mars affray in 1791, three persons were arrested who had previously been acknowledged as "victors" of the Bastille; four of them were among those who, a year later, were killed or wounded in the assault on the Tuileries; and many more experienced militants, trained in the clubs and *armées révolutionnaires,* were among the several thousand arrested and disarmed after the popular rising of May 1795.[12]

As yet exceptional, such cases became far more frequent in both France and England after 1830. In 1832 in France, we saw that industrial workers were already taking part in successive economic and political disturbances; and we noted the highly sophisticated radicalism of George Loveless, leader of the Dorchester farm laborers, who not only was deported as a militant in 1834 but returned one three years later.° With the spread of radical and socialist ideas and the growth of working-class movements this process would, of course, go much further; and one of the many features of the new industrial society was the emergence from the crowd itself of its own militants and leaders, no longer occasional, sporadic, and anonymous, but continuous and openly proclaimed.

There remains a final set of questions relating to the crowd's behavior. What truth is there in Le Bon's assertion that the crowd (and he frequently equates "crowd" with "masses") tends to be fickle, irrational, violent, and destructive?[13] The fickleness or "mobility" of the crowd is, of course, a shibboleth that has become sanctified by constant repetition: the very word "mob" is derived from the Latin *mobile vulgus,* and it is not surprising that the possessing classes, wherever they were unable to control its energies, should have looked on the crowd as a fickle monster,

° See pp. 165 and 223 above.

lacking in both rhyme and reason. How far is the view confirmed by our study of the pre-industrial crowd? There can obviously be little to be said for it in the case of the more highly organized or ceremonial occasions when the crowd assembled to hear speeches or to carry out the specific instructions of its leaders: this is so evident, perhaps, that it is hardly worth repeating. But even such demonstrations might be transformed by the intrusion of a sudden panic: at "Peterloo," for example, when the yeomanry broke up the disciplined ranks of the weavers and their families; or at the Tuileries in 1792, where a sudden cry of treachery led to the massacre of the Swiss Guards defending the palace. Under rather different circumstances, we saw how the French peasants in 1789 abandoned their plans to deal with mythical "brigands" for the more fruitful operation of dealing with their landlords; and how Rebecca's peaceful parade through Carmarthen was transformed, after the entry of "the rabble of the town," into a violent attack on the local workhouse.*

In short, the intrusion of the unexpected might create a panic or otherwise divert the crowd from its original purpose: in such cases, the charge of fickleness would appear to have some substance. But, in general, such "mobility" of behavior was not typical of the riotous crowd. We have already quoted numerous instances that illustrate the very opposite: the remarkable single-mindedness and discriminating purposefulness of crowds, even those whose actions appear to be the most spontaneous. We saw how the Gordon rioters in London and the "Church and King" rioters in Birmingham, having carefully earmarked their victims, took meticulous care to avoid destroying or damaging the properties of their neighbors. The machine wreckers of 1830 appear to have discriminated between one type of farmer and another; the Réveillon rioters in Paris looted shops, but only food shops; Ned Ludd and Rebecca invariably chose their targets with deliberate care; the crowds that burned the Paris customs posts spared those belonging to the Duc d' Orléans; the September "massacrers" despatched only such victims as had been found guilty by improvised tribunals; and the reader may remember those Cleehill colliers of 1766 who, the *Annual Register* wrote, "entered the town [of Lud-

* See p. 160 above.

low] in a very orderly manner, proceeded to the house, pulled it down, and then returned without offering any other violence to any person whatever."[14] In fact, the study of the pre-industrial crowd suggests that it rioted for precise objects and rarely engaged in indiscriminate attacks on either properties or persons.

Equally, though riots might spread, by "contagion" or other means, beyond the rural or urban boundaries within which they started, they rarely spread to areas untouched by the grievances that gave them birth. We may take the example of Wiltshire, which was affected successively by the southern counties riots of 1830 and the Chartist agitation of 1839. In 1830, the rick-burning farm laborers stopped short of the traditionally riotous textile centers in the western parts of the county; whereas in 1839, when old grievances had been replaced by new, it was the textile centers that were stirred by "physical force" Chartism, while now rick burning was at its lowest ebb for a whole decade.[15] This merely shows, once more, the need to study the behavior of crowds, like the leaders and the crowds themselves, in its social and historical context. Such illustrations suggest, too, that the crowd was by no means "irrational" in the wider meaning of the term. It might be diverted or provoked by panic, as it might be stirred by Utopian pipe dreams or millenarial fantasies; but its purposes were generally rational enough and often led it, as we have seen, to choose not only the targets but the means most appropriate to the occasion.°

But if the pre-industrial crowd was not remarkable either for its fickleness or its irrationality, it was certainly given to acts of violence, above all to the violent and methodical destruction of property. This happened with such almost unfailing regularity in strikes, riots, and rebellions that we can hardly attribute the fact to chance, accident, or sudden panic. Such violence might result from the deliberate plans of "outside" leaders, as in the Rebecca and Luddite riots in England; it might occur against the wishes of the "outside" leaders, as in the Wilkite or "No Popery" disturbances in London; and, above all, it might occur where the crowd was acting on its own, as in strikes, food riots, the Réveillon affair in Paris, and (most spectacularly) in the "Swing" riots of 1830 in England. On several of these occasions, as we saw, the entry of new and

° See p. 240 above.

unexpected elements changed the course of disturbance and led to indiscriminate attacks beyond the range of the selected targets; yet, even without these intrusions, the toll of destroyed and damaged houses, chapels, fences, toll gates, machinery, and mills would have been remarkable enough.

Destruction of property, then, is a constant feature of the pre-industrial crowd; but not the destruction of human lives, which is more properly associated with the *jacqueries*, slave revolts, peasant rebellions, and millenarial outbursts of the past, as it is with the race riots and communal disturbances of more recent times. In our particular context, the famous "blood-lust" of the crowd is a legend, based on a few carefully selected incidents. Let us look at the record. In the great English riots of the 1730's to 1840's, whether urban or rural, there were remarkably few fatal casualties among the rioters' victims. There were none at all in the Wilkite, Birmingham, Bristol, anti-Irish, "No Popery," and "Swing" and other rural disturbances; and not even in the armed rising at Newport in 1839. Food riots were singularly free from injury to life or limb: no farmer, miller, magistrate, or forestaller appears to have been fatally injured in the riots of 1766. On the other hand, the Porteous riots at Edinburgh (1736), the Luddite riots, and the Rebecca riots each claimed one fatal victim. Murder may have been more frequent in industrial disputes: a sailor was killed by coal heavers at Shadwell in 1768 and a soldier by Spitalfields weavers in 1769. This record contrasts sharply with the toll of life exacted among the rioters by the military and the law courts. Twenty-five Gordon rioters were hanged in 1780, a dozen or more food rioters in 1766, 8 London coal heavers and 2 (or maybe 3) weavers in 1769, 37 or more Luddites in 1812-13, and 19 "Swing" rioters in 1830. The military took a far heavier toll: 5 rioters were shot at Norwich in 1740; 10 were killed and 24 wounded in the West Riding turnpike riots of 1753; over 100 colliers were killed or wounded at Hexham in 1761; 8 rioters were shot dead at Kidderminster, 8 at Warwick, 2 at Frome, and 1 at Stroud in the food riots of 1766; 11 demonstrators (they were hardly rioters) were shot dead in St. George's Fields in London in 1768; 285 were killed outright or died of wounds in the Gordon Riots; 8 were shot dead in the Luddite disturbances of 1811–1812 and 7 in the battle of Bossenden Wood; 110 were killed or wounded at the Bristol toll-gate riots of 1793; 24 died at Newport in 1839; and, twenty years earlier, the Lancashire yeomanry killed 11 and wounded 420 or more in the massacre at "Peterloo."[16]

French rural riots, like the English, were also directed against property rather than against persons; and there were no fatal injuries among the rioters' numerous victims in the disturbances of 1775. It was not, in fact, until the great wave of disturbance in 1789 that food riots were accompanied by the murder of a number of bakers and millers. Yet the French Revolution in Paris, for all the destructive violence that attended it, was not particularly marked by murderous violence on the part of crowds. In the pro-*parlement* riots of 1788, the crowds killed none but the troops killed 8 at least and wounded 14. In the Réveillon riots of April 1789, the crowds wrecked properties but took no lives; the troops killed "several hundred" (the exact number is not known) and 3 alleged ringleaders were hanged after the event. At the siege of the Bastille, 150 assailants were killed or wounded by the defenders; after it fell, crowds massacred 6 or 7 Swiss Guards; the governor of the fortress, de Launay; and a municipal officer. Between July and October 1789, 4 more persons (including a baker) were lynched by crowds, and 5 rioters were hanged for these and other offences. In all the peasant disturbances of the summer of 1789, 3 victims (or at most 4) were recorded. At Versailles, in October, the crowd killed 2 of the Guards who had shot down one of their number. In the Champ de Mars affair of July 1791, 2 men were lynched by the crowd and upwards of 50 demonstrators were shot dead by Lafayette's National Guard. There were no fatal casualties on either side in the Paris food riots of February 1792 and 1793, nor in the insurrections of May-June and September of that year. In the final armed uprising of the sans-culottes in May 1795, the crowds invading the Convention killed the deputy Féraud; in the reprisals that followed 36 persons, including 6 Jacobin deputies, were guillotined by order of a military tribunal.*

From this balance sheet of violence and reprisal it would appear, then, that it was authority rather than the crowd that was con-

---

* See *The Crowd in the French Revolution*, pp. 37-8, 56, 67-75, 89, 96-8, 116-17, 155-6; G. Lefebvre, *La Grande Peur de 1789* (Paris, 1932), p. 242; K. Tönnesson, *La défaite des sans-culottes* (Oslo and Paris, 1959), p. 330. I have omitted the royalist rising of October 1795, when 200-300 were killed on each side (*The Crowd in the French Revolution*, p. 173), as this was not strictly a popular outbreak.

spicuous for its violence to life and limb. Yet there were the two exceptional incidents of August and September 1792. In the first, 376 anti-royalist insurgents were killed or wounded by the defenders, while the assailants, in the reprisals that followed, slaughtered 600 of the Swiss Guards after they had been ordered to lay down their arms. In the second, no fewer than 1,100 to 1,400 prisoners, most of them common law offenders rather than aristocrats or priests, were dragged from the jails and massacred after sentence by hastily improvised tribunals.[17] These are the incidents on which Taine's and Le Bon's case against the "murderous mob" largely rests. Yet revolting as such incidents must seem, neither can be said to be typical of the crowd's behavior. The first was largely a military operation carried out by men acting under the orders of their commanders and the newly installed Revolutionary Commune of Paris. The second case was somewhat different. It was a civilian and not a military affair; yet it occurred as the result of a panic induced by a military defeat, by the Prussian breakthrough at Verdun and the conviction that the advancing enemy, in league with the inmates of the jails, would exact a bloody vengeance on the Parisian population. While the approving majority stood by, the actual executions were carried out by small bands of *massacreurs* operating (or so it would appear) under the orders of members of the Commune and the Paris Sections.[18] Can the crowd then (in the sense in which we have so far used the term) be called an active or a passive agent in the affair? It is a debateable point; yet, in either event, the incident stood on its own and was not typical of the actions and behavior of the pre-industrial crowd.

In short, the crowd was violent, impulsive, easily stirred by rumor, and quick to panic; but it was not fickle, peculiarly irrational, or generally given to bloody attacks on persons. The conventional picture of the crowd painted by Le Bon and inherited by later writers is not lacking in shrewd and imaginative insight; but it ignores the facts of history and is, in consequence, overdrawn, tendentious, and misleading.

REFERENCES

1. G. Le Bon, *The Crowd* (London, 1909), p. 26; G. Lefebvre, "Foules révolutionnaires," in *Etudes sur la Révolution française* (Paris, 1954), p. 273.

2. Lefebvre, *op. cit.*, p. 272.

3. *Middlesex Journal,* April 13-15 and 20-22, 1769.

4. Hardy's *Journal,* VIII, 475; E. P. Thompson, *The Making of the English Working Class* (London, 1963), pp. 681-2.

5. Raffaello Carboni, *The Eureka Stockade,* ed. G. Serle (Melbourne, 1963), p. 179.

6. G. Rudé, *The Crowd in the French Revolution* (Oxford, 1959), pp. 220-21.

7. G. Vauthier, "Le choléra à Paris en 1832," *La Révolution de 1848,* XXV (1928-9), 234-41; L. Chevalier, *Classes laborieuses et classes dangereuses* (Paris, 1958), p. xix.

8. Le Bon, *op. cit.,* pp. 133-4.

9. See *The Crowd in the French Revolution,* pp. 48-9, 73-7, 229.

10. Archives Nationales, Z² 4691 (July 29, 1789).

11. *The Crowd in the French Revolution,* pp. 230-31.

12. See my *Wilkes and Liberty* (Oxford, 1962), pp. 101-102; and *The Crowd in the French Revolution,* pp. 108, 230-31.

13. Le Bon, *op. cit.,* pp. 16-17, 42, 73.

14. *Annual Register,* IX (1766), 149.

15. E. J. Hobsbawm, "Economic Fluctuations and Some Social Movements since 1800," *Economic History Review,* 2nd series, V, i (1952), 8.

16. See my *Wilkes and Liberty,* pp. 51, 203-204; R. W. Wearmouth, *Methodism and the Common People of England of the Eighteenth Century* (London, 1945), pp. 19-91; D. Williams, *The Rebecca Riots* (Cardiff, 1953), p. 253; F. O. Darvall, *Popular Disturbances and Public Order in Regency England* (London, 1934), pp. 104, 120, 130; E. P. Thompson, *op. cit.,* p. 687; M. Hovell, *The Chartist Movement* (Manchester, 1959), p. 180; and pp. 59, 70, 76, 86, 89, and 155 above.

17. *The Crowd in the French Revolution,* pp. 104-105, 110.

18. P. Caron, *Les massacres de septembre* (Paris, 1935), pp. 76-102.

SIXTEEN

The Success and Failure
of the Crowd

One final and important question remains. Did all the vigor, heroism, and violence recounted and dissected in these chapters lead to any positive results? In this phase of its history in France and England, what did the crowd achieve? In terms of immediate gains, it must be admitted that it achieved comparatively little. In strikes and wage movements, as long as trade unions were weak and scattered and proscribed, workers could only hope to win short-lived and limited results. The Parisian workers of 1794, who struck work at a time of war and labor shortage, won considerably higher wages, but they were more than swallowed up by the inflation of the following months. The Luddites, though they failed to stop the steam loom, wrung some temporary concessions from the clothiers of Yorkshire and the hosiers of the midlands counties; yet these, too, were withdrawn or eclipsed in the depression that continued long after their riots had been suppressed. In English rural riots, weavers, miners, cottagers, freeholders, and laborers made their social protest for a day or two: they broke down fences, "pulled down" farms or mills, and imposed their price controls on wheat, flour, meat, and butter—until the militia arrived, opened fire, and arrested the "ringleaders," who were hanged, imprisoned, or transported; and "normality" reigned once more. The French grain riots of 1775 thoroughly alarmed the government because of their scope and their threat to the security of the capital; but Turgot mustered a strong military force and brought the rioters to heel, without making the slightest concession to the small consumers whose hardship had provoked them.

In fact, of all the many food riots of the period it was probably only those of the French Revolution—particularly those of 1793—that achieved the aims with which they started.

Outside revolutions, urban riots were no more strikingly successful than the rural. In the Gordon Riots, London's "No Popery" crowds held the streets for a week on end; but the Catholic Relief Act, which had prompted them, remained. After the riots of 1791, Priestley felt compelled to leave Birmingham and take refuge in the United States; but this was due as much to the continued hostility of the authorities as to the destructiveness of "Church and King." French city riots, before 1787, were minor explosions and achieved less than the English. And the results of such outbreaks as those at Bristol and Nottingham in 1831 and at Birmingham and in the pottery towns in 1839-42 are impossible to assess because they were part of wider movements: of the Reform Bill agitation in the first case and of Chartism in the second.

But besides its failures the crowd had its indisputable successes. Not only did the Rebecca riots destroy the hated turnpikes, which were not rebuilt, but tolls were reduced in number and County Boards were set up to administer the old unpopular Trusts. "Swing's" successes were less sensational; but, in some districts, the collusion of the farmers ensured that the threshing machines smashed by the laborers were not restored. The Wilkite disturbances in London not only achieved a remarkable series of personal victories for Wilkes himself but contributed substantially to the growth of a mass radical movement in England. Chartism, though a failure at the time, was hardly so in the long run, since five of its Six Points were adopted by a succession of Parliaments over the next hundred years. And, finally, it would be tedious to recount the profound influences exerted on French national life, and beyond France herself, by the revolution of 1789 and, to a lesser degree, by those of 1830 and 1848.

But why should some "hostile outbursts" be successful and others be so patently failures? Of course, in its wider aspects, this question raises a whole host of problems—some social and ideological, others political and administrative—arising both before and after the point of explosion.° But, in this short final chapter, we

° See N. J. Smelser, *Theory of Collective Behavior* (London, 1962), pp. 261-8, 364-79, for what the author terms the "social control" of tension and disturbance.

shall be concerned mainly with those arising after the outbreak itself. First, as to the outbreak and the initial "break-through." Here, unless numbers were overwhelming, early success might depend on such factors as a rapid thrust, seizing the initiative, or exploiting the advantages offered by geography. In rural riots, for example, it was comparatively easy to effect an early "break-through" before the militia could be summoned or the army mustered. Thus, in 1775, the French grain rioters had been running loose in the markets and villages for a whole week, and had actually entered Versailles and Paris before Turgot was able to summon an armed force adequate to check them. Again, in London in March 1768, crowds celebrating Wilkes's first election victory in Middlesex got off to a good start while the constables were at Brentford, where the election had taken place; and similarly, in the Paris food riots of February 1793, crowds were able to occupy the grocers' shops without opposition because the National Guard was on that day engaged on other duties at Versailles.

At other times, the almost simultaneous outbreak of disturbances over a wide area would make it impossible for even the most astute and determined of police chiefs or military commanders to make an effective disposition of the forces at his disposal. This was certainly the case in the initial stages of the Rebecca and Luddite riots in England; and in April 1848, the Chartist Convention, prompted by Ernest Jones, quite deliberately planned to divert the authorities' attention from London, where the main operation was to take place, by organizing simultaneous demonstrations in the provinces, "so that the myrmidons of power in the country might be kept in check by the brave men there."[1]

Yet, of course, such devices could do no more than win a temporary respite, unless there were other, more solid, reasons for success. And this was so only in one of the cases that I have cited. In London, in 1768, even when the constables returned from their other duties, the forces of law and order were quite inadequate to curb the noisy display of enthusiasm among Wilkes's supporters. In Paris, in February 1793, on the other hand, the return of the National Guard, with the brewer Santerre at its head, brought the riots to a speedy close; and, in the other examples quoted, the authorities only needed time to muster their forces in order to quell disturbance. In 1775, Turgot set two whole armies afoot, the one under the Marquis de Poyanne in the Ile de France and the other under the veteran Duc de Biron in Paris; after which, the riots were over within a week. In England, in the summer of 1812, as we have seen, the Luddites were overawed by an army of 12,000 men, which was larger than any that had previously been called upon to cope with civil disorder.° In the main years of Chartist agitation in England, large forces of regular troops were mustered in the disaffected areas: 10,500 in 1839 and 10,000 in 1842; and in April 1848, to meet the last Chartist threat, nearly 170,000 special constables were enrolled and 7,123 "regulars" and 1,290 armed pensioners were assembled in the capital alone.[2]

Such numbers were impressive; yet, in the final reckoning, it was not so much the numbers in themselves that might prove decisive as the willingness or the ability of the authorities to use them. Much might depend, as we have seen, on the speed and efficiency with which they were assembled, and even more depended on the determination of magistrates, constables, and troops to crush disturbance. In English riots, there were numerous occasions when swift action by justices who commanded respect brought local outbreaks to a speedy close.[3] In June 1848, the troops stationed in London to overawe the Chartists were said to be "so savage that Lord Londonderry told the Duke of Wellington he was sure, if a collision took place, the officers of his regiment would not be able to restrain their men."[4] Even more remarkable, that same month, was the ferocity with which the Parisian Gardes Mobiles, though themselves recruited from young workers and unemployed, mowed down the June insurgents on the barricades. In 1830, it was to a somewhat different social group that the Duke of Wellington appealed in order to break up the "Swing" rioters in Hampshire:

I induced the magistrates [he wrote] to put themselves on horseback, each at the head of his own servants and retainers, grooms, huntsmen, game-keepers, armed with horsewhips, pistols, fowling pieces and what they could get, and to attack in concert, if necessary, or singly, these mobs, disperse them, and take and put in confinement those who could not escape. This was done in a spirited manner, in many instances, and it is astonishing how soon the country was tranquillised, and that in the best way, by the activity and spirit of the gentlemen.[5]

° Before the end of the Gordon Riots of 1780 there were 10,000 troops encamped in the parks and squares of London (P. de Castro, *The Gordon Riots* (London, 1926), p. 263).

Such "spirited" appeals to class might indeed, as in this instance, prove highly effective in mobilizing resistance to disturbance; but there were occasions when the hatreds thus aroused, by alienating or outraging the noncommitted, might rebound on the heads of their sponsors and prove more of a liability than an asset. This was certainly the case with Lafayette and the Parisian National Guard, whose zeal in shooting down unarmed demonstrators in the Champ de Mars in July 1791 stirred passions that were not easily abated. Results similar though not so drastic flowed from the "massacres" of Wilkite supporters in St. George's Fields by the Foot Guards in 1768 and of the Lancashire weavers by the yeomanry at "Peterloo" half a century later.

Yet it was not so much excessive zeal as its direct opposite that was liable to endanger authority and to undermine its defenses. For every vigorous, respected, or over-zealous magistrate in English disturbances, there could usually be found another whose fatuity, arrogance, timidity, or caution would estrange supporters or confuse and paralyze the constables and military commanders at his disposal. Moreover, the antiquated machinery of order, in particular the anomalies surrounding the operation of the Riot Act, led to endless confusion; and the Englishman's boasted "right of resistance" to oppression, particularly when the parliamentary opposition chose to exploit it, might almost be construed as a right of rebellion.[6] There were occasions, too, when magistrates (and this applied as much to France as to England) not only were cautious and timid in summoning troops but openly or secretly sympathized with the rioters' cause. Even in the French grain riots of 1775, which were actively repressed, some magistrates, while not openly flouting Turgot's authority, were inclined to meet the rioters half-way. In the Gordon Riots in London, many City magistrates were even more half-hearted in carrying out their duties: being as hostile to Catholic relief as the crowd itself, they virtually condoned their activities until the rioters became a menace not only to Catholic properties but to property as a whole. Such collusion between magistrates and rioters might go even further: in France, in 1788, the *parlements* could hardly be expected to take firm measures against those who rioted on their behalf; and in Birmingham, three years later, there was a strong suspicion that some of the chief instigators of the Priestley riots would be found, if authority felt so disposed, among the magistrates themselves.*

But it was only in exceptional circumstances, such as those attending the French "aristocratic revolt" of 1788, that the insubordination or collusion of magistrates could yield more than a temporary advantage to rioters or rebels: generally, it could ensure their complete success only in such limited and negative operations as those undertaken in the name of "Church and King." In the last resort, it was always the army on which authority in both France and England relied to defend itself against popular disturbance; and as long as the army remained substantially loyal any serious threat to the government or the established order was negligible or nonexistent. In theory, it was possible to imagine that vast numbers of civilians, if they had access to weapons and ammunition, might arm themselves and seize power with such speed that the army had time neither to offer resistance nor to become disaffected; but, in fact, this never happened and never has happened since. In England, the army remained stubbornly loyal to King and Parliament throughout this period—though there were moments in 1839 and 1840 when General Napier, who held the northern command, expressed fears that his troops were being infected by Chartist propaganda.[7]

In France, for all the unpopularity of ministers, the army never seriously wavered in its allegiance to the King until the autumn of 1787—so much so that Sébastien Mercier, writing in 1783, thought it was inconceivable that a city as well policed as Paris should ever be exposed to such tumults as London, for lack of such defenses, had suffered during the Gordon Riots.[8] But, of course, as he was soon to discover, it was not just a matter of simple arithmetic: the effectiveness of armies in civil disturbance depended far less on numbers than on their willingness to obey. And this is precisely what the French army, in 1788 and still more in 1789, was not prepared to do. Disaffection started not among the rank and file but among the officers. These, drawn largely from the small provincial *noblesse,* had long-standing grievances concerning their status and opportunities for promotion, and the

* See pp. 29, 59, 94, and 146 above.

"aristocratic revolt" provided an admirable occasion to voice them. In Brittany, Dauphiné, and other provinces, they ordered their troops not to fire on demonstrators, refused to arrest rebellious magistrates, and generally set their soldiers, who had grievances of their own, an example of disobedience which they were not slow to emulate.

In February 1789, even before the Revolution had started, Necker advised the King that the army was already too disaffected to be relied on as an instrument for suppressing civil disorder; and from now on it was mainly foreign levies or troops from distant provinces that were brought to Versailles to defend the Court, and later to overawe the capital. In Paris, the Gardes Françaises were loyal enough to shoot down the Réveillon rioters in April; but, by June, they were parading to shouts of *Vive le tiers état!*, and in July they played a crucial part in the capture of the Bastille.[9] After this, a new national army emerged, which proclaimed its allegiance to the nation and the new revolutionary authorities; but it was kept out of Paris, whose defense was entrusted to the National Guard. The Guard, at first solidly *bourgeois,* was effective, as we have seen, in suppressing the demonstration of July 1791; but it gradually became the instrument of the sans-culottes as much as of the Assembly; and it was only when the army was called in again, in May 1795, that the long series of popular disturbances that had marked the whole course of the Revolution in Paris was brought to a close.

In 1830 and 1848, the defection of the armed forces was once more decisive in assuring the defeat of the royal government and the success of the revolutionary challenge. Yet the pattern was not the same as that of 1789. The outbreak of 1830 was a short-lived affair and, after three days' street-fighting, Charles X was driven out and Louis Philippe was installed for the next eighteen years. In February 1848, it was the defection of the National Guard in Paris, even more than that of the army (which was passive rather than openly rebellious), that drove Louis Philippe, in his turn, into exile. This time, the popular forces that challenged the authority of the new revolutionary government and Assembly were far stronger and more efficiently organized than they had been in 1789. Yet they were brought to heel not after six years but after a mere four months. This was due partly to the building of railways, which made it possible to summon troops more quickly to the capital; and it was due, perhaps even more, to the loyalty of the bulk of the National Guard and the Mobile Guards, who were the real victors of the June insurrection.

It would seem, then, to be almost a truism that the key factor in determining the outcome of popular rebellion and disturbance is the loyalty or disaffection of the armed forces at the government's disposal. "It is obvious," writes Le Bon, "that revolutions have never taken place, and will never take place, save with the aid of an important faction of the army";[10] and Professor Crane Brinton is saying much the same when he writes "that it is almost safe to say that no government is likely to be overthrown until it loses the ability to make adequate use of its military and police powers."[11] Such assertions are true enough as far as they go; yet they are not the whole truth and they even tend, when presented in such baldly military terms, to beg the further and more important question of why the army refuses to obey or why the government loses control of its means of defense. Essentially, this is a social and political rather than a military question. For if magistrates condone riots or soldiers fraternize with or refuse to fire on rebels, it is because the ties of class or of political affiliation are at that moment stronger than allegiance to the established order or government.

We have already seen evidence of this in the actions of the French aristocratic officers in 1788 and of their troops in the following year; and, in February 1848, the National Guard that deserted Louis Philippe clearly showed—in fact, they said so in so many words—that they had, like their fellow tradesmen out of uniform, become infected by the prevailing middle-class demand for political reform. But this could not in itself assure the success of the February revolution: that depended not only on the National Guard but on its cooperation with the middle-class radical journalists and the very different social elements that composed the revolutionary crowd. For social and political reasons, the alliance was short-lived, and in June the popular insurrection failed because it found little or no support among its allies of February. Similarly, in 1789, the great insurrections and popular upheavals of the day were carried through as a joint operation of the sans-culottes—the main elements composing the revolutionary crowd —and a varying combination of middle-class, and even liberal-aristocratic, groups. When this combination of social forces broke down, as it finally broke down in the spring of 1795, the Parisian common people stood no more chance of winning victories by street demonstrations and riots than the small peasants and petty consumers of 1775.

In England, as we have seen, such victories were far less frequent than in France; and England probably stood near to revolution only in 1831, when Irish unrest, rural disturbance, and popular and middle-class excitement over the first Reform Bill combined to bring the country to the brink of civil war. This was not because Methodism or any other religious movement turned men away from earthly strife and thus averted a revolution; but, until the 1840's at least, no insurrectionary movement of the English "lower orders," whether of town or countryside, stood any chance of success without the support of some combination of other social groups. And in England this was rarely forthcoming; when it was, it was too short-lived to yield more than limited results. In the Wilkite movement of the 1760's and 1770's, popular radicalism won some victories; but this was only so as long as the agitation of the crowd in the streets was supported by that of Middlesex freeholders and London craftsmen, shopkeepers, and merchants. Similarly, in the Gordon Riots the crowd could hold the streets just as long as the City magistrates and householders condoned their activities; but once this sanction was withdrawn, the movement had no future. In Birmingham, in 1791, it is doubtful if the "Church and King" crowd would have succeeded in wrecking Priestley's house and driving him out of town without the active or tacit approval of a number of its magistrates. The "daughters of Rebecca" owed their success not to any defection of the military, which was eventually mobilized in sufficient numbers to suppress them, but to the support they enjoyed among the whole farming population—and even, in part, to the willingness of the government to remove the main abuses which had prompted them to riot. The Chartists failed in their immediate aims because their numbers, though considerable, were insufficient to compensate for their lack of middle-class support; and yet, in the long run, most of their Six Points were realized precisely because that support, refused in the 1840's, was forthcoming later.

But, finally, should we judge the crowd's importance in history purely in terms of its record of success or failure? It is indisputable that its impact on events was far more marked in some cases than in others. In this sense, the revolutionary crowds of 1789 and 1848, in respect both of their maturity and their achievement, may justly claim a precedence over those engaged in the more primitive, and often seemingly futile, pursuits of destroying houses in the name of "Church and King," of wrecking toll gates and machinery, or of imposing short-lived price controls in food riots. Such distinctions are valid enough; yet there is a broader sense in which the pre-industrial crowd, irrespective of its immediate failures or successes, marks an important stage in the historical process. As society has changed, so the crowd has changed with it and, in changing, has left its legacy to succeeding generations. As the sans-culotte, small freeholder, and cottager have given way to the factory worker and farm laborer, so the machine wrecker, rick burner, and "Church and King" rioter have given way to the trade unionist, labor militant, and organized consumer of the new industrial society. New wine has certainly on occasion been poured into old bottles; but, in general, it is perhaps not unreasonable to see these earlier, immature, and often crude, trials of strength, even when doomed to failure, as the forerunners of later movements whose results and successes have been both significant and enduring.

REFERENCES

1. Cited by F. C. Mather, *Public Order in the Age of the Chartists* (Manchester, 1959), p. 22.
2. E. Lavisse, ed., *Histoire de France depuis les origines jusqu'à la Révolution* (9 vols. Paris, 1911), IX, 33; F. O. Darvall, *Popular Disturbances and Public Order in Regency England* (London, 1934), pp. 259-60; F. C. Mather, *op. cit.*, pp. 152, 163; M. Hovell, *The Chartist Movement* (London, 1918), p. 290.
3. See, for example, Darvall, *op. cit.*, pp. 244-5; and Mather, *op. cit.*, pp. 60-61.
4. Mather, *op. cit.*, p. 180.
5. Cited by D. Williams, *John Frost* (Cardiff, 1939), pp. 59-60.

6. E. Halévy, *A History of the English People in 1815* (3 vols. London, 1937), I, 193-8.

7. Mather, *op. cit.*, pp. 177-81.

8. L. S. Mercier, *Tableau de Paris* (12 vols. Amsterdam, 1783), VI, 22-5.

9. See my chapter on "The Outbreak of the French Revolution," shortly to appear in *The New Cambridge Modern History,* vol. VIII.

10. G. Le Bon, *The Psychology of Revolution* (New York, 1913), p. 49; cited by N. Smelser, *Theory of Collective Behavior* (London, 1962), p. 372.

11. Crane Brinton, *The Anatomy of Revolution* (New York 1960), pp. 266-7.

BIBLIOGRAPHY

The documentary materials on which this book is based have already been discussed in the Introduction, and it is not proposed to set them out fully here. Some primary sources, including contemporary printed journals and occasional manuscripts, are noted in the references at the end of chapters; others may be sought in the secondary works (books and articles) consulted, of which the more important are listed below.

Amann, P. "The changing Outlines of 1848," *American Historical Review*, LXVIII (1963), 938-53.

Agulhon, M. *La République au village* (Paris, 1973).

Ashton, T. S. *Economic Fluctuations in England 1700-1800* (Oxford, 1959).

Barnes, D. G. *A History of the English Corn Laws from 1660 to 1846* (New York, 1961).

Beloff, M. *Public Order and Popular Disturbances 1660-1714* (London, 1938).

Bendix, R. "The Lower Classes and the 'Democratic Revolution'," *Industrial Relations*, I, i (Oct. 1961), 91-116.

Bernard, L. L. Articles on "Crowd" and "Mob" in *Encyclopedia of Social Sciences* (15 vols, 1931-5), IV, 612-13; X, 552-4.

Bezucha, R. *The Lyons Uprising of 1834* (Camb., Mass., 1974).

Briggs, A. "The Language of 'Class' in Early Nineteenth-Century England," in A. Briggs and J. Saville (eds.), *Essays in Labour History in Memory of G. D. H. Cole* (London, 1960).

———(ed.) *Chartist Studies* (London, 1959).

Brinton, Crane. *The Anatomy of Revolution* (New York, rev, edn, 1960).

Brown, R. W. "Mass Phenomena," in *Handbook of Social Psychology* (2 vols, Camb., Mass.), II, 847-58.

Burke, E. *Reflections on the Revolution in France* (London, 1951).

Canetti, E. *Crowds and Power* (London, 1962).

Caron, P. *Les massacres de septembre* (Paris, 1935).

Charlesworth, A. *Social Protest in a Rural Society*, Hist. Geography Research Series, No. 1 (Liverpool, Oct. 1979).

Chevalier, L. *Laboring Classes and Dangerous Classes in Paris During the First Half of the Nineteenth Century* (New York, 1973).

Cobb, R. C. *The Police and the People, 1787-1820* (London, 1970).

Cole, G. D. H. and Postgate, R. *The Common People, 1746-1938* (London, 1945).

Darvall, F. O. *Popular Disturbances and Public Order in Regency England* (London, 1934).

Gurr, Ted, *Why Men Rebel* (Princeton, 1970).

Hay, D. *et al. Albion's Fatal Tree* (London, 1975).

Hill, C. "The Norman Yoke", in J. Saville (ed.), *Democracy and the Labour Movement* (London, 1945), pp. 11-66.

——*The World Turned Upside Down* (London/New York, 1972).

Hobsbawm, E. J. *Labouring Men. Studies in the History of Labour* (New York, 1965).

——*Primitive Rebels* (Manchester, 1959).

——and Rudé, G. *Captain Swing* (London, 1969).

Hoggart, R. *The Uses of Literacy* (London, 1957).

Jones, D. *Before Rebecca. Popular Protests in Wales, 1793-1835* (London, 1975).

Kitson Clark, G. "Hunger and Politics in 1842," *Journal of Mod. History*, XXV (1953), 355-74.

Knight, F. *The Strange Case of Thomas Walker* (London, 1957).

Lefebvre, G. "Foules révolutionnaires," in *Etudes sur la Révolution française* (Paris, 1954), pp. 271-87.

——*The Great Fear of 1789* (London, 1973).

Marx, K. *Class Struggles in France, 1848-50* (London, n.d.).

Mather, F. C. *Public Order in the Age of the Chartists* (Manchester, 1959).

Merriman, J. (ed.). *Consciousness and Class Experience in Nineteenth-Century Europe* (New York, 1979).

——(ed.). *1830 in France* (New York, 1975).

Mornet, D. *Les origines intellectuelles de la Révolution française* (Paris, 1933).

Mousnier, R. *Peasant Uprising in 17th-Century France, Russia and China* (London, 1971).

Peacock, A. J. *Bread or Blood. The Agrarian Riots in East Anglia in 1816* (London, 1965).

Perry, T. W. *Public Opinion, Propaganda and Politics in Eighteenth-Century England. A Study of the Jew Bill of 1753* (Camb., Mass., 1962).

Pinkney, D. "The Crowd in the French Revolution of 1830," *Am. Hist. Rev.*, LXX (1964), 1-19.

——*The French Revolution of 1830.*

Porchnev, B. *Les soulèvements populaires en France au XVIIIe siècle* (Paris, 1972).

Price, R. *The French Second Republic. A Social History* (London, 197).

Recollections of Alexis de Tocqueville, ed. J. P. Mayer (New York, 1959).

Richards, E. "Patterns of Highland Discontent 1790-1860," in J. Stevenson and R. Quinault (eds), *Popular Protest and Public Order* (see below).

Rogers, P. G. *Battle in Bossenden Wood. The Strange Story of Sir William Courtenay* (London, 1961).

Rose, A. G. *The Plug Riots* (Lancs and Cheshire Antiquarian Society, 1957).

Rose, R. B. "Eighteenth-Century Price Riots, the French Revolution and the Jacobin Maximum," *Internat. Review of Social History*, III (1959), 432-45.

——"Eighteenth-Century Price Riots and Public Policy in England," ibid., VII (1961), VI (1961), Pt 2, 277-92.

————"The Priestley Riots of 1791," *Past and Present*, Nov. 1960, pp. 66-88.

Rudé, G. *The Crowd in the French Revolution* (Oxford, 1959).

————*Ideology and Popular Protest* (London, 1980).

————*Paris and London in the Eighteenth Century. Studies in Popular Protest* (London/New York, 1970).

————*Wilkes and Liberty* (Oxford, 1962).

Shelton, W. "The Role of the Local Authorities in the Hunger Riots of 1766," *Albion*, V, i (Spring 1973), 50-56.

Smelser, N. J. *Theory of Collective Behaviour* (London, 1962).

Smith, F. B. "The Plug Plot Prisoners and the Chartists," *ANU Hist. Journal* (Canberra), Nov. 7 (Nov. 1970).

Soboul, A. *The Parisian Sans-Culottes and the French Revolution 1793-4* (Oxford, 1964).

————"Sentiment religieux et cultes populaires pendant la Révolution," *Archives de sociologie des religions*, no. 2, July-Dec. 1956, pp. 73-87.

Stevenson, J. and Quinault, R. (eds.). *Popular Protest and Public Order 1790-1920* (London, 1974).

————(ed.). *London in the Age of Reform* (London, 1977).

Thomis, M. *The Luddites. Machine-Breaking in Regency England* (Newton Abbot, 1970).

Thompson, E. P. "Eighteenth-Century English Society: Class Struggle without Class?", *Social History*. III, ii (1978), 33-65.

————*The Making of the English Working Class* (London, 1963).

————"The Moral Economy of the English Crowd of the Eighteenth Century," *Past and Present*, no. 50 (May, 1971), 76-136.

————*Whigs and Hunters: The Origin of the Black Act* (London, 1975).

Vovelle, M. "Les taxations populaires de février-mars, et novembre-décembre 1792 dans la Beauce et sur ses confins," *Mémoires et documents*, XIII (Paris, 1958), 107-59.

Wearmouth, R. W. *Methodism and the Common People of England in the Eighteenth Century* (London, 1945).

Williams, D. *The Rebecca Riots: A Study in Agrarian Discontent* (Cardiff, 1953).

Index

3-8-96, Midwest, 24.20, 63116